R. H. Blyth: Haiku, Vol. IV

Yuki yande   ki ni akane sasu   yūhi kana

The snow ceases to fall,
The ruddy sun glows on the trees:
The evening scene.

雪やんで
木に
茜さす
夕日かな

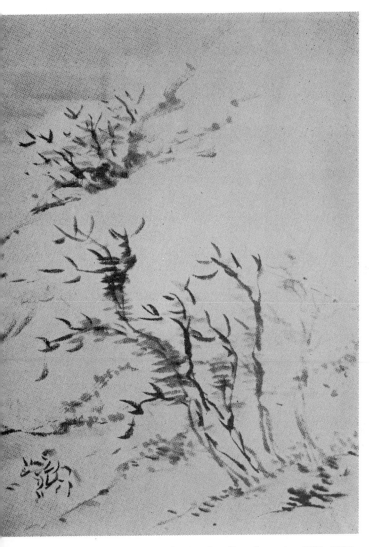

Verse and picture by Otsuji, 乙字, 1881–1920

HAIKU

BY
R. H. BLYTH

Volume Four: Autumn—Winter

(Pp. 977–1300)

(Reset in paperback edition)

1982
THE HOKUSEIDO PRESS
Tokyo

Haiku, Volume Four © by R. H. Blyth 1952, 1982
Paperback edition, fourth printing 1992

Complete set   ISBN 4-590-00571-9
Vol. IV   ISBN 4-590-00575-1

Published by The Hokuseido Press
3-32-4, Honkomagome, Bunkyo-ku, Tokyo

VOL. IV   AUTUMN—WINTER

Preface **980**

Page

SEASONAL INDEX

AUTUMN (Continued)

WINTER

APPENDICES

ILLUSTRATIONS

HAIKU

IN FOUR VOLUMES

VOL IV

AUTUMN – WINTER

Winter Seclusion

Verse and picture by Teiga, 定雅, 1755–1825, a pupil of Buson.

閑さを我か
相手なり冬ごもり

Shizukasa wo   waga aite nari   fuyugomori

Making quietude
My only companion:
Winter seclusion.

To the right, books; to the left, a tea-cup. In front of me, the fire-place; behind me, the post. There is no greater happiness than this.

右にふみ左に茶わん
前に一炉うしろに
はしら
たのしみこれに過る事
なし

THE PUBLICATION OF THIS VOLUME

WAS MADE POSSIBLE

THROUGH THE KINDNESS AND PATRIOTISM

OF

NAOTO ICHIMADA

GOVERNOR OF THE BANK OF JAPAN

PREFACE

Japanese Literature stands or falls by haiku, in my opinion, but its unique characteristic makes it a difficult matter to assess its position in world literature. It is not merely the brevity by which it isolates a particular group of phenomena from all the rest; nor its suggestiveness, through which it reveals a whole world of experience. It is not only in its remarkable use of the season word, by which it gives us a feeling of a quarter of the year; nor its faint all-pervading humour. Its peculiar quality is its self-effacing, self-annihilative nature, by which it enables us, more than any other form of literature, to grasp the thing-in-itself. Just as we are to be in a state of *muga*, self-lessness, when we compose haiku, so the haiku is not a thing of beauty and a joy for ever, but a finger-post, a raft unwanted when the river is crossed. If, like waka, the haiku itself has literary charm and value, we are distracted from the real region of haiku, the experience, the mutual, reunited life of poet and things.

The position which haiku has or should have in world literature may be brought out by comparing and contrasting Bashō with Shakespeare, Homer, Dante, Goethe and Cervantes. If he can hold his own with these, the 17-syllabled haiku may well claim an equality with the world masterpieces of epic, drama, and lyric.

Bashō has not the grim strength of Dante, but he also sees how

> The little flowers, bent and shut by the chill of night,
> Soon as the sunlight whitens them,
> Erect themselves quite open on their stems.
>
> *Inferno II, 127–129*

He has not Shakespeare's power to create forms more real than living man, but has the universality of

> Truly, sir, I am a poor fellow that would live,

as applied to all the things in the world, animate and inanimate:

よく見ればなづな花咲く垣根哉
Yoku mireba nazuna hanasaku kakine kana

Looking carefully,—
There is a shepherd's-purse
Blooming under the hedge.

He has not Homer's grasp of the primitive nobility of men and women, but he has his pleasure in the plain and elemental things of life:

身にしみて大根からし秋の風
Mi ni shimite daikon karashi aki no kaze

In the bitter radish
That bites into me, I feel
The autumn wind.

Goethe's understanding of science was to Bashō unknown, but he shares with him the knowledge that there is nothing behind phenomena; "they are themselves the meaning." On the other hand, Bashō is an idealist like Cervantes, but he does not tilt at windmills either real or symbolical; he does something just as destructive however, in taking away from things their (apparent) heavy, stupid meaninglessness, and shows us them as the world of grace and nature in one.

In what point is Bashō equal or superior to these great men? In his touching the very nerve of life, his unerring knowledge of those moments in time which, put together, make up our real, our eternal life. He is awake in the world that for almost all men exists as a world of dreams.

Bashō gives us the same feeling of depth as Bach, and by the same means, not by noise and emotion as in Beethoven and Wagner, but by a certain serenity and "expressiveness" which never aims at beauty but often achieves it as it were by accident. This comparison between Bashō and Bach may seem to be far-fetched. They have little in common except their profound understanding of vital inevitability, and the meaning of death. As Confucius implies, he who understands either life or death, understands both. The hymn says, in its rather sentimental way,

Days and moments, quickly flying,
Blend the living with the dead,

and Bach and Bashō felt this so deeply that the average mind finds the one too intellectual and difficult, the other too simple.

Many people must have had the experience of reading haiku which have not seemed very good or striking, and yet, for some strange and unknown reason, were unforgettable. To take some examples; the first by Bashō:

六月や峯に雲おく嵐山
Rokugatsu ya   mine ni kumo oku   arashiyama

In the Sixth Month,
Mount Arashi
Lays clouds on its summit.

To explain the poetic point of this would be very difficult. It lies partly, no doubt, in the personifying of the mountain, or rather, in realizing the "life" of it, but the simple sublimity of the verse is Homeric; it is that of the cloud-capped mountain.

稲妻や昨日は東今日は西
Inazuma ya   kinō wa higashi   kyō wa nishi

Summer lightning!
Yesterday in the East,
Today in the West.

There could be nothing less "poetical" than this bald statement of meteorological fact by Kikaku, and yet we feel the vastness of nature, together with the underlying willing acceptance of man. The same is true of the following, by Yayu:

二つ三つ星見出すや啼く蛙
Futatsu mitsu   hoshi miidasu ya   naku kawazu

A few stars
Are now to be seen,—
And frogs are croaking.

Two or three stars have come out, dusk falling; a few frogs are croaking. The unity of nature is seen without a word about it; without, indeed, a glance at it.

There is a short poem by Robert Frost, *The Pasture*, that expresses to me almost the whole meaning of human life,— and with it the nature of haiku:

I'm going out to clean the pasture spring;

I'll only stop to rake the leaves away
(And wait to watch the water clear, I may):
I shan't be gone long.—You come too.

I'm going out to fetch the little calf
That's standing by the mother. It's so young
It totters when she licks it with her tongue.
I shan't be gone long.—You come too.

We see these things, the pasture spring and the water clearing, the cow and her wabbly calf, and in them our life is fulfilled, —but not entirely; you, the other person, humanity, must come too; myself and Nature and man, the tender and strong relation between us.

There are two elements in this relation, a systole and a diastole. There is eternity and infinity, and there are the "minute particulars." In life and art it is as well perhaps to allow the eternity and infinity to be overheard, overseen. Where haiku is unrivalled is in its power of expressing the whole world of inanimate, or animate, or human life, and at the same time entering into the minutest details of fact or feeling. The following example, by Bonchō, of this delicacy applies to visual sensations:

灰捨てゝ白梅うるむ垣根かな
Hai sutete   shiraume urumu   kakine kana

Throwing away the ashes,
The white plum-blossoms
Became cloudy.

This does not mean that the blossoms became dirtied by the grey ash, nor does it mean that they became more beautiful. It is something between the two, leaning towards the second, but more indefinite, more hesitating than it. Not so delicate and more a matter of sensation, but still revealing the whole through the parts, a verse by Sodō:

春もはや山吹白く苣苦し
Haru mo haya   yamabuki shiroku   chisha nigashi

Spring soon to be over,
The yellow rose whitening,
Lettuce becoming bitter.

Another example of the delicacy of the haiku poet is the
following verse by Buson, where the feeling is quite a nameless
one, without words to express it in any language, yet expressed,
faultlessly and unequivocally:

梅遠近南すべく北すべく
Ume ochikochi minami subeku   kita subeku

Plum-blossoms here and there,
It is good to go north.
Good to go south.

There is here a feeling of the newness of spring, and yet of
the luxury, the bounty, the universality of the season; in truth,
anywhere will do in these days of renewed life and beauty.
One more example, also by Buson, in which the delicacy is so
great as to require the maximum of effort on the part of the
reader:

菜の花や法師が宿は訪はで過ぎ
Na no hana ya   hōshi ga yado wa   towade sugi

Rape-flowers;
Not visiting the priest,
But passing by.

Buson is walking along a road on both sides of which rape-
flowers are blooming. For some reason or other he passes by
the monk's house he intended visiting. To say that he chooses
nature instead of religion, the rape-flowers rather than talking
with the monk,—this is not only saying too much, it is de-
stroying the very life of the poetry which is in a realm that
transcends (while including) this "Shall I, or shall I not?" of
hesitation and dubiety. There is a similar verse by Taigi:

欺いて行きぬけ寺やおぼろ月
Azamuite   yukinuke tera ya   oborozuki

Pretending it is on purpose,
And passing through a temple,—
The hazy moon.

Going out for a walk in the evening, the poet mistook the
way and found himself in such a place that, to avoid going
round a long way, he had to go through the temple grounds,

so going in the gate, and bowing to the main temple and to the Buddhas enshrined in other buildings, he went out of the back gate, feeling that his religious actions had been more than usually spiced with practical requirements and hypocritical observances. And the moon, quite properly, is hazy. The tenderness of mind which is the most prominent characteristic of the writer of haiku is distinctly (almost too distinctly) seen the following verse by Shiki:

鉈あげてきらんとすれば木の芽かな
Nata agete   kiran to sureba   konome kana

Lifting up the hatchet
To cut it down,—
It was budding

This has been compared to the verse by Meisetsu, composed thirteen years later:

鎌をとげばあかざ悲しむ景色あり
Kama wo togeba   akaza kanashimu   keshiki ari

Sharpening the sickle,
The goose-foot[1]
Looks as if grieving.

Though haiku are so restricted in their subject matter, we have no feeling of monotony as we read them. There are however five main types: verses that record sensations; pictures of life; self-portrayals; verses that express human warmth; and romantic verses.

1.   Examples of sensation:

朝寒や旅の宿たつ人の声
Asasamu ya   tabi no yado tatsu   hito no koe

Morning cold;
The voices of travellers
Leaving the inn.

The voice of the men who are setting out early this autumn morning, and the coldness of the air, reinforce each other.

[1] Named from the shape of the leaves.

The sound is clearer, chillier; the cold has a human meaning.
There is another verse by the same author, Taigi, but the
time is evening:

旅人や夜寒問ひ合ふねぶた声
Tabibito ya   yosamu toiau   nebutagoe

Travellers,
Asking about the cold at night,
In sleepy voices.

結ぶよりはや歯にひゞく泉かな[1]
Musubu yori   haya ha ni hibiku   izumi kana

On the point of scooping up the water,
I felt it in my teeth,—
The water of the spring.

To Bashō, it was not merely the sight of the cold water but
the action of putting the hands together to scoop it up that
caused the strength of the sensation of chill in his teeth. The
following is by Shikō:

馬の耳すぼめて寒し梨の花
Uma no mimi   subomete samushi   nashi no hana

The horse lays back his ears;
Flowers of the pear-tree
Are chill and cold.

The flowers of the pear, unlike those of the cherry and plum,
have no brilliancy or gaiety, but rather some loneliness and
melancholy. The horse on his way home this cold spring
evening puts back his ears, and they are in momentary accord
with the flowers.

梅の花赤いは赤いはあかいはな
Ume no hana   akai wa akai wa   akai wa na

These flowers of the plum,—
How red, how red they are,
How red, indeed!

---

[1] This has a variant:
結ぶよりまづ歯にひゞく清水哉
The clear water, I felt it first in my teeth.

Also by Izen, a contemporary of Bashō famous for his doctrine of spontaneity, the two following verses:

磯ぎはにざぶりざぶりと波打ちて
Isogiwa ni   zaburi zaburi to   nami uchite

Along the sea-shore
Fall the waves, fall and hiss,
Fall and hiss.

杉の木にすうすう風の吹き渡り
Sugi no ki ni   sū sū kaze no   fukiwatari

Through the cedars
Whew, whew, whew,
Whistles the breeze.

The next two are by Issa:

二つなき笠ぬすまれし土用かな
Futatsu naki   kasa nusumareshi   doyō kana

The hottest day of the year;
The only *kasa* I had,—
Stolen!

We have here the inhumanity of man added to the inhumanity of nature. Issa nearly always gives us this, and in the following also:

暑き夜の荷と荷の間にねたりけり
Atsuki yo no   ni to ni no aida ni   netarikeri

A hot night;
Sleeping in between
The bags and baggages.

2.   Pictures of life.

名月やふな虫はしる石の上
Meigetsu ya   funamushi hashiru   ishi no ue

The bright autumn moon:
Sea-lice running
Over the stones.

This verse, by Tōrin, is peculiarly vivid and mobile. The moonlight is so bright that we can see even the sea-lice running about on their business over the stones left dry by the falling tide. But in some way or other we feel that the moonlight has itself come alive in the silvery creatures that move so smoothly here and there. The stones too share in this light-life. The first of the two following verses is by Raizan, the second by Bashō:

春風や白鷺白し松の中
Harukaze ya   shirasagi shiroshi   matsu no naka

In the spring breeze
The snowy heron flies white
Among the pine-trees.

雀と声なきかわすねずみの巣
Suzume to   koe nakikawasu   nezumi no su

Baby mice in their nest
Squeak in response
To the young sparrows.

The young mice in the ceiling and the young sparrows under the eaves are both chirping. These so different forms of life have the same pathos and faint humour of all incomplete things. Bashō, like Wordsworth, is saying,

I have heard the call
Ye to each other make.

The following verses, the first by Gojō, the second by Kozan, go beyond mere pictures; they have three or more dimensions.

夏草や山寺道の石佛
Natsugusa ya   yamadera michi no   ishibotoke

Summer grasses;
Along the path to the mountain temple,
Stone images of Buddha.

Stone Buddhas line the path to the temple in the mountains, almost unseen until we turn a sharp corner, and one of the images gives us a profound impression of the divine in nature, part of it, and yet above and beyond it.

ほととぎす夜は木をきる音もなし
Hototogisu yoru wa ki wo kiru oto mo nashi

A *hototogisu* sings
Among the evening shades;
No sound of the woodcutter.

This absence of things never fails to deepen the meaning of those that remain. The verse actually says: "No sound of wood-cutting."

青海苔や石の窪みの忘れ汐
Aonori ya ishi no kubomi no wasurejio

Green seaweed;
In the hollows of the rocks,
The forgotten tide.

This verse belongs to spring; the following, also by Kitō, to summer:

山寺や縁の下なる苔清水
Yamadera ya en no shita naru koke shimizu

A mountain temple;
Clear water running under the verandah,
Moss at the sides.

For a poet, or a child, this is the ideal dwelling place. The following, by Seira, has the simplicity of W. H. Davies:

角上げて牛人を見る夏野哉
Tsuno agete ushi hito wo miru natsuno kana

Lifting up their horns,
The cattle look at people,
On the summer moor.

The grass is rank, the day hot, the cattle moving slowly with their heads down. When someone approaches them they raise their heads, or rather, they raise their horns above the tall grasses, and we feel something menacing yet mild that tells of the wonder and power and danger of nature.

耕すや鳥さへ啼かぬ山かげに

Tagayasu ya   tori sae nakanu   yamakage ni

Tilling the field,
Not even a bird cries,
In the shadow of the hill.

In this verse, by Buson, we feel the season, the beginning of
April, the lateness of the coming of warmth here under the
hill-side, the young leaves unfolding, no breeze, complete
silence,—and with all this, the softly-harsh sound of the hoe.
The following verse, by Shirō, is at the opposite extreme:

たうたうと瀧の落ちこむ茂り哉

Tō tō to   taki no ochikomu   shigeri kana

The waterfall
Thunders down
Into the rank leaves.

The tremendous rush of water and tumultuous sounds have
their correspondence in the wildly growing plants and weeds
and trees all around.

蝶の羽のいくたび越ゆる塀の屋根

Chō no ha no   ikutabi koyuru   hei no yane

How many butterflies
Winged their way across
This roofed wall!

What struck Bashō was not merely the contrast between the
wings of the lightly flying butterflies and the heavily tiled
earthen wall, but the way in which they appear from the
unknown, and disappear into it with that levity and aimless
purposefulness that characterise them. The following, by Gyō-
dai, is a wonderful and powerful verse:

暁や鯨の吼える霜の海

Akatsuki ya   kujira no hoeru   shimo no umi

In the dawn,
Whales roaring;
A frosty sea.

The beginning of day, the spouting of the whales, the sea, ·the

frost,—all these have something primitive and primaeval in
them.

小夜時雨隣の臼は挽きやみぬ
Sayo shigeru   tonari no usu wa   hikiyaminu

The people next door
Have stopped grinding the mortar:
Cold rain at night.

The connection between one thing and another is always in-
credibly strange, even when it is simple cause and effect. How
much more so here, where the mere cessation of one sound
causes Yaha now to understand the meaning of the rain that
has been falling all the time. Compare the following by Bonchō:

灰汁桶の雫やみけりきりぎりす
Akuoke no   shizuku yamikeri   kirigirisu

The drip-drip
Of the lye-bucket ceases:
The voice of the cricket.

The following three verses, by Uryū, Gusai, and Kikaku, bring
out well the vitality and variety of haiku:

鯉の音水はのぐらく梅白し
Koi no oto   mizu honoguraku   ume shiroshi

The sound of the carp,
The water faintly dark,
The plum-blossoms white.

大寺のとびらあけたる春日かな
Ōdera no   tobira aketaru   haruhi kana

A spring day;
They open the folding-doors
Of the great temple.

こゝかしこ蛙鳴く夜やほしのかげ
Kokokashiko   kawazu naku yo ya   hoshi no kage

Here and there,
Frogs croaking in the night,
Stars shining.

The following small picture of country life by Bashō is more
of sound than of sight. The next, by Gyōdai, is larger:

雞 の 聲 に し ぐ る ゝ 牛 家 か な
Niwatori no   koe ni shigururu   ushiya kana

Winter rain falling
On the cow-shed;
The voice of the cock.

日 暮 れ た り 三 井 寺 下 る 春 の 人
Hi kuretari   miidera kudaru   haru no hito

The day darkening,
They come down from Mii Temple,
People of the spring.

We see here the shades of evening fall over a wide scene, Lake
Biwa in the distance, the Temple above, the long flight of
stone steps, and in ones and twos, people who are reluctantly
leaving the cherry-blossoms behind, so aptly termed "people
of the spring."

人 も 見 ぬ 春 や 鏡 の う ら の 梅
Hito mo minu   haru ya kagami no   ura no ume

A spring unseen of men,—
On the back of the mirror,
A flowering plum-tree.

This verse by Bashō is one that Keats would have appreciated.
There is a world of art which hardly belongs to this world
except as a kind of perversion of it, a sort of back-of-the-mirror
which our mind holds up to nature. This is the world that
Bashō was also drawn to, but like Wordsworth, the real world
was the one he earnestly desired to live in.

鶯 や 下 駄 の 齒 に つ く 小 田 の 土
Uguisu ya   geta no ha ni tsuku   oda no tsuchi

The *uguisu*!
Earth of the rice-fields sticks
On the supports of the clogs.

Two extremes of the whole of spring are given here by Bonchō, the heavenly voice of the *uguisu,* and the mud on the two "teeth" of the *geta,* or wooden clogs.

蜀魂なくや木の間の角櫓
Hototogisu   naku ya konoma no   sumiyagura

A *hototogisu* cries;
Between the trees
A corner turret.

The bird suddenly cried, and looking round, Shihō saw through a gap in the trees, the white corner of the donjon silhouetted against the blue sky of summer.

豆植る畑も木べ屋も名所哉
Mame ueru   hata mo kibeya mo   meisho kana

Fields for sowing beans,
Firewood sheds,—
All famous places.

This was written by Bonchō at Rakushisha, 落柿舎, in Saga, Kyorai's villa, where Kobori Enshū,[1] a great landscape gardener, had his tea-ceremony house. These fields sown with beans, sheds for firewood, were once scenes of splendour and of the cultural life of the community. Both the glory and the misery of human existence are powerfully contrasted.

凩やまばたきしげき猫の面
Kogarashi ya   mabataki shigeki   neko no tsura

In the winter storm
The cat keeps on
Blinking its eyes.

This by Yasō is on the one hand a vivid picture of the cat, its hatred of wind and confusion, the ears back, head down, blinking its half-shut eyes. On the other hand it is a description of one aspect of the essential nature of the winter wind, its make-cats-blink-ness.

---

[1] See page 1004.

わか鮎や谷の小笹も一葉行
Waka-ayu ya   tani no kozasa mo   hitoha yuku

With the young trout in the valley
A leaf of the dwarf bamboo
Floats away.

If we take this as a real experience of Buson, we cannot help admiring the presence of mind (of Mind) that could seize such a moment, such a world of meaning in miniature. If we take it, as some do, as pure imagination, we shall be even more struck by Buson's power of pictorial creation.

しずかさや湖水の底の雲のみね
Shizukasa ya   kosui no soko no   kumo no mine

The stillness;
Peaks of cloud
In the bosom of the lake.

We are reminded of Wordsworth's lines:

that uncertain heaven received
Into the bosom of the steady lake.

In Issa's verse we have rest only; in Wordsworth there is both motion and rest.   The next is by the same author.

なでしこや地蔵菩薩の後先に
Nadeshiko ya   jizōbosatsu no   atosaki ni

Before and behind
Jizō Bosatsu,
Pinks are blooming.

Jizō is the patron of travellers and children, and his statue is often found at cross-roads and other lonely places. His relation to the pinks may be taken in either of two ways: the sweetness of Jizō and the pinks; and the contrast between his calm indifference and their eager little faces.

白露や芋の畑の天の川
Shiratsuyu ya   imo no hatake no   amanogawa

White dew;
Over the potato field,
The Milky Way.

The Milky Way is the dew of heaven; the dew on the potato leaves is the stars of this earth. But as so often, there is something a little dead about Shiki's still-lifes. The next is better.

夕立や砂につき立つ青松葉
Yūdachi ya   suna ni tsukitatsu   aomatsuba

A summer shower;
Green pine-needles
Stick in the sand.

We feel here the force of the shower, that breaks off the pine-needles and thrusts them into the sand, so that they stand up in it.

桐の葉は落ちつくすなるを木芙蓉
Kiri no ha wa   ochitsukusu naru wo   mokufuyō

The leaves of the paulownia
Having all fallen,—
The tree-lotus in bloom.

When the great leaves of the paulownia have all fallen, it is late autumn, but just at this time the flowers of the tree-lotus bloom. There is sometimes an unnaturalness about nature which makes her akin to us.

The above and all the remaining verses of this second section are by Buson.

池と川ひとつになりぬ春の雨
Ike to kawa   hitotsu ni narinu   haru no ame

In the spring rain,
The pond and the river
Have become one.

We have here the omnipresence and omnipotence of water; and realize that what seemed three different things, lake, stream, and rain, are intrinsically one.

野分止んで鼠のわたる流かな
Nowaki yande   nezumi no wataru   nagare kana

The autumn storm
Stopped blowing;
A rat swam over the stream.

Though he has not Bashō's mysticism or Issa's humanity,
Buson is not shallow however. It is Nature without God or
man, but not that of science. As so often in Thoreau, Nature
speaks for herself.

古井戸の暗きに落つる椿かな
Furuido no   kuraki ni otsuru   tsubaki kana

A camellia;
It fell into the darkness
Of an old well.

This has something deeply symbolical in it,—but we are not
to think of what, just to be feel it so, and stop there.

岸根行く帆はおそろしき若葉哉
Kishine yuku   ho wa osoroshiki   wakaba kana

Passing the bank,
The sail fearful
The young leaves!

This literal translation of the original shows the way in which
the speed of the boat and the luxuriance of the young leaves
are seen as aspects of one awful energy of nature.

動く葉もなくておそろし夏木立
Ugoku ha mo   nakute osoroshi   natsu kodachi

How awesome!
Not a leaf stirs
In the summer grove!

The feeling seems to belong rather to tropical forests; it
reminds one of W. H. Hudson's stories of South America.

短夜の夜の間にさける牡丹哉
Mijika yo no   yo no ma ni sakeru   botan kana

The short night;
The peony opened
During that time.

In this verse Buson has expressed the power of nature that
can make the great flower bloom in such a short time as the
summer night.

青梅をうてばかつ散る青葉哉
Aoume wo   uteba katsu chiru   aoba kana

> Beating down the green plums,
> As the same time,
> Green leaves fall.

This is a good example of how nothing escapes the eye of the haiku poet, and how this slight accompanying fact of some leaves being knocked down too is perceived as deeply significant of the way in which purpose and accident are mingled in our world.

底見えて魚見えて秋の水深し
Soko miete   uo miete aki no   mizu fukashi

> The bottom seen clearly,
> The fish seen clearly,—
> Deep is the water of autumn.

Not only is the sky of autumn high, the water is deep. These seems to be a double infinity in this season, one above us, one below. Compare the following; the season is summer:

一口に足らぬ清水の尊さよ
Hitokuchi ni   taranu shimizu no   tōtosa yo

> The clear water,
> Not enough for a mouthful,—
> But how wonderful!

Thoreau says: "The shallowest still water is unfathomable."

静かなるかきの木はらや冬の月
Shizuka naru   kaki no ki hara ya   fuyu no tsuki

> How calm
> The persimmon orchard,
> Under the wintry moon!

Dorothy Wordsworth notes in her *Journal*, 24th March, 1798:

> The crooked arm of the old oak-tree points upwards
> to the moon.

立枯の木に蟬鳴きて雲の峯
Tachigare no   ki ni semi nakite   kumo no mine

A tree stands withered,
And on it a cicada crying;
Billowing clouds.

This verse seems to be one of contrast, contrast between the bare, wintry angularity of the tree with the shrill-crying insect, and the softly-swelling clouds that rise up in the summer sky; or perhaps the cicada unites with its hard warmth the tree and the clouds.

卯の花のこぼるる蕗の廣葉哉
U-no-hana no   koboruru fuki no   hiroha kana

The flowers of the *u*
Spill on the broad leaves
Of the bog-rhubarb.

The small, white, snow-like flowers of the *u* fall on the round, dark leaves of the bog-rhubarb.

をし鳥や鼬の覗く池古し
Oshidori ya   itachi no nozoku   ike furushi

Mandarin ducks;
A weasel is peeping
At the old pond.

Compare Shiki's verse, which seems a more homely version:

菊荒れて鶏ねらふ鼬かな
Kiku arete   niwatori nerau   itachi kana

The chrysanthemums withering,
A weasel is watching
The hens.

There are two more verses by Buson that we may give here; the first belongs to summer, the second to spring:

飯ぬすむ狐追ひ打つ麥の秋
Meshi nusumu   kitsune oiutu   mugi no aki

Driving away with blows
A fox stealing the rice;
The autumn of barley.

Everyone is out in the summer fields, and the fox comes to
the kitchen. In the following there is a contrast between the
fine threads of rain and the broad expanse of water, and a
harmony in their mild vagueness:

春雨の中を流るゝ大河かな
Harusame no   naka wo nagaruru   taiga kana

Flowing through the midst
Of the spring rain,
A great river.

3.　In the following verses, the poets are speaking to some
extent of themselves; Onitsura's haiku is well-known:

行水の捨てどころなし蟲の聲
Gyōzui no   sutedokoro nashi   mushi no koe

The bath water,—
Where can I throw it away?
The voices of insects.

The hesitation and at-a-loss-ness of the poet is heightened by
the fact that he cannot see the insects, he can only hear their
sweet voices trilling out from every bush and plant. The im-
material conquers the material, men do not live by bread alone.
There is a waka by Kageki, 景樹, 1768-1843, very similar in
meaning, but more aristocratic in mind-colour:

いづくより駒うち入れむさほ川の
さざれにうつる白菊の花

Whence shall I ride my horse
Into the River Saho?
White chrysanthemums
Are reflected
On the pebbles.

瘦臑の毛に微風あり衣更
Yasezune no   ke ni bifū ari   koromogae

A breeze blowing
On the hairs on thin shanks:
The change of clothes.

This, by Buson, is one of those verses which make us wonder at the delicacy of the poetical mind of the Japanese, and their faith in what is small and insignificant. In *Moby Dick*, Melville says:

> We expand to bulk. To produce a mighty volume you must have a mighty theme. No great and enduring volume can be written on the flea, though many there be who have tried it.

This is true, but it is not the only truth. The hairs on the legs of the man who has put on his new spring clothes has a meaning, a slender rapier-like meaning that is not as big as a barn door,—but 'twill suffice. Toho says:

片花飛減却春。

When one petal flies away, spring is over.

鳥もろとも野に出し我も霞むらん

Tori morotomo   no ni deshi ware mo   kasumuran

Out in the fields
Together with the birds,
I will be surrounded with mist.

Chora walks the fields. He also could say, no doubt,

> Casting the body's vest aside
> My soul into the boughs does glide;
> There like a bird, it sits and sings,
> Then whets and claps its silver wings,

but to say so seems somehow to spoil it. Together with the birds he will be surrounded by the morning mist. That is enough.

大の字に瘦て涼しさよ淋しさよ

Dai no ji ni   nete suzushisa yo   sabishisa yo

Lying with arms and legs outstretched,
How cool,—
How lonely!

When we are alone, we can do as we like, lie as we please; but this is, as Issa says, because we are alone.

世 の 夏 や 湖 水 に う か ぶ 浪 の 上
Yo no natsu ya   kosui ni ukabu   nami no ue

Summer in the world;
Floating on the waves
    Of the lake.

This verse by Bashō reminds us of Thoreau, with his power
of feeling and portraying the present and the past, the near
and the far, in one place, at one moment.

我 死 な ば 墓 守 と な れ き り ぎ り す
Ware shinaba   hakamori to nare   kirigirisu

Grasshopper!
Be the keeper of the grave-yard,
    When I die.

This verse contains everything of Issa, his feeling of imper-
manence, of kinship with other creatures, and the all-pervading
humour. The same may be said of the following, but the
humour is fainter.

生 き て ゐ る ば か り ぞ わ れ と け し の 花
Ikite iru   bakari zo ware to   keshi no hana

Just simply alive,
Both of us, I
    And the poppy.

Issa was the most democratic man (or should one say "bio-
cratic"?) who ever lived. More implicit still is the next verse:

蝶 が 來 て つ れ て 行 き け り 庭 の 蝶
Chō ga kite   tsurete yuki keri   niwa no chō

A butterfly came,
And flew off
    With a butterfly in the garden.

茸 狩 り や 頭 を 擧 ぐ れ ば 峯 の 月
Takegari ya   tō wo agureba   mine no tsuki

Mushroom-hunting;
Raising my head,—
    The moon over the peak.

This verse of Buson, which shows that dusk has fallen unawares, is quite different from Ritaihaku's:

擧頭望山月、低頭思故鄉。

I raise my head, and gaze at the moon over the mountains;
I lower my head, and think of my native place.

Buson's verse simply describes the two worlds, that of minute particulars near the eye, and that of the vast and distant.

こちらむけ我も淋しき秋の暮
Kochira muke   ware mo sabishiki   aki no kure

> Turn this way;
> I also am lonely,
> This evening of autumn.

Unchiku, a monk of Kyōto, seems to have painted a picture of himself with his face turned away, and asked Bashō to write a verse on it. Bashō said, "You are sixty and I nearly fifty already. Both of us, in a dream-world, are portraying a dream. To this (picture of a dream) I add this somniloquy." In this verse we see more strongly than in perhaps any other verse the intense subjectivity of Bashō's mind. Even a few smears of ink on a piece of paper, and he feels our loneliness, our isolation in the sea of life,

> The unplumb'd, salt, estranging sea.

So he begs the monk in the picture not to turn his face from him in the evening twilight.

4. Bashō and Issa are the poets of humanity. The following is by the former:

月代や膝に手をおく宵の内
Tsukishiro ya   hiza ni te wo oku   yoi no uchi

> The moon about to appear,
> All present tonight
> With their hands on their knees.

This is a verse praising the moon through a picture of the poets and moon-lovers who are gathered to gaze at it. The moon has not yet risen, but all are sitting waiting. Bashō glances mildly round, and notices that each man has his hands on his knees, a form of polite deportment. In the hands is seen the minds of those present; in the hands the moon too is seen, the yet invisible moon that whitens the horizon above the dark mountains in the distance. Hardy's *The Oxen* strongly reminds us of Bashō's haiku.

> Christmas Eve, and twelve of the clock.
> "Now they are all on their knees,"
> An elder said as we sat in a flock
> By the embers in hearthside ease.
>
> We pictured the meek mild creatures where
> They dwelt in their strawy pen,
> Nor did it occur to one of us there
> To doubt they were kneeling then.

玉あられ夜たかは月に歸るめり

Tama-arare　yotaka wa tsuki ni　kaerumeri

> Hail-stones on the ground;
> The "night hawks" come back home
> In the moonbeams.

"Night-hawks" were the lowest kind of prostitute in Edo. They appeared after dark carrying straw-mats. Issa is sleeping alone in the cold, and hears them walking by or talking. He also knows what cold and hunger and suffering mean, and the softness of the language he uses, *kaerumeri*, shows his compassionate feeling.

木がくれて茶摘も聞くやほとゝぎす

Kogakurete　chatsumi mo kiku ya　hototogisu

> Do the tea-pickers also,
> Hidden in the bushes,
> Hear the *hototogisu*?

The tea-trees are quite high, and women picking the tea-leaves can hardly be seen, only the towels on their heads, or their faces and hands occasionally visible. The *hototogisu* is singing, and Bashō is thinking, not of himself, but of humanity, of those hardly-to-be-seen workers in the bushes,—are they too entering into their heritage of poetic life as the notes of the *hototogisu* ripple over the field?

傾城の畠見たがるる菫かな
Keisei no   hata mitagaruru   sumire kana

These violets!
How the courtezans must want
To see the spring fields!

The courtezans of Edo were never allowed out of the enclosure.
Ryōto sees a distant connection of grace between the violets
and the women.

五月雨や色紙へぎたる壁の跡
Samidare ya   shikishi hegitaru   kabe no ato

Falling summer rain;
Walls with their remaining
Pictures peeling.

This verse comes in the *Saga Diary*, 1691, being written after
Bashō had looked through each room of a small house for the
Tea-Ceremony, Rakushisha, "falling persimmon hut," built by
Kobori Enshū;[1] it was a temporary residence of Bashō's pupil
Kyorai. On the walls of these rooms were once put paintings
and sketches. Now faded and stained they are seen in the
half-darkness of the summer rains. Bashō and the rain and
the dark, damp rooms with their discoloured walls are indeed
in harmony. The following five verses are by Buson, showing
the humanity of the artist-poet, much greater than usually
supposed:

行く我にとゞまる汝に秋二つ
Yuku ware ni   todomaru nare ni   aki futatsu

I go;
Thou stayest:
Two autumns.

The Japanese has seventeen syllables, the English only eight,
but the whole of life is given here, our meetings, our partings,

[1] Kobori Masakazu, 1579–1647, whose name Enshū, 遠州, is the Chinese
name of Tōtōmi, 遠江, from his name Tōtōmi no Kami. He was famous
in all the arts of Japan.

the world of nature we each live in, different yet the same.

商人に行き違うたる夏野かな
Akindo ni   yukichigōtaru   natsuno kana

The travelling pedlar;
Passing each other
On the summer moor.

Buson here expresses, (by not expressing) that faint feeling of sympathy and respect we have for man in his struggle with heat and weight and loneliness and poverty.

名月やあるじを問へば芋掘に
Meigetsu ya   aruji wo toeba   imohori ni

The harvest moon;
Calling on the master of the house,
He was digging potatoes.

The bright moon, the dark earth, the dully gleaming potatoes, and his friend who is enjoying the moon in the English way, digging the field in the moonlight. A stage lower:

剛力は徒に見過ぎぬ山ざくら
Gōriki wa   tada ni misuginu   yamazakura

The mountain guide
Simply takes no notice
Of the cherry-blossoms.

There is something good in this too, the animal indifference that takes beauty for granted.

病人の駕籠も過ぎける麥の秋
Byōnin no   kago mo sugikeru   mugi no aki

A palanquin passes,
With a sick man in it:
The autumn of barley.

"Barley's autumn" is summer. The farmers are cutting and threshing and stacking the barley; all is bustle and energy and healthy activity in the sunshine. But as the pale, sick man is slowly carried through their midst, they realise that the world is larger and darker than they thought.

涼風や力一杯きりぎりす
Suzukaze ya   chikara ip-pai   kirigirisu

A cool breeze,
The grasshopper singing
With all his might.

What is interesting here is Issa's conscious subjectivity. He attributes his own feeling of coolness to the grasshopper, who sings so joyfully "under some pleasant weed."

5. Examples of romantic verses. The following is by Bashō, whose verses are more various than usually thought:

蝶鳥の知らぬ花あり秋の空
Chō tori no   shiranu hana ari   aki no sora

A flower unknown
To bird and butterfly,—
The sky of autumn.

In *The Story of My Heart*, Richard Jefferies writes:

The rich blue of the unattainable flower of the sky drew my soul towards it, and there it rested, for pure colour is rest of heart.

かぎりある命のひまや秋のくれ
Kagiri aru   inochi no hima ya   aki no kure

Autumn evening:
Life has its limits,
But its moments too of leisure.

We live in time, but also in eternity. This short autumn evening is for Buson one of these moments, moments of vision, "spots of time" Wordsworth calls them.

Now chiefly is my natal hour,
And only now my prime of life.
I will not doubt the love untold,
Which not my worth nor want has bought,
Which wooed me young and woos me old,
And to this evening hath me brought.[1]

[1] Thoreau.

蘭 の 香 や 蝶 の つ ば さ に 薫 さ す
Ran no ka ya   chō no tsubasa ni   kaori-sasu

> The butterfly is perfuming
> Its wings, in the scent
> Of the orchid.

This verse was composed by Bashō in response to a request by a Miss Butterfly of a tea-house he stopped at on the way back from visiting Ise Shrine. It was once the custom of ladies of high rank to perfume their clothes in the smoke of certain scented trees such as sandal-wood.

聲 か れ て 猿 の 歯 白 し 峯 の 月
Koe karete   saru no ha shiroshi   mine no tsuki

> Its voice hoarsening,
> The white teeth of the monkey,
> In the moon over the peak.

This was written by Kikaku about a place in China, Hakō, 巴 江, famous for its screaming monkeys. Its romantic, "poetical" flavour may be contrasted with Bashō's homely, everyday verse:

鹽 鯛 の 歯 ぐ き も 寒 し 魚 の 店
Shiodai no   haguki mo samushi   uo no tana

> In the fish-shop,
> The gums of the salt bream
> Look cold.

In the next example, however, Bashō is once more romantic:

月 い づ こ 鐘 は 沈 み て 海 の 底
Tsuki izuko   kane wa shizumite   umi no soko

> Where is the moon?
> The bell is sunk
> At the bottom of the sea.

This was written on the fifteenth of the month, at the time of the full moon, when it was obscured by rain, at Tsuruga. The host told them that there was a story that in the sea a temple bell had sunk and that it could not be raised because it had sunk upside down. Bashō uses this legend, found in various parts of the world, to bring out the unseen beauty and mystery of the moon in the poetical mind.

戀ひ死なば我塚でなけほとゝぎす
Koi-shinaba   waga tsuka de nake   hototogisu

Should I die of love,
O *hototogisu*,
Cry at my tomb!

This verse is well-known from its being written by a woman, Ōshu, said to have been a courtezan of the Yoshiwara in Edo. There is something Elizabethan about it, reminding one of

Come away, come away death,

and other lyrics. This haiku belongs to the world of the mind rather than that of the body, and is about to bid adieu to the real, the poetical world, but with such a pang as moves us in spite of ourselves.

Enough examples have been given perhaps to show that haiku are infinitely varied within their very limited scope. Somehow or other, when we read them, all the important things they omit, sex, war, and the struggle for existence generally, do not seem to matter quite so much after all. There is a repose, a serenity about them which makes the tragedies of life and art seem somewhat hysterical, somewhat vulgar.

To conclude this over-long preface, I would like to say something about the translation of haiku into English, taking as an example the most famous of all, Bashō's *Furu-ike ya kawazu tobikomu mizu no oto.* This was translated in Volume 2, page 540, as follows:

The old pond;
A frog jumps in,—
The sound of the water.

The three-line translation used in these volumes obscures something fundamental in the originals, something that belongs to the Japanese mind, the Japanese language and the literature it produced and which produced it. We see it in linked poems, in the puns of the language of Nō, in the empty spaces of pictures, the absence of things in rooms, the silences of conversation. This "something" is a certain continuity, a lack of

division, a feeling of the whole when dealing with the parts.
In the present haiku, the first line, that is, the first five
syllables are "end-stopped" by the particle *ya*, which we can
represent only by a semicolon, since "ah" is sentimental, "yes"
too much like smacking the lips, and an exclamation mark just
ridiculous. But the second and third lines, that is, the middle
seven and final five syllables, may either be divided, as in the
above translation, or taken continuously. The verb *tobikomu*,
"jumps in," has also an adjectival function, qualifying *oto*,
"sound," thus meaning, "the water jumped into by a frog."
We may therefore translate the verse as follows:

> The old pond;
> The sound
> Of a frog jumping into the water.

But besides looking a bit odd, this translation, though undoubt-
edly nearer to the original than the former one, isolates the
sound from the rest of the elements of the experience and
makes it subsidiary to them. A point of interest and importance
is whether the verse is one of sound only, or of sight and
sound. Did Bashō see the frog jump in, and hear the sound
of the water? This seems rather matter-of-fact. Did he hear
the sound, and deduce the frog from past experience, or a
balance of probabilities? This is too rational and logical. Ba-
shō's real, that is, ideal experience must have been that re-
presented by the following:

> The old pond;
> The-sound-of-a-frog-jumping-into-the-water.

But even this is too exact, too definite, too much of a complete
and grammatical whole. The original haiku is more fragmen-
tary; it is indeed just a link or two of what Pater calls "the
great chain wherewith we are bound."
This fourth volume concludes an anthology of what seem to
me to be the best haiku from the beginnings to Shiki. In a
supplementary volume I wish to bring together in the same
way all the finest haiku that have been written since Shiki,
(died 1902,) up to the present time. I must "testify" in con-
clusion that haiku, together with the music of Bach and Chinese

paintings, have given me the greatest, purest, and most constant pleasure of my life.

R. H. BLYTH,
Tōkyō, 3 Dec. 1951

秋
AUTUMN
(Continued)

地 理 FIELDS AND MOUNTAINS

夕晴や浅黄に並ぶ秋の山　　　　　　　　　　　一 茶
Yūbare ya　asagi ni narabu　aki no yama

Clearing up in the evening;
In the pale blue sky,
　　　Row upon row of autumn mountains. Issa

This, for Issa, is an unusually objective verse. Not only Issa
but no other person, nothing human, is present here. It is
nature as it was before the advent of man, as it will be when
man has disappeared from the face of the earth.

立去る事一里眉毛に秋の峰寒し　　　　　　　蕪 村
Tachisaru koto ichiri　mayuge ni aki no　mine samushi

One league away,
And to the eyebrows
　　　The autumn peaks are cold. Buson

This has the postscript Myōgisan, 妙義山, a mountain of three
peaks in Gumma Prefecture. Buson is walking away from the
mountain. When he has reached a point about three miles
from the foot, he looks back and up, and the cold autumn
breeze strikes his hot forehead. He feels the coldness of the
distant mountain with his eyebrows. They are the link between
him and the heights far away.

Buson has several verses in which hairs play an important
part. Another example, besides that on page 999:

しら露やさつ男の胸毛ぬるゝほど
Shiratsuyu ya　satsuo no munage　nururu hodo

The white dew,—
Enough to wet the hair
　　　On the chest of the hunter.

家二つ戸の口見えて秋の山   道 彦
Ie futatsu   to no kuchi miete   aki no yama

Two houses,
The doors are open:
The autumn mountains.   Michihiko

These two black, mouth-like open doors have some strange meaning. There are invisible existences which enter and come out of them, though not a soul is to be seen, not a sound is heard.

秋の山ところどころに煙立つ   曉 臺
Aki no yama   tokorodokoro ni   kemuri tatsu

The autumn mountains;
Here and there
Smoke rising.   Gyōdai

This is of an extreme simplicity but combines with it a sense of mystery in the unportrayed details. The smoke, of that mysterious blue that Spengler would call Faustian, rises from unknown depths of mountain valleys to unknown heights of autumn sky. One cannot help recalling a water-colour by Turner, called The Crook of the Wye.

野路の秋我がうしろより人や來る   蕪 村
Noji no aki   waga ushiro yori   hito ya kuru

The road over the autumn moor:
Someone is coming along
Behind me!   Buson

It is interesting to compare this to a verse from *The Ancient Mariner*, Part VI:

> Like one that on a lonesome road
> Doth walk in fear and dread,
> And having once turned round, walks on
> And no more turns his head,
> Because he knows a frightful fiend
> Doth close behind him tread.

Coleridge's verse expresses the exceptional occurrence which is the foundation from which arises the general state of mind portrayed in Buson's poem. We are always surrounded by a multitude of witnesses, sometimes frightful, but there is always something, if only Time's chariot, hurrying near.

人に逢ひて恐ろしくなりぬ秋の山　　　子 規
Hito ni aite　osoroshiku narinu　aki no yama

Meeting someone,—
How fearsome
The autumn mountains!　　　Shiki

When we are alone with nature, that is, nature of the temperate Zones, we feel something lacking, but when a man, unknown and questionable, is seen passing by, the whole mountain is full of the evil influences which emanate from the mind of man alone. Man is the most ferocious of all the animals, man is the measure, the limit, the beginning and the end of all things. Mountains are in themselves only lumps of earth and stone; it is the mind of man, of this man, which makes them teachers, comforters, monsters, enemies.

Another interesting point is the fact that it is the mountains of *autumn* that cause this vague feeling of apprehension on his meeting with someone among them. It is perhaps the receding of life that we feel also within ourselves. There is something in the ebb, the evening of the year that disturbs us. The mountains are so silent the heart is constricted with something like fear.

門を出て十歩に秋の海廣し　　　子 規
Mon wo dete　juppo ni aki no　umi hiroshi

Going out of the house,
Ten paces,—
And the vast autumn sea.　　　Shiki

The ocean often looks boundless, and especially so in autumn, when not even a far-off swell lessens the distance of the horizon. But what strikes Shiki is the contrast between the expanse of

sea and the few paces he makes to survey it. At one moment
the four walls of a small room. A moment or two after, and
the whole scene of the illimitable ocean pervades the mind.

村々の寝ごゝろ更ぬ落し水 蕪 村
Mura mura no negokoro fukenu otoshimizu

In every village,
Sleep grows deeper;
Falling water. Buson

The rice is ripening and the surplus water is being run off
from the rice-fields. The farmers feel relieved for the moment.
"Grows deeper" contains two ideas, that of sounder sleep, and
the passing of time. It is midnight, and Buson listens to the
trickling sound of the water which has a lulling effect on the
mind, as though it were making sounder the sleep of the
villages. The meaning of the sound of the falling water is not
that of Keats'

The poetry of earth is never dead.

It is far deeper, less intellectual, neither explanatory nor ex-
plicable.

田に落ちて田を落ち行くや秋の水 蕪 村
Ta ni ochite ta wo ochiyuku ya aki no mizu

Falling into the fields,
Falling from the fields,
The water of autumn. Buson

This is what a haiku should be, perfectly clear without any
admixture of intellectual elements. At the end of autumn,
after the rice has been reaped, the water is run off from each
field into the next until it is all gone. This water, which you
may think is merely water, is not. It is the water of autumn.
Contrast this with a verse on the same subject by the same poet:

落し水田毎の暗となりにけり
Otoshimizu   tagoto no yami to   narinikeri

The water run off
Becomes the darkness
Of each field.

This is obscure and intellectual. It is a kind of poetical
thinking, a semi-verbal mysticism. At night, the shining ex-
panse of water in each field becomes the black mud, that is,
the water of light becomes the field of darkness.

神 佛 GODS AND BUDDHAS

まざまざといますが如し魂祭   季 吟
Mazamaza to imasu ga gotoshi tama-matsuri

Vividly present,
As though here before us,
The Feast of All Souls.   Kigin

This is an echo of *The Analects*, 3, 12:

祭如在、祭神如神在。子曰、吾不與祭、如不祭。

He sacrificed as if they were present; he sacrificed to
the spirits as if they were there. Confucius said; "If I am
not myself present at the sacrificing, it is the same as not
sacrificing at all."

The Feast of All Souls is from July 7 to July 16. In every
house the *tamadana*, literally, "spirit-shelf," is set out with
various symbolical offerings, and the spirits of the dead in that
household are comforted with a ceremony, reading of sutras,
etc. The common Japanese expression for All Soul's Day, *O
Bon*, お盆, is an abbreviation of *Ullambana*, 盂蘭盆. The masses
said for the sake of souls in purgatory are first heard of in the
6th Century A.D., and are of course opposed to the general
teaching and spirit of Hinayana Buddhism of the primitive type.
The official attitude of Zen is hard to get at; unofficially, it is
agnostic in theory and orthodox in practice. Its attitude might
be better described as the poetic one with which we are to
read the present verse. Christ also tells us,

God is not the God of the dead, but of the living, for unto
him all live.

魂祭けふも焼場のけぶりかな   芭 蕉
Tama-matsuri kyō mo yakiba no keburi kana

The Feast of All Souls;
Today also arises smoke
From the burning-ground.   Bashō

Today is the Festival of the Dead, but even today brown smoke is rising from the crematorium out in the fields, away from the town. This verse is rather intellectual, not so much in content as in the relations of the ideas; poetry transcends these cause-and-effect, is-or-is-not ideas. Also, Bashō seems to have remembered a passage from the *Tsurezuregusa*:

> あだし野の露消ゆる時なく、鳥邊山のけぶり立ち
> さらでのみ住み果つるならひならば、いかに物の
> 哀もなからん、世は定めなきこそいみじけれ

If human beings did not disappear like the dews of Adashino, if they did not vanish like the smoke of Toribeyama, how could there be any pathetic beauty? How good the changeableness of the things of the world!

> 蓮池やをらで其まま玉まつり　　　　　芭 蕉
> *Hasu-ike ya　orade sono mama　tama-matsuri*

The lotus pond;[1]
Just as they are, unplucked,
For the Feast of All Souls.　　　Bashō

Instead of picking the lotus flowers, and placing them on the altar, Bashō wishes to leave them where they are in the small pool as offerings to the spirits of the dead. He may have remembered a waka by the Empress Kōmyō:[2]

> 折りつればたぶさに汚るたてながら
> 三世の佛に花たてまつる

Should I pluck it,
My hands
Would defile the flower;
I offer it, as it stands,
To the Buddhas of the Three Worlds.

---

[1] Lotuses belong really to summer.
[2] 701–760. She personally washed one thousand beggars.

魂棚は露も涙も油かな   嵐 雪
Tama-dana wa   tsuyu mo namida mo   abura kana

The table of the spirits;
Dew, and tears,
These are the oil.   Ransetsu

These three things are thrown together in this verse in the same indifferent, half-accidental way that they are in fact. The dew is the dew on the flowers that are offered. The tears are those for near and dear children and fathers and mothers that have died not long ago. The oil is in the lamps that are lit to console the spirits of the dead.

魂棚をほどけばもとの座敷哉   蕪 村
Tama-dana wo   hodokeba moto no   zashiki kana

The table of the spirits;
Taking it down,
The same room as before.   Buson

At the time of the Festival of the Dead, a shelf is put up in front of the Buddhist altar, and on it various offerings to the spirits of the dead are made. At this time an ordinary room becomes a kind of Buddhist chapel, and everything done in it is done in a kind of religious atmosphere. When the shelf is taken down again, everything relapses into the normal again, and we realize, with a shock, what a simple room really is.

秋來ぬと知らぬ狗が佛かな   一 茶
Aki kinu to   shiranu koinu ga   hotoke kana

The puppy that knows not
That autumn has come,
Is a Buddha   Issa

This is Issa's poetical version of the 1st Case of the *Mumon-kan*; it has the prescript:

狗子有佛生,[1]

"The dog has the Buddha nature." The puppy even more than the mature dog takes each day, each moment, as it comes. It does not

> look before and after
> And pine for what is not.

When it is warm, it basks in the sun; when it rains, it whimpers to be let in. There is nothing between the sun and the puppy, the rain and the whimper.

　　　　玉棚や上座して鳴くきりぎりす　　　　一　茶
　　　　Tama-dana ya　jōza shite naku　kirigirisu

> At the altar,
> In the chief place,
> Cries a cricket.　　　　　　　　　Issa

The *tamadana*, more correctly written 魂棚, is a kind of shelf put up in front of the Buddhist altar at the time of the Ullabon, All Souls' Day. Rush matting is spread upon it and various herbs of autumn consecrated there.

By chance, a cricket has hopped in, and, occupying the place of honour, is chirping quietly to himself. Issa knew that the crying of crickets and the chirping of men are the same: he also knew that they are different. It is in this region of the sameness of difference, this different sameness, that religion and poetry lie.

　　　　稲積んで地蔵わびしや道の端　　　　子　規
　　　　Ine tsunde　jizō wabishi ya　michi no hata

> The rice being stacked up by him,
> *Jizō* looks forlorn
> At the side of road.　　　　　　　Shiki

While the rice was standing in the field, Jizō in his shrine

[1] This should be 性.

at the side of the road looked complacent, as befitted a patron of the life of the people. Now that the rice has been reaped and piled up, leaving bare and desolate fields, Jizō also looks neglected and wretched, perhaps a little uncomfortable.

人 事 HUMAN AFFAIRS

梶の葉を朗詠集のしほり哉　　　　　　　蕪 村
Kaji no ha wo   rōeishū no   shiori kana

The leaf of the *kaji*-tree,
As a book-mark
In the *Rōeishū*.　　　　　　　　　　　Buson

This has the prescript 七夕, Tanabata, Seventh Night. On the sixth day of the Seventh Month, hawkers went round the streets selling leaves of the *kaji*-tree, a species of mulberry. The next day, seven leaves were taken and poems written on them as offerings. Another name for the star Shokujo (there are seven names) is 梶葉姫, "Kaji Leaf Princess."

The *Rōeishū*,[1] an anthology of Japanese and Chinese poetry arranged in seasonal order, was formed during the Heian Era, 794–858. There is a section in it devoted to the Tanabata, and it is possible that the leaf of the *kaji*-tree was used to mark this place in the book. Anyway, it is clear that Buson used the leaf, on which was probably written some verse or other, to mark the place where he was reading. There is a subtle pleasure in marking with a leaf those poetical words which deal with mountains and rivers and leafy trees. It is as if one were marking the poem with the thing itself, the subject of the verse. And the leaf of a *kaji*-tree, with its poetic and human relations, the *Rōeishū*, so well-thumbed,—these have overtones of meaning which we can hardly realize. Compare a modern verse, by Kyoshi:

七夕の歌書く人に寄り添ひぬ
Tanabata no   uta kaku hito ni   yorisoinu

The Festival of the Weaver;
One is writing a poem,
The other leans towards him.

This is as charming as something from the *Tale of Genji*. One of the two people, the man probably, is writing a poem, a *waka*. The other, a woman, leans towards him watching the

[1] See Vol. 1, pages 103–4.

brush move down the paper. The appropriateness of the first line, "The Festival of the Weaver," is perhaps a little overdone, but not according to Japanese ideas, since every season and festival has its fixed observance. The following is the story connected with the *Tanabata*.

The daughter of the Master of Heaven, 天帝, lived East of the Milky Way, 天の川, and passed her time weaving cloth, whence the name of 織女, weaver, which was given to her. Her father chose a husband for her in the person of Kengyū, 牽牛, (herdsman) who ruled on the other side of the Milky Way. But their honeymoon lasted so long that the young couple neglected work altogether. The Master of Heaven condemned them to be separated. They were allowed to see each other only once a year, on the 7th night of the 7th month, and when the time arrived a raven extended its wings over the Milky Way to enable them to meet. This feast is especially kept by young girls who ask the Weaver Star to make them as skilful as she was in the art of sewing, and perhaps also, one day to be united to a husband as faithful as Kengyū. According to popular belief, the petitions made on this day are sure to be fulfilled in a space of less than three years. This feast is also called 乞巧奠, *Kikōten*, and was celebrated for the first time in the Imperial Palace in the year 755 A.D., whence it gradually spread over the whole country. It is one of the Five Fête Days, 五節句.

戀さまざま願の絲も白きより　　　　蕪 村
Koi samazama　negai no ito mo　shiroki yori

All kinds of love;
The petitioning threads
Were white at first.　　　Buson

This verse also belongs to the Tanabata festival. Besides the verses written on the leaves of the *kaji*-tree, there are offered up variously coloured threads. It is women especially who keep this festival, and their petitions are usually for a certain man as their lover or husband. Their feelings, their states of mind are of various kinds, corresponding to the different colours of the threads, but the threads, like the minds

of the women, are originally white, simple and pure. Buson
is probably thinking of the *Tsurezuregusa*, 26, where there is
a reference to Motsu, 墨子, who said, "when I see white threads
I weep, because they can be made yellow or black," 見練絲而
泣之, 爲其可以黄可以黑. This verse is allusive and fanciful, with
a kind of tenderness, a grief for lost innocence far away behind
it, that fits the feminine subject and the myth it is based on.

もうもうと牛なく星の別れかな　　　　子 規
Mō mō to　ushi naku hoshi no　wakare kana

The cow goes
Moo! Moo!—
The parting of the stars.　　　Shiki

This also is a fanciful verse, yet it has some effect in bringing
out the meaning of the lowing of the cow. The relation between
the voice of the cow and the parting of the star lies of course
in the fact that one of them is the herdsman. The lowing of
the cow seems to have the same function here as the crowing
of the cock in the case of ghosts.

燈籠をともして留守の小家かな　　　　子 規
Tōrō wo　tomoshite rusu no　koie kana

Having lit the garden lantern,
The people of the small house
Have gone out.　　　Shiki

As he walks by the house, the poet notices that all is dark
within; the occupants are absent. But in the lantern in the
small garden a light is burning, shedding its beams and shadows
on the winding stepping-stones, the shrubs and small trees. In
the small yellow light is shown the will of man to persist in
spite of change. But more deeply, it shows the indifference of
things to other things. The light will burn, sink, gutter and
go out whether the human beings who lighted it return or
not. It burns for itself, just as the Thames for Wordsworth
glided "at its own sweet will."

燈籠消えて芭蕉に風のわたる音　　　　子規
Tōrō kiete   bashō ni kaze no   wataru oto

The lantern having gone out,—
The sound of the wind
Passing through the *bashō*.　　　Shiki

Just as when the sun is obscured for a moment by a cloud
the wind seems to blow more chill, so when the light of the
garden-lantern goes out, the soughing of the wind in the broad
leaves of the banana plant seems to grow louder and more
melancholy. (See also page 1105.)

縁はなや二文花火も夜の體　　　　　一茶
En hana ya   nimon hanabi mo   yoru no tei

On the edge of the verandah,
A penn'orth of fireworks also,
Gives the feeling of night.　　　Issa

Issa has bought a few fireworks to please his wife and family,
and they all sit on the verandah watching the feeble spluttering
things with bated breath and eyes as big as saucers. The
brightness of the fireworks brings out, somehow or other, the
meaning of the darkness.

人かへる花火のあとの暗きかな　　　子規
Hito kaeru   hanabi no ato no   kuraki kana

The fireworks over,
The people all gone,—
How dark it is!　　　Shiki

This is no mere psychological observation. The darkness
was felt by the poet in a physical way. We may explain the
matter as a physiological reaction, but what Shiki is telling us
is something about the absence of two things and the presence
of one as a unity of deep experience.

There is a verse by Shōha, who died in 1771, that Shiki may
have remembered:

花火船遊人去つて秋の水
Hanabibune   yūjin satte   aki no mizu

In a boat seeing the fireworks;
When the spectators had gone,—
The water of autumn.

To see the darkness of the water, the fireworks were necessary.
To see the meaning of the water of autumn, its loneliness and
inevitability, its silence, the sightseers were necessary. Water
has all the seasons in it; and in solitude when all have departed
we see it under the aspect of autumn.

淋しさや花火のあとの星の飛ぶ   子 規
Sabishisa ya   hanabi no ato no   hoshi no tobu

Loneliness;
After the fireworks,
A falling star.   Shiki

The "loneliness" that Shiki speaks of here is a feeling, a
weltschmerz, a cosmic emotion that is at the back of most great
poetry and much great literature, but unnamed in the English
language. This "loneliness" denotes an unnameable state of
mind that has only a distant and biological connection with
feeling lonesome and wanting someone to talk to. The falling
star that glides so silently across the autumn sky, without
meaning, without object, gives us the feeling of nature as
opposed to that of man. Instead of the fireworks with their
many-coloured lights, we have a single faintly curved, faintly
bluish line of light. It is

The night in its silence,
The stars in their calm.

The real meaning of "calmness" here and that of *sabishisa* is
the same.

炭竈に手負の猪の倒れけり   凡 兆
Sumigama ni   teoi no shishi no   taorekeri

A wounded boar
Fell down
By the charcoal kiln.   Bonchō

This subject is a very unusual one for haiku, which avoids
anything vast, anything violent or heartrending. Shot by some
hunter, the great animal plunges out of the thicket, seeks
shelter beside the charcoal-kiln, stumbles and falls. Charcoal-
kilns are usually found in the recesses of deep mountains, and
here we have that always impressive combination of nature,
living creatures, and the works of man.

一家みな[1]白髪に杖や墓参り   芭 蕉
Ikka mina   shiraga ni tsue ya   haka-mairi

All the family visiting the graves,
White-haired,
And leaning on their sticks.   Bashō

Graves are visited and flowers offered in the Seventh Month,
between the 13th and 15th. As the group walk along, we
notice that most of them are aged, grey-haired, and using
sticks. Even while we go to the grave of others we move
towards our own. In the womb or in the grave, in this life
or in any other, piety never leaves us. It is not something for
the young and not for the old:

Truly thy goodness and mercy shall follow me all the
days of my life.

In the following verse, by Issa, we have the same picture but
with the interest focussed on the other end of human life:

末の子や御墓参りの箒持
Sue no ko ya   ohaka mairi no   hōki-mochi

Visiting the graves;
The youngest child
Carries the broom.

[1] Another form is 家はみな.

Another of Issa's goes further and deeper still, by bringing in the lower creation:

古犬が先に立つなり墓参り
Furu-inu ga   saki ni tatsu nari   haka-mairi

Visiting the graves;
The old dog
Leads the way.

There is something deeply pathetic in the unknowing knowledge of the old dog. We feel, by inference, the shallowness of our own understanding of the meaning of life and death. The dog's attitude towards the visit to the graves is not far from that expressed in another verse by Issa:

月影にうかれ序や墓参
Tsukikage ni   ukare tsuide ya   haka-mairi

Carried away by the moonlight!
Incidentally
Visiting the graves.

聲聞けば古き男や音頭取   太 祇
Koe kikeba   furuki otoko ya   ondo-tori

Listening to the voice
Of the leader of the singing,—
He was an old-timer.   Taigi

The old man's voice takes us back to the past. We feel, without knowing it, the past is present, and the present is future. It is timeless, and yet it is a thing of this moment. Besides this, we see in the voice of the leader, his wrinkled, leathery face. It is like the House that Jack built. In his voice, we see his past life; in his past life, we feel what Arnold describes in *Resignation*:

Before him he sees life unroll,
A placid and continuous whole;
That life, whose dumb wish is not miss'd
If birth proceeds, if things subsist.

なまぐさき漁村の月の踊かな   子 規
Namagusaki gyoson no tsuki no   odori kana

A fishing village;
Dancing under the moon
   To the smell of raw fish.   Shiki

When we read this verse, we may feel a tendency towards
cynicism, and check this with some philosophic thoughts con-
cerning human life being composed of two elements, the real
and the ideal, the mundane and the beautiful, fish-guts and
moonlight. But neither of these states of mind, the emotional
and the intellectual, has anything to do with this verse. It is
to be read with a kind of "blank" mind in which the intellect
is subsumed and the emotions universalized. There is dancing
and there is the smell of fish; the dancing in the moonlight
is "poetical", and the smell of raw fish is disagreeable and
"unpoetical", but both are as they are, that is, poetical, because
they are seen so.

一長屋錠をおろして踊哉   其 角
Hito-nagaya jō wo oroshite   odori kana

The whole tenement house,
Having locked their doors,
   Are dancing and dancing.   Kikaku

There is an unmentioned contrast between the dark, shadowy,
silent hovel, and men, women and children dancing in the
bright moonlight. They dance because they must:

To tunes we did not call, our being must keep chime.[1]

四五人に月落ちかゝる踊かな   蕪 村
Shi go nin ni   tsuki ochikakaru   odori kana

The moon beginning to fall
On four or five people,
   Dancing!   Buson

[1] Arnold, *Empedocles on Etna.*

A great many people, men and women, have been dancing since dusk, but the moon declines, time goes on, and one by one the dancers leave for home. Now the moon, increasing in size and deepening in colour, hangs upon the horizon. Only four or five people are left still unsatisfied in their dancing. They take upon themselves something unearthly, something immortal, eternal. The last line reminds one of Cory's *Heraclitus*:

> I remembered how often you and I
> Had tired the sun with talking, and sent him down the sky.

Buson's verse has the prescript: 英一蝶が畫に賛望されて. "Being asked to write a verse for a picture by Hanabusa Itchō." (A celebrated painter, 1652–1724, a friend of Bashō and Kikaku.) The picture must have represented several people dancing.

盆踊あとは松風蟲の聲   素月尼
Bonodori ato wa matsukaze   mushi no koe

After the dancing,
The wind in the pine-trees,
The voices of insects.   Sogetsu-ni

We oscillate between man and Nature, and it is right that we should do so, for we belong to both. On the one hand we may say that man is everything and Nature is nothing, but this is false in experience and false in theory. Though Buddhism teaches that without man there are no things, it is also true to say that without things there are no men. And so the poet, after he has seen and heard the dancers, their songs and rhythms, listens to the quieter sounds and pulsations of nature, and finds something deeper in them.

追剝を弟子に剃りけり秋の旅   蕪 村
Oihagi wo   deshi ni sorikeri   aki no tabi

He tonsured the highwayman,
And made him his disciple,
On a journey in autumn.   Buson

There are many stories of such incidents both in China and Japan. One form is the following: A robber met a high priest in a deserted spot and demanded everything he had. The priest gave all willingly, all but the Buddhist robe he was wearing. This alone he firmly declined, and when threatened with death, calmly stretched out his neck to receive the sword. The robber, knowing the meaning and value of courage, was overcome with remorse, and falling on his knees, begged to be admitted to the Buddhist life. The priest, realising the depth of his en-lightenment, made him a monk and shaved his head.

Poetically speaking, the interesting point is Buson's choice of the season for this incident. Spring might at first sight seem a suitable time in which to place the rebirth of a soul, but it is autumn, the season when we feel most deeply the transitoriness of things, that leads us to the painful serenity of the life of truth.

聲すみて北斗に響く砧かな   芭 蕉
Koe sumite   hokuto ni hibiku   kinuta kana

The clear voice
Of the fulling-block echoes up
To the Northern Stars.   Bashō

Thoreau, listening to a similar sound, the thud of the oars, felt the same relation to the stars of the sky,

a sort of rudimental music suitable for the ear of night, and the acoustics of her dimly lighted halls;

Pulsae referunt ad sidera valles,

And the valleys echoed the sound to the stars.

Both Thoreau and Bashō have that remarkable objective-sub-jective quality that is not a mixture of the two. The mind that composed Bashō's verse and the passage from Thoreau, is that which Ikkyū speaks of in one of his *Songs of the Way*, 道歌:

心とは　いかなるものを　いふやらん
すみ繪にかきし　松風の音

　　The mind,—
　What shall we call it?
　　It is the sound of the breeze
　That blows through the pines
　In the indian ink picture.

小路ゆけば遠く聞ゆる砧かな　　　　　　　　蕪　村
Koji yukeba tōku kikoyuru kinuta kana

　Walking along the narrow path,
Listening to the far-off
　　Fulling-block.   Buson

　　Distance is that through which we realize infinity. Infinite
space is unknowable as such, in fact, does not exist as such,
for us. The infinite and the finite are mutually dependent.
Without the whole there would be no part; without the part
there would be no whole. There is no apparent reason, other
than the constitution of our minds, why great distances should
lend themselves especially to the perception of infinity, but it
is so, and as an artist, Buson felt the open spaces of his canvas
to be of greater meaning, of quite other meaning, than those
that he filled in. That space between the fulling-block and the
listener, only perceptible in the clear ringing sound of the
mallet, stands for the otherwise non-existent infinite. Other
verses of his which show this continual nostalgia for something
which we have not only never experienced but in itself has no
reality (the essence of all poetry and religion), are the following:

落葉に遠くなりけり臼の音
Rakuyō ni tōku narikeri usu no oto

　　The leaves having fallen,
　The hand-mill sounds
　　　Far off.

待人の足音遠き落葉かな
Machibito no ashioto tōki ochiba kana

　　The longed-for footsteps
　Are distant,
　　　On the fallen leaves.

閑に座して遠き蛙を聞夜かな
Kaku ni zashite   tōki kawazu wo   kiku yo kana

> Seated in the palace,
> Listening at night
> To the distant frogs.

留守もりの鶯遠く聞く日かな
Rusumori no   uguisu tōku   kiku hi kana

> Left in charge of the house all day,
> Listening to the *uguisu,*
> Afar off.

憂我にきぬたうて今はまた止ミね   蕪 村
Uki ware ni   kinuta ute ima wa   mata yamine

> Beat the fulling-block for me,
> In my loneliness;
> Now again let it cease.   Buson

It is late evening. The sound of the fulling-block increases
the poet's feeling of the value of life, its meaningless meaning,
until he begins, in a vague way, to wish the hollow, echoing
sound to stop. It ceases, and the current of his life moves
once more at its wonted pace. There is in life, in experience,
in poetry, a certain limit of human endurance, both in time
and intensity, beyond which our mortal nature does not allow
us to go.

一つ家に泣聲まじる砧かな   子 規
Hitotsuya ni   nakigoe majiru   kinuta kana

> In one house,
> A voice of weeping,
> The sound of the fulling-block.   Shiki

Who is it that weeps, and why? For what reason does the
beating of the fulling-block continue in spite of the voice raised
in tears? Grief and woe, with the ordinary things of life going
on all the time,—this is human existence, and it is heard in
the mingling of wailing and rythmic beating of the mallet,

heard directly without moralizing, heard not with the head,
but with the belly, with "bowels of compassion."

寝よといふ寝覺の夫や小夜砧   太　祇
Neyo to iu   nezame no tsuma ya   sayo-ginuta

"Why not come to bed?"
The husband, awakening, says:
　　The sound of the fulling-mallet in the night.
　　　　　　　　　　　　　　　　　　　　　　Taigi

　　The wife is working late at night, perhaps at needlework.
Her husband, tired out, has been asleep some time, and waking,
says to her compassionately, "Come to bed, and get some sleep."
At this moment, through the night comes the sound of the
fulling-mallet, bringing the eternal note of sadness in.

猿引は猿の小袖を砧かな   芭　蕉
Saruhiki wa   saru no kosode wo   kinuta kana

The monkey showman
Beats the tiny jacket
　　On the fulling-block.   Bashō

　　This verse is of course half-fanciful. Bashō imagines that
the man looks upon the monkey as his own child, and in the
autumn evening will sit "ironing" the monkey's clothes.

よの中は稲かる頃か草の庵   芭　蕉
Yo no naka wa   inekaru koro ka   kusa no io

My thatched hut;
In the world outside
　　It is harvest time?   Bashō

　　The life of retirement is one way of living, and it is not
perhaps wise to attempt too many modes of existence. Bashō
looks out and sees the farmers cutting the rice. Under their
hands the whole aspect of the scene is changing. As a result
of their work, the world is fed. What has the poet to offer?

He is to give meaning to their work by his all-embracing, life-giving gaze over their activities from the door of his thatched cottage. Emerson says in *The Apology*:

> Tax not my sloth that I
> Fold my hands beside the brook.

落穂拾ひ日あたる方へあゆみ行   蕪　村
Ochibohiroi hiataru hō e   ayumiyuku

Gleaning the fallen ears,
Moving towards
The sunny part.   Buson

This is a simple picture of rural life, of poor people, in the style of Millet. A woman and her children are picking up the ears of rice that have remained. The mother puts them in her apron; the youngest child is picking flowers. They move unconsciously towards that part of the field not in the shade, for it is the end of autumn and the wind is cold. As Meisetsu the best of Japanese commentators says, we are not to take this too heavily. It is not a picture of poverty, but of poor people, a reaped field, the sun low in the sky. As contrasted with the grinding poverty of *The Man with a Hoe*, the atmosphere of humanity overwhelmed with toil and privation, we have the softness of the Japanese scene, conveyed through the echo of the sounds *hiroi, hiataru; ataru, ayumi*.

道くだり拾ひあつめて案山子かな   桃　隣
Michikudari hiroi atsumete kakashi kana

Picked up on a pilgrimage
And put together,—
The scarecrow.   Tōrin

This describes the nature, not the origin of the scarecrow. Like so many haiku, this has the appearance of causality, but the relation is a poetic, not a scientific one.

拵へし時から古きかゝしかな   如 風
Koshiraeshi toki kara furuki kakashi kana

From the day it is made,
It is ancient,—
   The scarecrow.   Nyofū

The scarecrow knows no youth; it is born old. A broken
kasa, an old stick taken from a fallen fence, some tattered
garment or other,—from such things it is made, and is an old
man from the day it begins to keep away the birds from the
field. It is at heart a melancholy object, and we feel in it the
faded sadness of things; Chigetsu-ni says:

蛬なくや案山子の袖の中
Kirigirisu naku ya kakashi no sode no naka

   A grasshopper is chirping
In the sleeves
   Of the scarecrow.

吾行けば共に歩みぬ遠案山子   三 允
Ware yukeba tomo ni ayuminu tō-kakashi

The scarecrow in the distance;
It walked with me
   As I walked.   San-in

This is a kind of illusion,—and yet the best are but shadows.
Men are trees walking, and a scarecrow is a good companion.
The verse also implies what it does not say, that when the
poet stopped still, the scarecrow also stopped still. (San-in is a
modern poet, born in 1879.)

足下の豆盗まるゝ案山子かな   也 有
Ashimoto no mame nusumaruru kakashi kana

   Under his very feet
The beans are being stolen,—
   What a scarecrow!   Yayū

God says,

> Thou shalt not steal,

and we steal the beans under his very nose. God says,

> The wages of sin is death.

We sin, and nothing happens. Most haiku show the power of things, but we perceive here the impotence of things. Life the unpredictable, subtle beyond the thought of man, life which indeed makes a man think as he does, lives in the mute out-stretched arms of the scarecrow, the hurried movements of the thief. Life takes off, for a moment, its mask of tragic dignity, and we see once more, in a corner of this very field, the cosmic Punch and Judy Show.

乳呑子の風除にたつかゝし哉   一 茶
Chinomigo no   kazeyoke ni tatsu   kakashi kana

> The scarecrow
> Stands there, keeping the wind
> From the sucking child.   Issa

The mother has put the baby to sleep under the scarecrow, and is working together with the father. The scarecrow holds out his arms as if protecting the child from the autumn wind that blows across the harvest field. In actual fact, of course, the scarecrow is of no use whatever as a shield from the wind, but Issa sees into the hearts of the parents, as from time to time they straighten their backs and look over towards the child. For them, in their feelings, in the poetic love they have for their offspring, the scarecrow is guarding it while they are at work. Another by Issa:

身の老や案山子の前も恥しき
Mi no oi ya   kakashi no mae mo   hazukashiki

> In my old age,
> Even before the scarecrow
> I feel ashamed of myself!

秋風の骨まで通る案山子かな   蝶 衣
Akikaze no   honemade tōru   kakashi kana

The autumn wind
Goes through into the very bones
Of the scarecrow.   Chōi

The clothes are tattered, the colours faded, the whole thing
wabbly, and the cold wind penetrates the scarecrow to its very
marrow. It is the poet who feels the cold for the scarecrow,
but it is the scarecrow that enables him to do it. Neither can
exist without the other.

かりてねむ案山子の袖や夜半の霜   芭 蕉
Karite nemu   kakashi no sode ya   yowa no shimo

Frost at midnight:
I would sleep, borrowing
The sleeves of the scarecrow.   Bashō

As he lies shivering in bed, Bashō thinks of anything he
might throw on it to keep him warm, and remembers the
ragged clothes on the scarecrow in the fields. Nearly all haiku
on scarecrows are good. This is because the subject, being a
naturally humorous one, does not lend itself to fanciful, "poet-
ical" treatment. The scarecrow is man himself with all the
stuffing knocked out of him, man as he one day will be, and
therefore as he now is. This is the thought of Onitsura in
the following:

骸骨の上を装うて花見かな
Gaikotsu no   ue wo yosōte   hanami kana

Their skeletons wrapt
In silk and satin,
They view the cherry-blossoms.

名月にけろりと立しかゝし哉   一 茶
Meigetsu ni kerorito tachishi   kakashi kana

The bright full moon,—
As if it were nothing special,
The scarecrow standing there.   Issa

The moon is nothing special, exactly as the scarecrow supposes. All truth is a simple, elemental suchness of things, and the poet perceives this through a self-identification with the scarecrow.

稲雀案山子に射られ海に入る　　　　子 規
Inasuzume   kakashi ni irare   umi ni iru

Harvest sparrows;
Shot by the arrow of the scarecrow,
They fall into the sea.　　　　Shiki

There is a rice-field that breaks down to the sea, and above it a crowd of sparrows is flying. They pass over the scarecrow that stands on the brink, a bow and arrows in his outstretched arms; they swoop down and are lost to sight over the edge of the field. Shiki fancies them to have been shot by the arrows the scarecrow holds. It is a fancy, but of such power that it becomes imagination, and the vital connection between scarecrow and sparrows and sea is grasped instantaneously where logic or intellect could only by painful and cumbrous endeavour abstract that relation from life. The difference between the creative imagination of this verse and the mirror-like reflecting character of most haiku may be seen by comparing the above with the following verses by Shōha and Setsugyo, 雪魚:

朝風に弓返りたる案山子哉
Asakaze ni   yumi kaeritaru   kakashi kana

The scarecrow's bow
Is turned the other way
In the morning breeze.

よその田へ弓引いて居る案山子かな
Yoso no ta e   yumi hiiteiru   kakashi kana

The scarecrow
Is stretching his bow towards
Another man's field.

御幸にも編笠ぬがぬ案山子かな   團　水
Miyuki ni mo　amigasa nuganu　kakashi kana

> Even before His Majesty,
> The scarecrow does not remove
> His plaited hat.   Dansui

This is hardly poetry, but brings out the nature of Royalty, of man, and of the scarecrow. We tend to see differences rather than identities, and the scarecrow corrects us, or rather, adds the other side of the matter. There is a somewhat similar verse by Shirao:

落る日に顔さへうとき案山子かな
Ochiru hi ni　kao sae utoki　kakashi kana

> To the rays of the setting sun
> The scarecrow
> Is indifferent.

Instead of lowering its *kasa* as the level rays of the sun strike its face, the scarecrow stands there quite philosophically.

人よりもかゝしの多き在所かな   茶　静
Hito yori mo　kakashi no ōki　zaisho kana

> Where I live,
> There are more scarecrows
> Than people.   Chasei

There is something naive and rustic about the simplicity of this verse. The scarecrows have a friendly, companionable air; there is nothing fearful about them.

畠主の案山子見舞ふて戻りけり   蕪　村
Hatanushi no　kakashi mimoute　modori keri

> The owner of the field
> Goes to see how the scarecrow is,
> And comes back.   Buson

These scarecrows have far more life than real people. Why

is this? It is because they obey all the Buddhist and Christian precepts naturally. They do not take care for the morrow; they let the dead bury the dead. And they are meek and pure in heart, merciful to all who seek a shelter in their rags and tatters. It is but right that owner of the field should go and pay his respects to this superior being, superior not in power or wealth, but in long-suffering and natural piety.

人に似て月夜の案山子あわれなり   子　規
Hito ni nite   tsukiyo no kakashi   aware nari

On a moonlight night
The scarecrows look like men,
So pitiful.   Shiki

It is hard to tell here whether Shiki is pitying the men for looking like scarecrows, or the scarecrows for looking like men. Certainly the scarecrow seems more alive, a more fearsome thing than in the light of day. Even the shadow looks human as it lies along the irregular ground.

Seibi has a different idea:

雨降れば人によく似る案山子かな
Ame fureba   hito ni yoku niru   kakashi kana

The scarecrow
Looks like a human being,
When it rains.

稲かれて化をあらわす案山子かな   蕪　村
Ine karete   bake wo arawasu   kakashi kana

The rice being reaped,
The scarecrow
Seems transformed.   Buson

While the rice was standing, the scarecrow looked like a man, but now the rice has been cut, the scarecrow only looks like a scarecrow, a patchwork of old clothes.

水落ちて細脛[1]高きかかしかな   蕪 村
Mizu ochite   hosozune takaki   kakashi kana

The water becoming lower,
How thin and long
The legs[1] of the scarecrow!   Buson

What is so remarkable is the contrast between the ordinari-
ness of the fact that as the water lessens more of the stick
supporting the scarecrow is visible, and the intensity of the
interest and depth of meaning of the impression it makes. In
this particular case, it is quite arithmetically "out of all pro-
portion," for poetry is seen where the relative eye sees nothing
but the relative.

夕日影道まで出づる案山子かな   召 波
Yūhikage   michi made izuru   kakashi kana

In the evening sun,
The shadow of the scarecrow
Reaches the road.   Shōha

The rays of the setting sun are almost level, and as the poet
walks along the country road, the shadow of the scarecrow is
seen extending from the middle of the hedgeless field right up
to the edge of the road. In the long shadows there is some
deep meaning, and when it is that of a scarecrow there is
something deeper still, almost of foreboding or warning.

人はいざ直な案山子も無かりけり   一 茶
Hito wa iza   sugu na kakashi mo   nakarikeri

The people, of course!—
But not even the scarecrows
Are upright.   Issa

The malignancy, the violence and bitter depth of contempt,
is strong enough to see all obliquity, whether moral or geomet-
rical, as obliquity, without discrimination, without respect of

[1] This is also given as 腰, "waist."

persons. Swift's writings are full of the contempt that clever
men feel for fools. And this feeling is not so reprehensible as
it seems, for it is in large part a rejoicing in the power we
feel within ourselves. Christ's "Thou hypocrite!" "Laughing
hyæna!" "Whited sepulchres!" belong to the same state of
elation, when the spirit of God is running freely through us.

The verse seems a kind of parody on a well-known waka of
Tsurayuki, 883-946:

人はいざ心もしらずふるさとは
花ぞむかしの香に匂ひける
I know not the mind
Of the man himself,
But in his old home,
The plum-blossoms
Smell as sweet as ever.

笠とれて面目もなき案山子かな   蕪 村
Kasa torete memmoku mo naki kakashi kana

His hat fallen off,
The scarecrow
Looks discomfited.   Buson

There are few more painful situations in public than being
compelled to run after one's hat. Looking serious is the mark
of a prig, and grinning like a fool is only contemptible. Even
God himself could not do run after his hat and keep his dignity.
The scarecrow, one would imagine, is too low in the scale of
created things to fall lower, but not so; even he suffers when
his hat is blown off, revealing a hairless poll.

大水を踏みてたへたる案山子哉   子 規
Ōmizu wo fumite taetaru kakashi kana

The scarecrow
Plants his feet in the flood,
Enduring it all.   Shiki

The heroism of the scarecrow is just the same as that of the heroic man. It consists in doing one's job thoroughly without thinking about its value or results. And so we need not resist a feeling of admiration, a fellow-feeling, for this insensible bundle of rags. Compare the following by Hagi-jo:

笠とれて雨無殘なる案山子哉
Kasa torete   ame muzan naru   kakashi kana

His hat fallen off,
How pitiless the rain
On the scarecrow!

案山子にも目鼻ありける浮世哉　　　子　規
Kakashi ni mo   mehana arikeru   ukiyo kana

In this fleeting world,
The scarecrow also
Has eyes and nose.   Shiki

In this world, all things are human. Whitman says:

I find I incorporate gneiss, coal, long-threaded moss, fruits, grains, esculent roots,
And I am stucco'd with quadrupeds all over.
And have distanced what is behind me for good reasons,
But call anything back again when I desire it.

Potatoes have eyes, and boats have noses; nature has a face.

どちらから寒くなるぞよかかし殿　　　一　茶
Dochira kara   samuku naru zo yo   kakashi-dono

From whence
Does the cold come,
O scarecrow?   Issa

The humour of this is light and shallow, but intimate. The scarecrow stands out here in the field in all weathers. It does not chatter or gossip but stores up its wisdom in silence. The cold comes from some mysterious place, and with no perceptible reason. Issa asks the scarecrow because he himself is no better than the scarecrow in his ignorance.

Shiki has a verse somewhat similar, but hard and contemptuous in feeling:

あるが中に最も愚なる案山子哉
Aru ga naka ni   mottomo gu naru   kakashi kana

Among existent things,
The stupidest
Is the scarecrow.

This is true, but "a truth that kills."

秋ふけて木の葉衣の案山子かな   乙　由
Aki fukete   ko-no-ha-goromo no   kakashi kana

Autumn deepens;
Scarecrows are clad
In fallen leaves.

Otsuyū

Such a simple verse as this brings us back to the purest and most elementary pleasures of life. Many leaves have fallen and the trees are beginning to show their bare branches. The scarecrows stand solitary in each deserted field, and the late autumn wind carries the dead leaves around them. Just a few leaves on the scarecrow and it wears a robe of fallen leaves. One word is uttered and the world is never the same again.

今朝見ればこちら向たる案山子哉   太　祇
Kesa mireba   kochira mukitaru   kakashi kana

Looking at it this morning,
The scarecrow
Has turned this way.

Taigi

The explanation of the fact is simple. The scarecrow stands upon a single stick and if this becomes loose, the scarecrow will turn this way or that, almost like a weathercock, according to the direction of the wind. But for the poet, it is a change of feeling, of his own feeling, because of the way in which the scarecrow has turned round, that strikes him.

近付きに成つて分かるる案山子哉　　　惟　然
Chikazuki ni　natte wakaruru　kakashi kana

　　We have been friends,
　And now we must part,
　　　Scarecrow.　　　　　　　　　　Izen

One scarecrow bids farewell to another, taking

　　Without more thinking, in good part,
　　Time's gentle admonition.

稲舟に乗後たる案山子哉　　　巳　百
Inabune ni　noriokuretaru　kakashi kana

　　The scarecrow,
　Too late
　　For the harvest boat.　　　Shihyaku

There is a tragic feeling hidden beneath the fancifulness of
this verse. The field has been reaped, the rice dried, and loaded
on the boat that floats on the canal-like stream nearby. As
the farmers look back they see the scarecrow still standing
there, keeping the absent birds away from the non-existent
grain. He has "missed the boat;" he is one of

　　The friends to whom we had no natural right.

案山子から案山子へ渡る雀哉　　　小　波
Kakashi kara　kakashi e wataru　suzume kana

　　The sparrows are flying
　From scarecrow
　　To scarecrow.　　　　　Sazanami

This is a very beautiful picture. The troop of sparrows first
one, the boldest, flying off and all the rest following, moves
in flying festoons from field to field, from scarecrow to scare-
crow, quite unafraid of them. There is a verse of Sōseki,
another modern poet, in which the scarecrow reproves the
familiarity of the sparrows in dignified terms:

それがしは案山子にて候雀どの
Soregashi wa　kakashi nite soro　suzume dono

"Your Honour the Sparrow;
It is The Scarecrow
Addressing you!"

冬來ては案山子にとまる烏かな　　　　　其　角
Fuyu kite wa　kakashi ni tomaru　karasu kana

Winter having come,
The crows perch
On the scarecrow.　　　　　　　　Kikaku

The value of things is in their use. All things may be used
for every kind of use. Modern Science may prove this before
it is generally accepted on the authority of the sages and poets.
All things have therefore infinite value. (This is not quite
syllogistic but 'twill suffice.) The crows, like the poet, perceive
that the scarecrow that can be called a scarecrow is not an
eternal scarecrow, the name that can be named is not an eternal
name.[1] What is the eternal scarecrow? The answer to this is
the poem itself.

The *picture* of the poem is a bare, colourless field, not an
"eye of green" in it, with one miserable scarecrow, almost
naked poles; a single crow on one arm of this scarecrow and
several on the ground nearby.

秋風のうごかして行く案山子哉　　　　　蕪　村
Akikaze no　ugokashite yuku　kakashi kana

The autumn wind
Moved the scarecrow,
And passed on.　　　　　　　　　Buson

In this verse there are many oblique meanings. There is
the unforgetfulness of the wind as it causes the scarecrow to
wabble, yet passes on indifferent and sways the grasses in the
next field already. There is the stolidity and yet the respon-

[1] 名可名非常名。

siveness of things, the scarecrow moving a little and then still again. There is the meaning of autumn in the instability and shakiness of the scarecrow, the dying down of vital energy, change and decay all around.

物の音ひとりたふるゝ案山子かな   凡 兆
Mono no oto   hitori taoruru   kakashi kana

A sound of something:
The scarecrow
Has fallen down of itself.   Bonchō

What the poet perceived here is what Wordsworth understood on Westminster Bridge: "The river glideth at its own sweet will." Besides all outside circumstances there is something in each thing, some inner necessity which is so secret that no one can express it, yet all may feel and know it. Bonchō has a prescript, the last line of a poem by Ōanseki, 王安石, 1021-1086, famous Chinese poet and statesman:

鍾　山

澗水無聲遶竹流。竹西花草露春柔。
茅簷相對坐終日。一鳥不啼山更幽。

MOUNT SHŌ

Soundlessly the valley stream winds round the bamboos;
The plants and grasses of Chikusei show their budding softness.
They and I sit facing each other, I under the thatched eaves, all day long;
Not a bird cries; the mountains grow yet more mysterious.

一番に案山子をこかす野分かな   許 六
Ichiban ni   kakashi wo kokasu   nowaki kana

The first thing
To be blown down by the tempest,
The scarecrow.   Kyoroku

The frailty of the scarecrow is one of its most human characteristics, and when the autumn wind rushes across the fields, the scarecrow tumbles down almost immediately

吹倒す起す吹かるゝ案山子哉   太 祇
Fukitaosu   okosu fukaruru   kakashi kana

> Blown over, set up,
> Blown over again,—
> The scarecrow!   Taigi

This verse is a triumph of condensation. We see the scarecrow down, and up and down again so quickly, that like the scarecrow himself we hardly know whether we are on our head or our heels. The speed of it, the way in which the standing and the falling are telescoped gives us that peculiar feeling of the contradictory nature of things that is the "ground" of poetry and religion.

立ちながら往生申す案山子かな   北 枝
Tachi nagara   ōjō mōsu   kakashi kana

> Giving up the ghost
> As he stands,—
> The scarecrow.   Hokushi

The scarecrow stands there on its last legs, doing his job and giving up his breath in that station in life to which it has pleased God to call him. The life of things, as opposed to that of animals or men, is a perfect one, for there is an undivided will to do what is done, until change and dissolution demand its cessation.

据風呂の下や案山子の身の終り   丈 草
Sueburo no   sita ya kakashi no   mi no owari

> Under the portable bath-tub,—
> That's the final resting place
> Of the scarecrow.   Jōsō

Even in his death he is more useful than most of us. The poet cannot withhold his unwilling admiration for the sterling qualities of endurance to which has now been added the final one, that of combustion.

There is, however, a verse by Shōshū, 正秀, which denies this:

薪ともならで朽ぬる案山子哉
Takigi tomo   narade kuchinuru   kakashi kana

No good for firewood,
It's rotting,—
This scarecrow!

動 物 **BIRDS AND BEASTS**

山寺や縁の上なる鹿の聲   一 茶
Yamadera ya   en no ue naru   shika no koe

A mountain temple:
The voice of the stag,
On the verandah.   Issa

The temple in this wild, out-of-the-way mountain is visited
by few people, and the wild deer come so near that when a
stag roars in the rutting season, it sounds as if it is standing
on the verandah outside. We feel the closeness of the world of
nature and the world of man. But here in the temple before
the images of Buddha, the animal world touches the divine.
The voice of the stag mingles with the chanting of the sutra
and the sound of the gong: Vox cervi vox dei.

神に火をあげて戻れば鹿の聲   子 規
Kami ni hi wo   agete modoreba   shika no koe

Having lighted a candle to the god,
On the way back,
The voice of the deer.   Shiki

The poet went to a nearby shrine in the early evening, lighted
a candle, prayed, and returned to his house through the gather-
ing autumn shadows. Now and again the cry of an unseen
deer was heard from the mountain side. What is this strange
harmony between the uprising yellow flame of the candle burn-
ing like a soul of fire in his mind, and the voice of the deer
that comes through the darkness and fades into the distance?
The light of the candle is the visible voice of matter, the cry
of the deer the audible flame of life. How then should they
seem anything but a two in one, a one in two, to the poetic
mind?

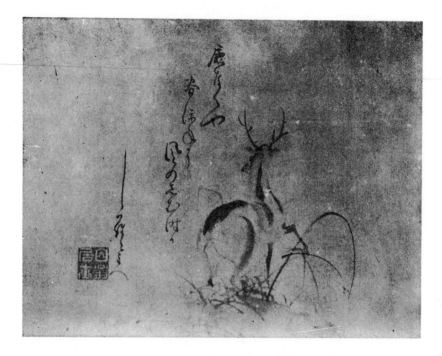

A Deer

by Rantei, 蘭亭, contemporary of
the poet, Shirara, し羅々, 1742-1827.

鹿
な
く
や

脊
ぼ
ね
に

風
の
し
む
時
か

Shika naku ya   sebone ni kaze no   shimu toki ka

The deer utters its mournful cry
When the cold autumn wind
Chills its spine?

三度啼て聞えずなりぬ鹿の聲　　　　蕪　村
Sando naite　kikoezu narinu　shika no koe

> Three times it cried,
> And was heard no more,
> The voice of the deer.　　　　Buson

From olden times the voice of the deer was deemed a poetic thing, chiefly from its association with love and its lack of fulfilment or sad satiety, but from the time of Bashō it began to have a deeper meaning, a returning to nature for its own sake, as we see in the following verse.

ひいとなく尻聲悲し夜の鹿　　　　芭　蕉
Hii to naku　shirigoe kanashi　yoru no shika

> Hee...the lingering cry
> Is mournful:
> The deer at night.　　　　Bashō

But even here the subjective element is too strong. Buson's verse attains that subjective-objective level in which we are left without any feeling of reaction against wallowing in our own feelings, and yet not left out in the cold by a pure and artificial objectivity. The voice of the deer has a meaning which is not merely a non-human one, yet it is nameless; it leaves us where we are, and yet enlarges our vision and power beyond this present place.

鹿ながら山影門に入日かな　　　　蕪　村
Shika nagara　yamakage mon ni　irihi kana

> The slanting sun:
> The shadow of a hill with a deer on it
> Enters the temple gate.　　　　Buson

This is a picture in the Japanese style, but the lines are not static; they have some latent motion. This verse is one of the best examples of Buson's dynamic objectivity.

汽車道に低く雁飛ぶ月夜哉   子 規
Kishamichi ni   hikuku kari tobu   tsukiyo kana

> Low over the rail-road,
> Wild geese flying;
> A moon-lit night.   Shiki

The word that gives life, that is, poetic meaning to the scene
is "low." The moon is high in the sky, but the moonlight,
the railway track, and the wild geese are far below. The rails
shine white in the light of the moon as they curve across the
plain. The geese fly also flat and silent on their long journey
towards the unknown and unseen. In this picture, we are
irresistibly reminded of a colour print by Hokusai or Hiroshige.
The following, by Yasui, belongs to spring. "Wild geese"
belong to autumn, but "Returning wild geese" to spring, when
they go back to northern regions.

麥喰し雁と思へど別れかな
Mugi kuishi   kari to omoedo   wakare kana

> The wild geese,—
> They ate barley, it is true,
> But departing—

All parting is painful, even from enemies and hateful things;
how much more so from the wild geese, which eat the young
barley, but whose discordant voices, as they wing their way
to other regions through the spring skies, strike on the ear
with a strange sadness and sorrow.

雁よ雁いくつのとしから旅をした   一 茶
Kari yo kari   ikutsu no toshi kara   tabi wo shita

> Wild goose, O wild goose,
> Your first journey,—
> How old were you?   Issa

This is a question that Gilbert White might have been able
to answer, but it is a question that Issa does not want answered,
though it is not merely his way of expressing interest in the
bird. It is the same with the following;

歸る雁淺間のけぶりいく度見る
Kaeru kari   asama no keburi   ikudo miru

Departing wild geese,
How many times have you seen
The smoke of Mount Asama?

落雁の聲のかさなる夜寒哉   許　六
Rakugan no   koe no kasanaru   yosamu kana

Wild geese coming down,
Their voices one upon another,
The cold of night increasing.   Kyoroku

No sooner do the cries of one group of wild geese become
faint than another approaches, and the cumulative effect of
their cries is to increase the feeling of cold.

The word *kasanaru* applies to three things: the coming down
of the geese, one group after another; the voices of each flock
of geese that sound across the cold fields and then cease when
they have come to earth; the cold that seems to increase with
each batch of geese.

一行の雁や端山に月を印す   蕪　村
Ichigyō no   kari ya hayama ni   tsuki wo insu

Under a passage of wild geese,
Over the foot-hills,
A moon is signed.   Buson

The word "passage" is to be taken in the sense of a line of
verse, which the geese resemble. On the edge of the picture,
like the seal of the painter, is the oval-irregular moon. There
is a similar play of fancy in the following:

苗代の色紙に遊ぶ蛙かな
Nawashiro no   shikishi ni asobu   kaeru kana

In the coloured slip
Of the rice seedling plantation,
The frogs are making merry.

The oblong pieces of field containing the young rice seedlings are the coloured slips of paper upon which the songs of the frogs are inscribed.

To take this as mere fancy, even the fancy of genius, is to do injustice to the poet and to one's own inner life. We term the imaginative power here exerted "fancy", because the two sets of objects are widely separated in the ratiocinative processes. It is difficult, it is true, to keep them together for long, but it is worth the effort.

鶴啼くや其聲に芭蕉破れぬべし　　　　芭　蕉
Tsuru naku ya   sono koe ni bashō   yarenu beshi

The crane screeches:
At its voice
The *bashō* will surely tear.　　　Bashō

This is an early haiku of Bashō. He has attempted here to resolve into one, sound and sight and texture, the voice of the bird and the rending of the broad leaves of the banana plant. This verse was actually written for and on a picture, evidently of a crane and a banana-plant. Bashō imagines the bird suddenly crying out; at its harsh strident note the tenderly brittle leaf of the plant will slit like calico.

鵙鳴くや入日差し込む女松原　　　　凡　兆
Mozu naku ya   irihi sashikomu   mematsu-bara

Rays of the setting sun pass
Through the red pine grove;
A shrike is crying.　　　Bonchō

The sharp cry of the shrike, or butcher-bird, the long slanting rays of the evening sun, and the red-barked pine-trees, all suggest a certain secret aspect of nature, a mystery which is seen and known but never understood.

鷹の目もいまは暮ぬと啼く鶉　　　　　芭 蕉
Taka no me mo ima wa kurenu to naku uzura

    Now that the eyes of the hawks
  Are darkened, in the dusk
    The quails are chirping.　　　　　Bashō

This might almost have come from White's *The Natural History of Selborne*; but it is not an ornithological observation. Still less does it manifest "the poet's sympathy for weaker birds." It simply says what Wilde wrote in *De Profundis*:

    One of the many lessons that one learns in prison is, that things are what they are and will be what they will be.

木啄の柱をたゝく住居かな　　　　　芭 蕉
Kitsutsuki no hashira wo tataku sumai kana

    Ah, this abode!
  Oft the woodpecker
    Will peck at its posts.　　　　　Bashō

Compare the verse on page 35, Vol. I, where Bashō says that the woodpecker will *not* peck his old teacher's hermitage.

Here also we have hyperbole, but of a peculiarly gracious kind, for it shows Bashō's deep love of solitude. This abode is Bashō's ideal home; living creatures are so much in harmony with his hermitage that Alexander Selkirk would say of them also,

    Their tameness is shocking to me.

Bashō himself living there has so tenuous an existence that he lives there as though he did not live there.

    This is the bell that never rang,
    This is the fish that never swam,
    This is the tree that never grew,
    This is the bird that never flew.[1]

---

[1] Jingle on Glasgow City Arms.

手斧うつ音も木深し啄木鳥　　　　　蕪　村
Teono utsu　oto mo kobukashi　keratsutsuki

> In the far depths of the forest,
> The woodpecker,
> And the sound of the axe.　　　　　Buson

The sound of the distant sea, the wind in a lofty pine-tree,
the echoing of the axe deep in the ravine of a forest, are things
too great for the ear of man. Buson stands listening and hears
nearby the tap-tap of the woodpecker; in the distance, faint
but clear, the ringing sound of

> the rude axe with heavèd stroke.

It is nature and man in their constructive-destructive, life-death
work, here and there and everywhere unceasing. We may
quote once more Shelley's lines from *To Jane*:

> Even the busy woodpecker,
> Made stiller by her sound
> The inviolable quietness.

木啄や一つところに日の暮るる　　　　　一　茶
Kitsutsuki ya　hitotsu tokoro ni　hi no kururu

> The woodpecker
> Keeps on in the same place:
> Day is closing.　　　　　Issa

Monotony and dreariness. Does Issa represent himself and
his life as a poet in this verse?

故郷も今は假寢や渡り鳥　　　　　去　來
Furusato mo　ima wa karine ya　wataridori

> Birds of passage;
> For also me now, my old home
> Is but a lodging for the night.　　　　　Kyorai

It is hard not to think that this verse was not written by
Bashō. It expresses that feeling of—not renunciation, but some-

thing deeper, an anguished acceptance of the instability and
non-ego, non-self nature of all things, ourselves especially.
Even our birth-place, to which we are linked by the most
sacred ties of blood and race, this too is only one of those

Homes that were not destined to be ours.[1]

鴫遠く鍬すゝぐ水のうねり哉   蕪 村
Shigi tōku   kuwa susugu mizu no   uneri kana

The snipe farther and farther away,
The ripples
Of the washed hoe.   Buson

The farmer goes to the river to wash his hoe, and snipe dart
up from behind the tall grass and fly off. The ripples caused
by the hoe also spread out farther and farther across the river.
Both birds and water are moving into the distance, near and far.

高土手にひはの鳴く日や雲千切れ   珍 碩
Taka-dote ni   hiwa no naku hi ya   kumo chigire

Siskins are crying
On the high embankment;
Cloudlets float above.   Chinseki

This verse gives a sensation of height, and of unseen ani-
mation.

小鳥來る音うれしさよ板びさし   蕪 村
Kotori kuru   oto ureshisa yo   itabisashi

The sounds of small birds
On the pent-roof,—
What a pleasure!   Buson

It is very quiet; not a deathly silence, but that of a hermitage
in the recesses of the mountains. Upon the pent-roof there are

[1] Arnold, *Human Life.*

sounds of scuffling, pecking, chirping, fluttering, hopping,—all the life of a little world. To live for a while in this world, though only through the imaginative ear, is an exquisite pleasure. Thoreau writes in his Journals, 1850, of

> Autumnal mornings, when the feet of countless sparrows are heard like rain-drops on the roof by the boy who sleeps in the garret.

秋の季の赤蜻蛉に定りぬ　　　　　　白　雄

Aki no ki no   akatombō ni   sadamarinu

The beginning of autumn,
Decided
By the red dragon-fly.　　　　　Shirao

This reversal of the common-sense order of cause and effect is found often in poetry, the song of the bird causing the sun to rise, the appearance of the red dragon-fly causing the advent of autumn. The dragon-fly and the autumn are thus confused and become the same thing. Compare the following, by Bakusui:

己が身に秋を染めぬく蜻蛉かな

Ono ga mi ni   aki wo somenuku   tombo kana

He has dyed his body
With autumn,—
The dragon-fly.

Another way of describing the appearance of the multitude of red dragon-flies flashing to and fro under the autumn sky, is the following by Gotei, 呉莚:

くれなゐのかげろふ走る蜻蛉かな

Kurenai no   kagerō hashiru   tombo kana

Fleeting, crimson
Gossamer-threads,—
The dragon-flies!

名
月
や
と
ん
ぼ
う
の
羽
の
動
き
な
き

A Dragon-fly

Verse and picture by Mōen, 孟遠.

Meigetsu ya   tombō no ha no   ugoki naki

Under the autumn moon
The wings of the dragon-fly
Are motionless.

Notes how the verse and
the picture are mingled.

蜻蛉やとりつきかねし草の上   芭 蕉
Tombō ya   toritsuki kaneshi   kusa no ue

> The dragon-fly,
> It tried in vain to settle
> On a blade of grass.   Bashō

One of the beautiful things about this is the fact that the
dragon-fly does not show, because it does not feel, any irritation
at the movement of the grass, blown by the wind, which pre-
vents the dragon-fly from alighting on it.

日は斜關屋の鎗にとんぼかな   蕪 村
Hi wa naname   sekiya no yari ni   tombo kana

> Dragon-flies
> On the spears of the barrier,
> In the slanting rays of the sun.   Buson

Towards the end of this afternoon of autumn, the travellers
passing through the barrier are few and far between. Upon
each of the spears or javelins standing there in case of emer-
gency, a single dragon-fly is resting, its wings glittering in the
level rays of the sun. Shadows are long, the wind sounds as
if it comes from far away; the great gate is in the shade, and
against this background the spears stand perpendicular to the
horizontal lines of light.

なき人のしるしの竹に蜻蛉かな   几 董
Naki hito no   shirushi no take ni   tombo kana

> On the bamboo
> That marks the place of a dead man,
> A dragon-fly.   Kitō

The indifference of things is continually striking us, and
striking us deeply before we think shallowly about it. The
dead man, the bamboo, the dragon-fly have come together at
this point of space, at this point of time. The same accidental-
inevitable, free-determined nature is seen also in the following
by Taisō:

往つては來て蜻蛉絶えず船の綱   太 巣
Itte wa kite   tombō taezu   fune no tsuna

> About the ropes of the ship
> The dragon-flies come and go
> Ceaselessly.

古墓や赤とんぼ飛ぶ枯樒
Furuhaka ya   akatombo tobu   kareshikimi

> Old graves;
> Red dragon-flies flitting
> Over the withered *shikimi*.

The author is unknown to me. The *shikimi* or Chinese anise
has a small white flower in summer. The plant smells sweet,
but is poisonous. Nevertheless, sprays are offered before the
Buddha. The old grave, its withered offerings, the dragon-flies
rustling to and fro,—what a scene of thoughtless significance?
Buson has a verse concerning the flower:

ゆかしさよ樒花さく雨の中
Yukashisa yo   shikimi hana saku   ame no naka

> What loveliness!—
> The *shikimi*
> Blooming in the rain.

There is a slightly similar verse by Kyoshi:

蜻蛉飛んで事無き村の日午なり
Tombo tonde   koto naki mura no   hiruma nari

> Dragon-flies
> In an uneventful village,—
> It is midday.

夕づく日薄きとんぼの羽影かな   花 朗
Yūzukuhi   usuki tombo no   hakage kana

> In the evening sunlight,
> The faint shadow of the wings
> Of the dragon-fly.

Karō

The poet, not content with the smallness of the insect goes as far as the faint shadow of its translucent wings. A man's shadow is homogeneous, but that of a dragon-fly differs. The shadow of the body is dark, but that of the wings is faint, a lace pattern traced on the ground.

出る月と入り日の間や赤とんぼ　　　　二　丘
Deru tsuki to   irihi no ai ya   akatombo

> Between the moon coming out
> And the sun going in,—
> 　　The red dragon-flies.　　　　Nikyū

This has a simplicity which is a good test of our poetical health. The same applies to the following by Senka:

蜻蛉の壁をかゝゆる西日かな
Tombō no   kabe wo kakayuru   nishibi kana

> The dragon-fly
> Clinging to the wall;
> 　　Sunlight from the west.

蜻蛉の舞ふや入日の一世界　　　　倚　菊
Tombō no   mau ya irihi no   ichisekai

> The dance of the dragon-flies:
> A world
> 　　In the setting sun.　　　　Kigiku

We feel of these dragon-flies what Lawrence writes of fish:

> And I said to my heart, there are limits
> To you, my heart;
> And to the one god.
> Fish are beyond me.

A more sober and less romantic but not inferior verse by Ryōta, which also shows us the world of the dragon-flies:

A Dragon-fly

Verse and picture by Kempū, 見風.

Tombō ya   mizu wo nabaeru   yūgeshiki

The dragon-fly
Slants over the water,
The evening sun on everything.

とんぼうや
水をなばへる
夕げしき

五六尺己が雲井の蜻蛉かな
Gorokushaku   ono ga kumoi no   tombo kana

The dragon-fly;
Five or six feet above,
Is his own sky.

遠山やとんぼついゆきついかへる   秋之坊
Tōyama ya   tombo tsui yuki   tsui kaeru

The dragon-fly,
Swift to the distant mountain,
Swift to return.   Akinobō

This expresses humorously the nature of the flight of the
dragon-fly. It suddenly darts off towards the far-off mountains,
as if it would never return, but in a moment it has turned
round and is coming swiftly back.

打つ杖の先にとまりしとんぼかな   康　瓢
Utsu tsue no   saki ni tomarishi   tombo kana

The dragon-fly
Perches on the stick
That strikes at him.   Kōhyō

This is a very simple kind of poetry, a mere description of
fact, an entomological observation. Whatever poetry it may
have is derived partly from the frustrated, non-plussed state of
mind of the man with the stick who is in the same position
as the executioner with the Cheshire Cat's head, and partly
from the innocence of the dragon-fly. Other verses that are
also practically descriptions of the nature of the dragon-fly, its
stupidity that is not so foolish after all, its "equal mind," are
the following by Kōjōdō and Eiboku:

蜻蛉や花には寄らず石の上
Tombō ya   hana ni wa yorazu   ishi no ue

The dragon-fly,
Not approaching the flowers,—
But on the stone.

杭 の 先 何 か 味 ふ と ん ぼ か な
Kui no saki   nani ka ajiwau   tombo kana

The dragon-fly
Is tasting something
On the top of that stake.

蜻蛉 の 顔 は 大 か た 眼 玉 か な   知 足
Tombō no   kao wa ōkata   medama kana

The face of the dragon-fly
Is practically nothing
But eyes.   Chisoku

This is what any child might say, but for that very reason, near to the kingdom of poetry.

お と な し く 留 守 を し て ゐ ろ き り ぎ り す   一 茶
Otonashiku   rusu wo shite iro   kirigirisu

Be a good boy
And look after the house well,
Cricket!   Issa

This may be taken in two ways, as an expression of unfeigned intimacy and equality with other living creatures, or as implying the poet's solitary and lonely life. But these are not, after all, two separate things. One springs from the other, the other from the one.   The same applies to another verse by Issa:

鷦鷯 き よ ろ き よ ろ 何 ぞ 落 し た か
Misosazai   kyoro-kyoro nan zo   otoshita ka

The wren
Looking here, looking there,—
"Dropped something?"

By the colloquial language Issa has got rid of that "wonder" which has so falsely coloured much English verse.

むざんやな甲の下のきりぎりす   芭 蕉
Muzan ya na   kabuto no shita no   kirigirisu

How piteous!
Beneath the helmet
    Chirps a cricket.   Bashō

This verse comes towards the end of *Oku no Hosomichi*, and
was composed after visiting the Tada Shrine, where the helmet
and fragments of the clothes of Sanemori were kept. "How
piteous!" comes from a Nō play called *Sanemori*, 實盛. There
was a battle between the Taira and the Minamoto at Shinohara,
1183, in which the former were defeated, and all fled except
Sanemori. He was killed, and the head brought to Yoshinaka.[1]
Sanemori was more than sixty, but had dyed his hair and beard
black, and the head was not recognized until,

樋口參りてただ一目見て、あなむざんやな
齋藤別當實盛にて候ひけるぞや。

Higuchi [Kanemitsu] came forward and with but one
glance said, "Ah, how pitiful! it is Saitō Betto Sanemori!"

This story comes from the *Heike Monogatari*. Bashō's verse
is remarkable in the way he had used the pathos of history
and the language of the Nō, and concentrated these in the cry
of the cricket[2] beneath the helmet before him.

白露の玉ふんがくなきりぎりす   一 茶
Shiratsuyu no   tama fungaku na   kirigirisu

Grasshopper,—
Do not trample to pieces
    The pearls of bright dew.   Issa

This is the natural attitude of the tender-minded poet, as
opposed to the tough-minded Zen adept who can enjoy cock-
fighting and bear-baiting, not to speak of scenes of carnage on
the field of battle. The poet, as such, disturbs nothing, not

[1] See Volume III, page 939.
[2] It should be noted that the present use of *kirigirisu*, grasshopper,
and *kōrogi*, cricket was exactly opposite in former times.

even the dew-drops on the morning grass. In addition, there is a kind of hyperbole; the grasshopper[1] is seen as of enormous size and power.

蜑の屋は小海老にまじるいとゞ哉   芭 蕉
Ama no ya wa   koebi ni majiru   itodo kana

In the fisherman's hut,
Mingled with dried shrimps,
Crickets are chirping.   Bashō

It is a kind of still-life, yet alive. The original does not say "chirping," only "crickets!"

出て行くぞ仲よく遊べきりぎりす   一 茶
Dete iku zo   naka yoku asobe   kirigirisu

Now I am going out;
Be good and play together,
Crickets.   Issa

Issa is not pretending or being fanciful. He wishes the lion to lie down with the lamb, and infuses all things with his own benevolence.

庵の夜や棚さがしするきりぎりす   一 茶
Io no yo va   tanasagashi suru   kirigirisu

My hut at night;
The cricket
Is rummaging about.   Issa

A human being may be sometimes quite a companion,—much more so a mouse or a cricket. Just the silent night, an empty room, the flickering lamp, a cricket invisible but chirping here and there,—and nothing is lacking, above all the "loneliness" which is so near the heart of things.

[1] In this verse, the modern meaning of *kirigirisu* seems more suitable.

きりぎりす自在をのぼる夜寒かな   蕪 村
Kirigirisu   jizai wo noboru   yosamu kana

A cricket climbing
The pot-hanger;
How cold the night!   Buson

The pot-hanger is a kind of long hook suspended over the
open fire-place. It often had an artistic form, valued by poets
and connoiseurs.

Buson is sleeping near the open fire-place, in which the fire
is going out. Night deepens, and it grows colder and colder.
Suddenly he notices, by the light of the night-lamp, that some-
thing is moving up the large hook over the fireplace. It is a
cricket, that somehow has thought fit to perch himself there.
It is a picture that would strike any poet or painter who can
see much in little, the cricket brownish-green, the pot-hanger
black, the embers still red.

寝返りをするぞ脇よれきりぎりす   一 茶
Negaeri wo   suru zo wakiyore   kirigirisu

I'm going to turn over;
Mind away,
Cricket.   Issa

In one sense this is "mere" gentleness of character, indeed,
gentlemanliness of the best kind, that wishes to avoid all un-
necessary pain. In another, it is the compassion of the Buddha,
the love of Christ, the realization that not only all men but all
things are equal. The truth is that we must have the second,
but it should appear, as it does in Issa's verse, as the first.

我が影の壁にしむ夜やきりぎりす   蓼 太
Waga kage wo   kabe ni shimu yo ya   kirigirisu

My shadow soaks into the wall
This autumn night,
A cricket chirping.   Ryōta

This verse expresses a somewhat unusual, almost abnormal

experience. Things of two dimensions seem almost to have three. In Bashō's haiku, it is the voice of the insects which soaks into the rocks:

閑さや岩にしみいる蟬の聲
Shizukasa ya   iwa ni shimiiru   semi no koe

> The stillness!
> The voice of the cicadas
> Sinks into the rocks.

In Ryōta's verse the crying of the cricket exacerbates the sense of sight so that it feels the pressure and penetrative power of the shadow on the wall.

秋の蚊や死ぬる覺悟で我れをさす   子 規
Aki no ka ya   shinuru kakugo de   ware wo sasu

> Autumn mosquitoes
> Bite me,
> Prepared for death.   Shiki

When autumn comes, and the air turns colder, mosquitoes become more sluggish in their movements, but more persistent in their biting, as though they knew their time on earth was short, and are determined at all costs to suck as much blood as possible before they die. The humour of this verse expresses something of the nature of autumn and of mosquitoes, something that could not be said except by way of the "pathetic fallacy."

A similar verse by the same author, in which he shows his likeness to Heine:

死にかけて尚やかましき秋の蟬
Shini kakete   nao yakamashiki   aki no semi

> Dying,
> All the more noisy,
> Cicadas of autumn.

蜘蛛何と音を何と啼く秋の風   芭　蕉
Kumo nan to   ne wo nan to naku   aki no kaze

> With what voice,
> And what song would you sing, spider,
> In this autumn breeze?   Bashō

Bashō is sitting under the eaves, watching a spider in its web
as it sways to and fro in the wind of autumn. It is a deep
mystery, this silence profound that some creatures preserve, in
contradistinction to the chattering and chirping of others. If
the spider had a voice, what would it be like? Would it not,
in its own unique, inimitable way, be singing now, in the
soughing of the breeze, of the loneliness and desolation of
autumn? This verse is prophetic of the poetry of Issa.

河鹿啼く袖なつかしき火打石   蕪　村
Kajika naku   sode natsukashiki   hiuchiishi

> The "river deer" is crying:
> In my sleeve,
> My dear old flint-stone.   Buson

The *kajika* is a kind of frog, small and black, that lives
between the boulders of valley streams. It cries in autumn,
in a voice slightly resembling that of a deer, hence its name.
Buson is climbing slowly up a ravine when suddenly,—the
sweet voice of a singing-frog! It may be as Ryōto, 涼菟, says
in the following verse:

川音につれて鳴出す河鹿かな
Kawa-oto ni   tsurete nakidasu   kajika kana

> Prompted by the sound of the river,
> The "river deer"
> Begins to sing.

The rippling, trickling water and the voice of the frog in this
green, secluded place,—Buson must sit down and listen to them.
Almost unconsciously his hand strays into his sleeve, and he
feels the well-known touch of the flint-stone he has used for
many years to light his short pipe. The beauty and delicacy
of the one and the warm, human homeliness of the other, give

him an ineffable feeling of perfection and bliss.

名 月 や 暗 き 處 は 蟲 の 聲　　　　　　汶　村
Meigetsu ya　kuraki tokoro wa　mushi no koe

    The bright autumn moon:
In the shadows,
    The voices of insects.　　　　　　Bunson

    Beneath the moon, all is calm and bright; under every tree
and bush it is dark, but all kinds of insects are chirping and
trilling: "all that we behold is full of blessings."

蟲 の 音 の 中 に 咳 き 出 す 寢 覺 か な　　　　丈　草
Mushi no ne no　naka ni seki dasu　nezame kana

    Waking in the night,
I mingle my coughs
    With the cries insects.　　　　　　Jōsō

    The coughing of the sick man and the chirping of the insects,
—how different! And yet, what is the difference? Does God
hear them differently? Do not they both accord in perfect
harmony with the soundless music of the spheres, the spirit
ditties of no tone? One is reminded of a verse by another sick
man, Shiki:

つ く づ く と 我 が 影 見 る や 蟲 の 聲
Tsukuzuku to　waga kage miru ya　mushi no koe

    Gazing steadfastly
At my shadow,—
    The voices of insects.

蟲 よ 蟲 よ 鳴 い て 因 果 が 盡 き る な ら　　　乙　州
Mushi yo mushi yo　naite inga ga　tsukiru nara

    Ah, insects, insects!
Can your Karma
    Be cried away?　　　　　　Otokuni

Literally, "If your karma is cried away by singing, [sing on!]." This has the idea of weeping away, by penitence, one's fate,—and a deeper one, that the insects are fulfilling their destiny, obeying their original nature by chirping, and by thus not opposing their lot; they are working it out and tending towards their ultimate Buddhahood.

にぎやかな乞食の床や蟲の聲   千代尼
Nigiyaka na   kojiki no toko ya   mushi no koe

The nightly couch of the beggar,—
How lively and gay,
With voices of insects!   Chiyo-ni

This has a heartlessness deeply akin to Zen, that is, to life itself. Whether we eat or whether we starve, the planets revolve around the sun, the seasons follow one after the other, insects chirp all around. But this verse is not saying such a thing; neither is it full of self-pity. It is heart-less, like Nature, like Destiny itself.

蟲ほろほろ草にこぼるゝ音色かな   樗良
Mushi horo-horo   kusa ni koboruru   neiro kana

The sound-colour
Of insects pattering down
On the leaves.   Chora

As the poet shakes the bushes in passing among them, he hears the insects drop onto the leaves below. The insects' bodies, soft and plump, or hard and light, falling on the thin, pulpy leaves, has a peculiar sound born of each yet different from each. This is what the sensitive ears of the poet catch, and in the timbre of the sound he hears the life of the leaves, he perceives with his ears the life of the insects. This is not a figurative way of speaking. We can hardly enter at all into the world of smell that a dog lives in, the world of touch inhabited by the ant, the mole, the fish. The world of sound known by birds and insects, we cannot even surmise. The poet, for an instant only, leaves this world of light that is permanently our world until the darkness of death receives us. He comprehends an aspect of the nature of things through hearing. But what he hears is of course inexpressible. Man has never even attempted to form a vocabulary for such experiences.

蟲聴くと話しを聞くと別つの耳   和　風
Mushi kiku to   hanashi wo kiku to   betsu no mimi

We listen to insects,
And human voices,
With different ears.   Wafū

This is a didactic verse, and as such is devoid of poetry. It expresses, however, a profound truth. We are to listen to men, to listen to the talking of men, their praising and blaming, as the chirping of insects.

Listen to the fool's reproach! it is a kingly title!

But a philosophic indifference is not what is inculcated here. The ear, like the eye, is to be single. Not to distinguish between Nature and Man,—this is the secret of living. And not to distinguish between Man and Nature and God,—this is to be a Buddha.

世の中はなく虫さへも上手下手   一　茶
Yo no naka wa   naku mushi sae mo   jōzu heta

Even among insects, in this world,
Some are good at singing,
Some bad.   Issa

Listening attentively to the insects singing in the garden (and in this "attentively" consists the whole of this experience), Issa hears differences in the chirping and trilling of the same species of insect. One is loud, another softer, one metallic, another mellow and subdued, one sprightly, another sad and weary. What a deep forgetfulness of self this distinction demands! This is a beautiful example of the paradox that only when the difference (between oneself and the insect) is

A Bagworm

by Suisui, 翠蓑, i.e. Hanabusa Itchō, 英一蝶, 1652-1724,
the verse by Bashō, his contemporary.

Minomushi no　ne wo kiki ni koyo　kusa no io

    The voice of the bagworms;
O come to my hut,
    And hear them cry!

みのむしの
音をきゝに
こよ
草の庵

forgotten, is the difference (between one insect and another) perceived.

虫鳴くやきのふは見えぬ壁の穴   一　茶
Mushi naku ya   kinō wa mienu   kabe no ana

Insects are crying;
A hole in the wall
Not seen yesterday.   Issa

What an odd place to find poetry,—in the fact of noticing a hole in the wall that had not been remarked before. There is a strange affinity between the timbre of the insects' voices and the broken plaster of the hole that is, as it were, seen with his ears.

蟲なくや月出でゝ尚くらき庭   子　規
Mushi naku ya   tsuki idete nao   kuraki niwa

Insects are crying;
The moon comes out,
The garden is yet darker.   Shiki

When the moon is behind a cloud, all things are dimly seen. When it comes out, the garden under the trees and bushes is in deep darkness, and we become aware of the darkness more strongly. And what of the insects? Their chirping so sweetly, so sadly, their melancholy-cheerful voices make our feelings more intense, they stimulate the organ of sight so that we can see the darkness.

蓑蟲の音をきゝに來よ草の庵   芭　蕉
Minomushi no   ne wo kiki ni koyo   kusa no io

The voice of the bagworms;
O come to my hut,
And hear them cry.   Bashō

There is no communion of saints without common union with

things. Sodō, 素堂, says of the *minomushi*, "Its faint, uncertain voice makes it pathetic," 聲のおぼつかなきを哀れむ. In actual fact, of course, it does not cry or make any noise at all.

古犬や蚯蚓の唄にかんじ貌   一 茶
Furuinu ya   mimizu no uta ni   kanji gao

The aged dog
Seems impressed with the song
Of the earth-worms.   Issa

In old Japan it was thought that worms made a chirping noise. It is said that this was a mistake made on hearing the voice of the mole-cricket under the ground.

The old dog lies in the autumn sun, his head on his paws, his eyes wide open as if listening to something, perhaps the song of the earth-worms that move in the earth under him.

うそ寒や蚯蚓の唄も一夜づゝ   一 茶
Usosamu ya   mimizu no uta mo   hitoyo zutsu

Getting colder,
The song of the earth-worm also
Dwindles every evening.   Issa

Autumn deepens, the nights grow chill; and every evening the voice of the earthworm grows feebler and feebler. This is all there is in this verse, yet it sums up the loneliness and a certain apprehensiveness of late autumn.

植 物 TREES AND FLOWERS

笑ふにも泣くにもにざる木槿哉   嵐 雪
Warau ni mo   naku ni mo nizaru   mukuge kana

It neither smiles
Nor weeps,—
This Rose of Sharon.   Ransetsu

The Rose of Sharon, a bush about ten feet high, is used as
an ornamental tree, and for fences. The flowers are purplish,
white, or pink, both single and double. They open in the
morning and close at night. Some say that the convolvulus of
the *Manyōshū* is really this flower. It is indeed a beautiful
flower, says the poet, and yet has something inhuman about it.
"It looks neither like smiles nor tears," is the literal translation.
It has a cold prettiness, without the tender charm of the violet
or the blowzy heartiness of the peony. This way of looking
at the Rose of Sharon reminds us somewhat of Lawrence in
Birds, Beasts and Flowers. Again, in *The Two Blue Birds* we
have the following:

> There is a certain nonsense, something showy and stagey
> about spring, with its pushing leaves and chorus-girl bowers,
> unless you have something corresponding inside you. Which
> she hadn't.

There is a similar critical spirit, an unwillingness to be pleased,
about the following by Senna:

高燈籠ひるは物うき柱かな
Takatōrō   hiru wa monouki   hashira kana

The Tall Stone Lantern,
In the day-time
Is a melancholy pillar.

At night when the light is lit in it, it is a thing of beauty in
itself, and adds to the beauty around it, but in the daytime it
is uninteresting and a thing of gloom. There are many varieties
of stone lantern, each having a special name. This particular
kind is the most funeral in appearance.

道 の べ の 木 槿 は 馬 に 喰 は れ け り   芭 蕉

Michinobe no   mukuge wa uma ni   kuwarekeri

A Rose of Sharon
By the roadside;
The horse has eaten it.   Bashō

There is an anecdote in connection with this verse, which,
even if not authentic, brings out its pure objectivity and perfect
directness. Bashō was once reproached by his teacher of Zen,
Butchō, for wasting his time on haiku. Bashō answered,

俳 諧 は 只 今 日 の 事 目 前 の 事 に て 候、

"Haikai is simply what is happening in this place, at this
moment," and then quoted the above verse as an example.
Butchō expressed his approval of this, saying:

善 哉、 善 哉、 俳 諧 も か ゝ る 深 意 あ る も の に こ そ

"Excellent! Excellent! In haikai also there is such a deep
meaning?" A verse of Issa's worthy to stand beside it:

さ を し か の 喰 ひ こ ぼ し け り 萩 の 花

Saoshika no   kuikoboshikeri   hagi no hana

The stag eats
And spills
The flowers of the lespedeza.

A verse by Shiki very similar to that of Bashō:

大 蓼 の 花 く ふ 馬 や 茶 の 煙

Ōtade no   hana kū uma ya   cha no kemuri

A horse eating
The flower of a kno_grass;
Smoke from under the tea-kettle.

代 々 の 貧 乏 垣 の 木 槿 哉   一 茶

Daidai no   bimbōgaki no   mukuge kana

From generation to generation,
The Rose of Sharon
Of this poor fence.   Issa

This has partly the idea of Tennyson's *The Brook*:

For men may come and men may go,
But I go on for ever.

But much more than this, and deeper, is the feeling of the natural piety of the plant, and filial piety in the family.

川音や木槿咲く戸はまだ起きず   北　枝
Kawa-oto ya   mukuge saku to wa   mada okizu

The sound of the river;
The door where the Rose of Sharon blooms
Is not yet opened.   Hokushi

Over the river the morning mist still hovers; the sound of the rapids is high and clear. Under the wall, white blossoms are blooming, faint with dew,—but the door of the farmer's house is still closed; no one is up yet. This closed door opens another in his mind. There is a certain remote harmony in the varied sensations of the early morning hour.

手をかけて折らで過ぎ行く木槿哉   杉　風
Te wo kakete   orade sugiyuku   mukuge kana

I laid my hand upon it,
And did not break it off, but passed on,—
The Rose of Sharon.   Sampū

The position of "The Rose of Sharon," is significant in the original (and in the translation). It remains at the end of the poem, just as the beauty of the flowering bush remains in his mind long after his refraining from breaking off a branch has been forgotten. Compare the verse by Buson on the next page.

柳ちり菜屑流るゝ小川かな   子　規
Yanagi chiri   nakuzu nagaruru   ogawa kana

The leaves of the willow fall,
Scraps of vegetables
Floating down the brook.   Shiki

A light wind sways the long hanging boughs of the willow-trees and the withered leaves fall, leaving the branches bare. Along the stream come flowing fragments from greens. Shiki has expressed almost unwittingly the "poetical" and the "un-poetical" of life, of human life and that of nature. The dry, curled-up, slender leaves fall from the hanging branches, fall on the surface of the water and float gracefully away down the current. From some unknown village, yellow, waterlogged leaves and stems of cabbages and greens come slowly down the stream, half-submerged, things of no value or beauty whatever, the refuse of human life, unwanted rubbish spoiling the pellucid water. Yet in their sadness they accord with the falling of the leaves of the willow-tree. They too express the melancholy season and share in the poet's life.

空家の戸に寝る犬や柳散る　　　　　子 規

Aki-ie no to ni neru inu ya   yanagi chiru

A dog sleeping
At the door of an empty house,
Leaves of the willow-trees scattering.　Shiki

The stray dog is sleeping where he knows no one comes in or out to drive him away. The house is empty, the shutters are up. Willow-trees are scattering their leaves in the wind. The whole creation "seems to bear rather than rejoice."

よらで過る藤澤寺のもみじ哉　　　　蕪 村

Yorade sugiru fujisawa-dera no   momiji kana

Not going in, but passing by:
The autumnal leaves
Of Fujisawa Temple.　　　Buson

The fact that Buson did not go in and worship at the temple (for some unknown, or rather, unstated reason) made the impression of the crimson and yellow leaves of the temple court-yard all the more unforgettable. In some ways, and at some times, we can enter into things and persons by holding aloof from them. It is said that the spectator sees most of the game, while the participants are aware only of a restricted portion of it. So in this verse, by not going into the temple, but walking by it, on looking back at the glowing leaves, distance lends a kind of enchantment to the view. The mind is not disturbed by details or inconsistent elements, and at the same time, the sense of remoteness, of something lost, strengthens the sensation of beauty. This comes out also in the following verse by the same author:

出家して親在す里の紅葉かな
Shukke shite   oya imasu sato no   momiji kana

Renouncing the world,—
The autumn leaves
In my parents' village.

The priest sees in his mind the scarlet and vermilion leaves of the little village where he was born, and where his old parents are still living,—far away, yet so near to the heart.

山くれて紅葉の朱をうばひけり   蕪 村
Yama kurete   momiji no ake wo   ubai keri

The mountain grows darker,
Taking the scarlet
From the autumn leaves.   Buson

This reminds one of Virgil's lines:

Ubi caelum condidit umbra
Juppiter, et rebus nox abslulit atra colorem.

When darkness hides the heavens,
And black night has taken away the colours of things.

紅葉する木立もなしに山深し   子 規
Momijisuru   kodachi mo nashi ni   yama fukashi

Of crimson foliage
There is none here,
Deep in the mountains.   Shiki

On the lower slopes of the mountains, autumnal leaves were glowing, scarlet and yellow colours gave animation and a false

Wild Boar

by Kakujō, 角上, 1664–1747. The verse is by Bashō:

Inoshishi mo tomo ni fukaruru nowaki kana

猪
も
と
も
に
吹
か
る
ゝ
野
分
か
な

The autumn tempest
Blows along also
Even wild boars.

Kakujō, a contemporary of Bashō, shows the wild boar in its lair in the bush-clover, blown by the rushing wind. See Kyoroku's comment, Vol. III, page 960.

happiness to the mind; but here, higher up the mountains, not
a red leaf is to be seen. All the trees are evergreen or leafless,
dark and silent, with not a bird or animal, not a human being
or a sign of habitation. There is not a touch of brightness or
hope, only a solemn fatality.

白露をこぼさぬ萩のうねりかな　　　　　芭　蕉
Shira-tsuyu wo   kobosanu hagi no   uneri kana

The flowers of the bush-clover
Do not let fall, for all their swaying,
Their drops of bright dew.　　　　　Bashō

The lespedeza, or bush-clover, is a graceful bush-like plant
whose stems rise from the ground and bend over all together
like the spray of a fountain. When the wind blows, the bushes
move in waves, but the white and red blossoms do not drop
the dew or rain that they hold. This verse is to some extent
a picture, but only a poet could paint it, and only a poet could
see it.

浪の間や小貝にまじる萩の塵　　　　　芭　蕉
Nami no ma ya   kogai ni majiru   hagi no chiri

In the surf,
Mingled with small shells,
Petals of the bush-clover.　　　　　Bashō

This verse comes towards the end of *Oku no Hosomichi*.
Accompanied by Tōsai, Bashō went to the beach of Iro to
gather small shells called *masuo*. The loneliness of the place
made a deep impression on Bashō:

寂しさや須磨にかちたる濱の秋
Sabishisa ya   suma ni kachitaru   hama no aki

The loneliness
Of the autumn of the beach,
More even than that of Suma.

The next verse, the present one, turns from this vague sadness
to the particularity of the small shells and the faintly red petals
of the bush-clover that are seen in the back-wash of the waves

as they recede. There is something of the sad loneliness of the autumn shore in these small shells and flower petals mingled together, the ones in their element, the others not, but both in the everlasting arms of nature.

たそがれや萩にいたちの高臺寺　　　　　蕪 村
Tasogare ya　hagi ni itachi no　kōdaiji

Kōdaiji Temple;
A weasel in the bush-clover,
At dusk.

Buson

Kōdaiji Temple was built in Kyōto in 1601 by Kita no Mandokoro, widow of Hideyoshi. A temple of the Zen sect, it is even now a very lonely place at the foot of a mountain where bush-clover grows profusely. The weasel, the temple, and the bush-clover are in an unintellectual harmony that may be the result of its being an imaginary scene. The same can be said of the following winter verse by Buson:

水仙に狐遊ぶや宵月夜
Suisen ni　kitsune asobu ya　yoizukiyo

Foxes playing
Among the narcissus flowers,
In the early evening moonlight.

折々や雨戸にさはる萩の聲　　　　　雪 芝
Oriori ya　amado ni sawaru　hagi no koe

From time to time,
Brushing against the shutters,
The voice of the bush-clover.

Sesshi

Bush-clover is growing so close to the poet's hut that when the autumn wind blows, the long stems tap and rustle on the sliding shutters. In such a quiet place, touch and sound come closer together to the poetic mind.

唐黍のうしろに低し寺の壁　　　　　子 規

Tōkibi no　ushiro ni hikushi　tera no kabe

Behind the Indian millet,
The low wall
Of a temple.　　　　　　　　　　Shiki

This is a poem that is quite inexplicable to anyone who has
not noted the peculiarly strong and beautifully-made walls of
country temples, that are yet low enough to vault over should
one be so inclined. There is something both symbolical and
characteristic about the strength and lowness of the wall, and
its relation of harmony with the "Chinese-millet" that looks as
if it also came from some far land in the south.

朝がほの花に鳴きゆく蚊の弱り　　　芭 蕉

Asagao no　hana ni nakiyuku　ka no yowari

Out towards the morning-glories,
Mosquitoes fly humming:
Their languor.　　　　　　　　　Bashō

Bashō got up early in the morning, opened the door, and as
he stood looking at the flowers of the morning-glories, mosqui-
toes slowly came from behind and flew out towards them.
Their voices were weak, the weather being cold. The ephem-
eral beauty of the flowers in his eyes, the languishing sound
of the mosquitoes in his ears, unite in giving him a physical
feeling of early autumn.

朝顔にあぶなき棒の稽古かな　　　　樗 良

Asagao ni　abunaki bō no　keiko kana

Single-stick practice:
I fear
For the morning-glories.　　　　　Chora

Literally the verse says: "The stick-practice is dangerous to
the morning-glories." Life means destruction. Without death
there is no birth. From the point of view of Zen, we must
say that damaging or destroying the morning-glories would be

giving them life, life more abundantly. But it is this which makes life a tragic thing, what gives to the word *destiny* its lugubrious sound.

朝顔や一輪深き淵の色　　　　　　　蕪 村
Asagao ya   ichirin fukaki   fuchi no iro

A single flower
Of the morning-glory:
　　The colour of a deep tarn.　　　Buson

There are three points to observe in this verse. There is the delight in the deep colour of the flower, infinite in meaning, contrasted with its smallness and ephemeral nature. This we see in the following, by Shiki:

三尺の庭に上野の落葉かな
Sanjaku no   niwa ni ueno no   ochiba kana

In three feet of garden,
The falling leaves
Of Ueno.

Besides this there is the delight in colour as such, a blessedness of pure sensation which Buson shows in so many of his haiku. To take two only:

つつじ咲て片山里の飯白し
Tsutsuji saite   katayama-zato no   meshi shiroshi

Azaleas blooming;
In this remote hamlet
The rice is white.

手燭して色失へる黄菊かな
Teshoku shite   iro ushinaeru   kigiku kana

The yellow chrysanthemums
Lose their colour
In the light of the hand-lantern.

Last we have to consider the prescript, which requires a long explanation:

澗水湛如藍

The valley water, accumulating, is like indigo.

This comes from the 82nd Case of the *Hekiganroku*:

僧問大龍、色身敗壊、如何是堅固法身。龍云、
山花開似錦、
澗水湛如藍。

A monk said to Tairyū, "The Body of Form suffers
annihilation; how about this Eternal Body of the Law?"
Tairyū replied, "The mountain flowers opening are like
brocade; the valley water accumulating is like indigo."

The monk speaks of the relative, and asks concerning the
absolute, but Tairyū's reply is not in either realm.

In his verse, Buson has most skilfully combined both lines of
Tairyū's answer, and his haiku is also the answer to the monk's
question and to all our questions. What is God? Is the soul
immortal? What is this world out of time that nevertheless
is in time; that is spaceless, and yet in this very room? Buson
answers, "Look at this fleeting flower: it is the colour of
eternity." But it is not an eternal colour.

看經の間を朝顔の盛哉　　　　　許六
Kankin no ma wo asagao no sakari kana

While I intone the sutras,
The morning-glories
Are at their best.　　　　　Kyoroku

As the poet sits reciting the Buddhist scriptures before the
altar in his house, he glances out and sees the convolvulus
flowers blooming in the soft early sunshine. He too is at his
best, but the flowers somehow excel him, not merely in their
beauty, but in their silent unselfconsciousness, their delicate
warmth; in their *living* they excel him, and his voice falters
as he chants. Nevertheless, his intoning of the sutra is a kind
of funeral service for the flowers.

塵塚に朝顔咲きぬ暮の秋　　　　　太　祇

Chirizuka ni   asagao sakinu   kure no aki

> From the rubbish-heap,
> A morning-glory has bloomed;
> Late autumn.　　　　　Taigi

In this verse we feel the "loneliness" of nature, each thing
living its own, solitary, secret life, of which the most profound
expression is, "My God! My God! Why hast thou forsaken
me?" But we feel, at the same time, the charm of the small
flower that sheds its sweetness on the desert air.

朝顔や人の顔にはそつがある　　　　　一　茶

Asagao ya   hito no kao ni wa   sotsu ga aru

> The morning-glories;
> In the faces of men
> There are faults.　　　　　Issa

The Japanese for morning-glory means "morning face." It
is a strange thing, when one thinks of it, that the countenances
of the morning-glories, however different they may be from
one another, are all perfect, faultless in line and balance, colour
and texture. There is no room for criticism, no point about
which we can find fault with them, nothing to irritate or
weary. A man who lived in a world of flowers would have no
difficulty in being a saint.

朝顔やこれもまた我友ならず　　　　　芭　蕉

Asagao ya   kore mo mata waga   tomo narazu

> The morning-glory too,
> Can never be
> My friend.　　　　　Bashō

Nothing transitory is fit companion for us,—and *all* is tran-
sitory; where then can we find rest? Emily Dickinson says,

> In insecurity to lie
> Is joy's insuring quality,

echoing Blake's

> But he who kisses the Joy as it flies,
> Lives in eternity's sunrise.

Yet somehow or other Bashō's verse is not so satisfying as a famous waka by the poet Tadanori:[1]

ゆきくれて木の下蔭を宿とせば
花やこよひのあるじならまし

> Overtaken by darkness,
> I make this cherry-tree
> My lodging place,
> The flowers, this night,
> My hosts, my friends.

A verse by Bashō similar to Tadanori's:

あさがほや晝は錠おろす門の垣
Asagao ya   hiru wa jō orosu   kado no kaki

> A morning-glory,
> On the fence of my gate,
> That is shut all day.

There is a verse by Ikkyū like the first of Bashō's verses, but it is a very grim waka indeed; we hardly care for the truth in quite such an unadulterated form:

世の中の生死の道につれはなし
たださびしくも獨死獨來

> There is no companion for us
> On the road of this world
> Of life and death;
> Only death in solitude,
> Birth in solitude.

朝顔の地を這ひわたる空家哉　　　　　　子 規
Asagao no   chi wo haiwataru   akiya kana

> The morning-glory
> Trails over the ground
> Of the empty house.　　　　　　Shiki

[1] 1143–83.

The house and garden look forlorn and neglected, and above all the convolvuluses creeping aimlessly and unrestrictedly on the ground brings out the lack of meaning, the uselessness of the house that no one is living in.

朝顔は下手の書くさへあはれなり　　　　芭蕉
Asagao wa　heta no kaku sae　aware nari

> The pathos,
> Even when painted unskilfully,
> Of the morning-glory.　　　　Bashō

Ransetsu, Bashō's pupil, painted a picture of morning-glories and asked Bashō to write a verse for it. The flower of the morning-glory has something pathetic in it, lasting only a few hours, and the unskilfulness of the artist has inadvertently, and thus all the more effectively, brought out the essential *aware*, the gentle beauty of the flower. It is the more moving because like the mathematician that Goethe speaks of, who

> is only complete in so far as he feels within himself the beauty of the true,

the philosopher attains his full height only when, like Plato, he is a poet. There is a passage in Spengler in which we see the botanist apprehending the flowers in a more than intellectual aspect:

> It is a sight of deep pathos to see how the spring flowers craving to fertilize and be fertilized, cannot for all their bright splendour attract one another, or even see one another, but must have recourse to animals, for whom alone those scents exist.[1]

朝露や薄は撓み萩は伏し　　　　　　　樗良
Asatsuyu ya　susuki wa tayumi　hagi wa fushi

> The morning dew:
> The pampas grass is drooping,
> The bush-clover lies prostrate.　　　　Chora

[1] Peoples, Races, and Tongues, 1.

Chora's verse gives us a feeling of wetness without mentioning it. The difference between the characters of the two plants is clearly seen.

山は暮れ野はたそがれのすゝき哉　　蕪　村
Yama wa kure　no wa tasogare no　susuki kana

On the mountain, day has closed;
On the moor, the pampas grass
In the twilight.　　Buson

The sun has set behind the mountain and it is dark and formless, of two dimensions only. But on the moor, it is still twilight, and the white plumes of the pampas grass float like ghosts in the dusk.

嵯峨中の淋しさくくる薄かな　　嵐　雪
Sagajū no　sabishisa kukuru　susuki kana

The pampas grass,—
It sums up all
The loneliness of Saga.　　Ransetsu

The subjective colouring of the desolate wilds of Saga is treated objectively in the pampas grass, that is both a symbol, and what is symbolized. It is a strange thing that a person to whom Saga is a name only should be able to get from this verse something which one who has lived there and knows its historical associations may receive. It is like "the farthest Hebrides" of Wordsworth's *Solitary Reaper*. To visit Saga or the Hebrides might be to break the spell.

穂芒や細き心のさわがしき　　一　茶
Hosusuki ya　hosoki kokoro no　sawagashiki

The plume of the pampas grass,—
The helpless tremblings
Of a lonely heart.　　Issa

The actor and the spectator have powers and functions which

are difficult to combine; action and contemplation are seldom
found united, at their highest, in one person. The love of
glory, the feeling of power in the guiding of the destinies of
a nation have been found in few of the poets. In spite of the
great names of Dante and Milton, it is not without good cause
that we think of poets as an effeminate, shrinking tribe. Of
them, sensitiveness and compassion are required to such a de-
gree that the possession and practice of the martial virtues
becomes well-nigh impossible. In Christ alone, we see them
combined in an almost unbearably poignant contrast, and even
in him, the feminine predominates.

武蔵野や畑の隅の花芒   子 規
Musashino ya   hatake no sumi no   hana-susuki

The plain of Musashino;
In the corners of the fields,
Flowering pampas grass.   Shiki

Anyone who has looked out of the railway windows in autumn
on his way from Tōkyō westward, will recognize the justness
of this description of the scenery. With this the picture is
complete, and all farther details unnecessary. The following
verse by the same poet is on the same subject, but the mere
picture has changed into poetry:

田の中や何にのこして花芒
Ta no naka ya   nani ni nokoshite   hana-susuki

In the fields,
Why have they left
The flowering pampas grass?

This is in the form of a question, but the poet is not asking
for the reason why the farmers did not cut down the pampas
grass. It is simply the feeling of wonder at the existence of
things; it has no ulterior motive. If we insist on an answer
to the question, it is given in a poem by Robert Frost, *The
Tuft of Flowers*:

A leaping tongue of bloom the scythe had spared
Beside a reedy brook the scythe had bared.

. . . .

The mower in the dew had loved them thus,
By leaving them to flourish, not for us,
Nor yet to draw one thought of ours to him,
But from sheer morning gladness at the brim.

槍立てゝ通る人なし花芒   子 規
Yari tatete tōru hito nashi hana-susuki

None passes
Bearing a javelin:
Flowering pampas grass.   Shiki

When the pampas grass blooms and the plumes sway in the
autumn breeze, one half expects to see once more the stately
train of a daimyō passing slowly along the road. But no, men
with up-pointing spears do not pass through the plumed pam-
pas grasses.

十丈の杉六尺のすすきかな   子 規
Jūjō no sugi rokushaku no susuki kana

The cryptomeria, a hundred feet;
The pampas grass,
Six feet.   Shiki

Though this seems to be but a lumberman's calculation, it
is really an etching in black and white, in which, however,
the figures given express the wonder of the poet as he gazes
up at the towering, age-old trees along the highway, and down
at the frail reeds that droop their plumy heads far below. In
their disparity of colouring, power, and form of life, is felt
some common element symbolized in the figures of their re-
spective heights. There is another and better verse by Shiki
resembling the above:

大木に並んで高し鶏頭花
Taiboku ni narande takashi keitō-bana

Together beneath a giant tree,
How tall
The cockscombs in flower!

穂芒やおれが小鬢をともそよぎ   一 茶

Hosusuki ya   ore ga kobin wo   tomosoyogi

Wisps of my hair
Quiver together with the plumes
Of the pampas grass.   Issa

The white wisps of hair at the sides of the poet's head are
shuddering in the autumn wind; at the same time, the white
plume of the pampas grass flutters and trembles, and with that
wanton impartiality which makes it a symbol of the spirit of
the universe, the wind sways both the grass and the man.
Perhaps Issa remembered here Sora's verse:

卯の花に兼房見ゆる白髪かな

U no hana ni   kanefusa miyuru   shiraga kana

In the flowers of the *u*
Are seen the white hairs
Of Kanefusa.

But this is a historical recollection; Issa's verse has in it a
feeling of the continuity of his own body with that of the earth
and the grass it produces. One wind trembles in himself and
in the pampas grass. Thoreau says:

We see men haying far off in the meadow, their heads
waving like the grass which they cut. In the distance the
wind seemed to bend all alike.[1]

茨老すゝき瘦萩おぼつかな   蕪 村

Ibara oi   susuki yase hagi   obotsukana

The wild rose growing old,
The pampas grass thinning,
    The lespedezas faint and weak.   Buson

Walking through the fields Buson notes the flowers and bushes
and weeds as they stand there declining from their summer
beauty, yet unceasingly full of a meaning that has a relation
to beauty but is not beauty itself. The wild rose belongs to
summer, but now it is only a leafy plant beginning to wither.

[1] *A Week on the Concord and Merrimack Rivers.*

The time of the pampas also is past; the bush-clover is fading and falling unsteadily. Each thing is leaning towards "its grave i'the earth so chilly," but each in its own way. Another translation:

> The wild rose grown aged,
> The pampas grass is sparse,
> The bush-clover hesitating.

米 の な き 時 は 瓢 に を み な へ し   芭 蕉
Kome no naki   toki wa hisago ni   ominaeshi

> When there is no rice,—
> The maiden-flower
> In the gourd.   Bashō

The *ominaeshi* flowers in autumn. The plant is three or four feet tall, and small grain-like yellow flowers appear on the group of stalks of deep yellow colour. These stalks are slender and look transparent, somehow reminding one of the horns of the snail.

Bashō was born of a samurai house, and learned that

> poem-composing pastimes are not to be engaged in by a samurai. To be addicted to such amusements is to resemble a woman. A man born a samurai should live and die sword in hand.[1]

The above verse shows that breeding will tell. Bashō, as a poet and a samurai, puts blessedness above happiness. His life of retirement is that of a verse in the *Zenrinkushū*:

拈 持 紅 葉 書 秋 思、
摘 得 黄 花 當 晚 食。

> Breaking off a branch of crimson leaves, and writing thoughts of autumn;
> Plucking the yellow flowers, and making them the evening meal.

There is a similar verse by Buson:

[1] From the *Code of Katō Kiyomasa*, famous general of the 16th century.

古郷や酒はあしくも蕎麥の花
Furusato ya   sake wa ashiku mo   soba no hana

> My old home;
> The wine is poor,—
> But the buck-wheat flower!

However, Buson may well be meaning that the flowers of the buck-wheat promise a good crop, and he will be able to eat noodles.

ひよろひよろ尚ほ露けしや女郎花　　　　　　芭 蕉
Hyorohyoro   nao tsuyukeshi ya   ominaeshi

> The maiden-flower,
> So slender,
> Seems the more dewy.　　　　　　Bashō

The maiden-flower, literally, "harlot-flower," has a soft, dewy appearance, and this is increased by the slimness of the stems. The mind of Bashō is here as slender and dewy as the flower itself. Further, the verse expresses in its rhythm and onomatopoeia the nature of the *ominaeshi* and its dew. Buson has the following verse:

女郎花そも莖ながら花ながら
Ominaeshi   somo kuki nagara   hana nagara

> The *ominaeshi*, ah!
> The stems as they are,
> The flowers as they are.

Taigi has made a similar attempt, but concerning the *yamabuki*, the yellow rose, expressing the multitude of green leaves and yellow blossoms mingled:

山吹や葉に花に葉に花に葉に
Yamabuki ya   ha ni hana ni ha ni   hana ni ha ni

> The mountain rose,—
> Leaves and flowers and leaves
> And flowers and leaves.

女 郎 花 あ つ け ら か ん と 立 て り け り   一 茶
Ominaeshi   akkerakan to   tateri keri

The maiden-flower
Stands there
Vacantly.   Issa

When we look at things we give them their value, (so Maha-
yana Buddhism tells us), but our experience is one of receiving,
not of giving. We receive the beauty of the flower; we do not
have any feeling of bestowing it. But in the above verse, Issa
stands looking at the maiden-flower, and knows the life of the
flower as its own, not his. It is standing there abstractedly,
with a slightly foolish air.

何 事 の か ぶ り か ぶ り ぞ を み な へ し   一 茶
Nanigoto no   kaburi kaburi zo   ominaeshi

What is it
You are nodding about,
Ominaeshi?   Issa

This again is a verse in which there is a frank attribution
of human feelings to an inanimate thing, but without the so-
called "pathetic fallacy." Issa feels that the *ominaeshi* is nod-
ding in him and he in it. Only when the poet and the flower
are taken as two things do we find the difficulty of attributing
personality to the flower and simple movement to the motion-
less poet.

芙 蓉 さ い て 古 池 の 鷺 や も め な り   子 規
Fuyō saite   furu-ike no sagi   yamome nari

Rose-mallows are blooming;
The widowed heron
Of the old pond.   Shiki

The *fuyō* has a white or pink flower, rather gorgeous in
character. In contrast to this, the pond is silent and deserted;
only a solitary heron, whose mate is dead, stands there motion-

less in the shallower water. There is another very similar verse by the same author:

廢館に鶏遊ぶ芙蓉かな
Haikan ni   niwatori asobu   fuyō kana

> Round the ruined mansion,
> Hens wander;
> Rose-mallows are blooming.

霧雨の空を芙蓉の天気かな　　　　　　　　芭 蕉
Kirisame no   sora wo fuyō no   tenki kana

> In the misty rain,
> The rose-mallows
> Make a bright sky.　　　　　　　　Bashō

This is a remarkable, if not remarkably good, verse. The great flowers of the hibiscus are so bright that the misty sky above is overpowered by them, and the weather there alone appears fine. The flowers have a kind of aura or halo. They exude a kind of light. They are like haiku, which shed beams out into our dark world and enlighten those that sit in its shadows.

痩草のよろよろ花と成にけり　　　　　　　一 茶
Yase-kusa no   yoro yoro hana to   nari ni keri

> The feeble plant,
> At last,
> Has a wabbly flower.　　　　　　　　Issa

This has pathos and humour, a colloquial expression of rare sympathy. Not only man but nature has its weedy plants, its distortions and stunted growths, its failures and monstrosities. The thin, helpless plant, with its flower too big and heavy for its stem, has an appeal for us that the perfect flower of health and strength can never have.

名はしらず草毎に花哀なり　　　　杉風
Na wa shirazu　kusa-goto ni hana　aware nari

 The names unknown,
But to every weed its flower,
 And loveliness.   Sampū

To walk in the country and see the myriad shapes and
colours of leaves and stems and flowers among the grasses is
one of the purest pleasures of life. When we are at our best,
that is, at our least, every green leaf, even the leaves of the
same plant in their different sizes and depths of tint, are the
different expressions of itself; and each of these weeds, though
nameless, has its flower of tender beauty.

The names are unknown, and best so. Walt Whitman says
something which Thoreau found out by experience:

> You must not know too much or be too precise or scien-
> tific about birds and trees and flowers and watercraft; a
> certain free-margin, and even vagueness—ignorance, cre-
> dulity—helps your enjoyment of these things.

名を聞てまた見直すや草の花　　　　低耳
Na wo kiite　mata minaosu ya　kusa no hana

 A flowering weed;
Hearing its name,
 I looked anew at it.   Teiji

The poet looked at it with quite different eyes after he knew
its name. Associations of all kinds, historical, poetical, medical,
now coloured his vision. But this does not necessarily mean
that his view was distorted by these associations. It might
have been so, but on the other hand the name might have
revealed to him the flower's true nature, causing him to know
what to look for, what to see. Blake says,

The fool sees not the same tree that a wise man sees.

百 な り や 蔓 一 筋 の 心 よ り   千代尼
Hyaku nari ya   tsuru hitosuji no   kokoro yori

A hundred different gourds,
From the mind
  Of one vine.

          Chiyo-ni

It is said that Chiyo, the most famous of women haiku writers,
was asked by the Zen Master of Eiheiji Temple to illustrate in
a haiku the teaching that a thousand meanings come from one
thought. The above verse is the parabolic expression of this
Zen principle, (which is that rather of Mahayana Buddhism).
The *Kegonkyō*, 華嚴經, says:

三界唯一心、 心外無別法、 心佛及衆生無差別。

In the three worlds,[1] all is Mind. Other than Mind,
nothing exists. Buddha, mind, sentient beings,—these three
are not different things.

Plotinus says:

In our realm all is part rising from part, and nothing
can be more than partial; but There, each being is an
eternal product of a whole, and is at once a whole and an
individual manifesting as part, but, to the keen vision
There, known for the whole it is.[2]

For haiku, a gourd is "a part rising from part," but it is
seen as a whole, though at the same time as a part. For
haiku, here is There, and There is here. The above verse of
Chiyo is of course not to be called haiku, but it is nevertheless
not disconnected with the state of mind which produces haiku,
for it is the one Poetic Mind which produces all haiku and all
poetry, and in so far as we share in It we are living There
and here now.

---

[1] This 三界 does not mean past, present, and future (which is 三世),
but 欲界, 色界, 無色界, the three worlds of desire, form, and no-form.
[2] V. 8, 4.

夜の蘭香にかくれてや花白し   蕪 村
Yoru no ran   ka ni kakurete ya   hana shiroshi

An evening orchid,—
It hid in its scent,
The flower white.   Buson

As it grew darker, nothing could be seen of the stem and
the leaves, but the fragrance was stronger than ever, and the
orchid hid in its own perfume, the white flower alone faintly
seen, palely gleaming through the darkness.

芭蕉植ゑて先づ憎む荻の二葉哉   芭 蕉
Bashō uete   mazu nikumu ogi no   futaba kana

Having planted a *bashō*,
I feel spiteful now
Towards the sprouting bush-clover.   Bashō

That spring,[1] Rika, 李下, a pupil of his had sent a banana-
plant, and Bashō had planted it in the garden of his hermitage,
a hut with a nine-foot square room and a tiny earth-floored
kitchen. Being near the river, the damp earth was suitable
for the *bashō*, but also for bush-clover and bulrushes that
grew all around luxuriantly. These rushes that looked pleasant
enough before, now began to take upon themselves a disagree-
able aspect, when Bashō thought they might choke and kill
the precious plant he had so carefully planted.

We are at this moment Buddhas, and at the same time
human beings with likes and dislikes. This "at the same time"
does not mean that we are partly human and partly divine.
Without these inscrutable preferences and this loving one above
another, we are not Buddhas; without pure indiscriminate love
of all things, we are not human beings.

[1] 1681. Gradually people began to call him Bashō.

隣から灯火うつる芭蕉かな　　　　　　　　　　子　規
Tonari kara　tomoshibi utsuru　bashō kana

The next-door lamp
Lights up
　　The *bashō*.　　　　　　　　　　　　　　　Shiki

The banana-plant stands there in the darkness, when suddenly a door is opened in the neighbour's house and the *bashō* becomes illuminated. The great translucent green leaves become full of light, as if themselves luminous. The poet and the *bashō* and the house next door immediately enter into a new and totally unexpected relation, whose outcome is the verse above. Another verse by Shiki, and one by Bashō, showing the power of the banana-plant:

廻廊の曲り曲りの芭蕉かな
Kairō no　magari magari no　bashō kana

　　　At every turn
　　Of the corridor,—
　　　The *bashō*!

此寺は庭一ぱいの芭蕉哉
Kono tera wa　niwa ippai no　bashō kana

　　　The garden
　　Of this temple is full
　　　Of the *bashō*.

青々と障子にうつる芭蕉かな　　　　　　　　子　規
Aoao to　shōji ni utsuru　bashō kana

　　The green shadow
Of the *bashō*
　　On the paper-screen.　　　　　　　　　　Shiki

The shadows of things are without colour, but the broad leaves of the banana-plant are translucent, and its reflection on the milky-white paper is a coloured one, a tender green.

燈籠消えて芭蕉に風のわたる音　　　子 規
Tōrō kiete　bashō ni kaze no　wataru oto

The garden lantern goes out;
The sound of the wind
Blowing through the *bashō*!　　　Shiki

The wind is blowing violently, and the light in the stone
lantern in the garden suddenly goes out. As the poet looks at
the darkness, he becomes aware of the rushing of the wind
through the great leaves of the banana-plant.

破れ盡す貧乏寺の芭蕉かな　　　子 規
Yare-tsukusu　bimbō-dera no　bashō kana

In the ruined,
Poverty-stricken temple,
A *bashō*.　　　Shiki

The temple is a small one, in a remote part of the country.
It has fallen into disrepair; the monk has died, his simple
grave is nearby. Though religion declines, Zen always flour-
ishes. The small courtyard in front of the temple is filled with
the green vigour of the huge leaves of the *bashō*.

野烏の上手にとまる芭蕉かな　　　一 茶
Nogarasu no　jōzu ni tomaru　bashō kana

The crow from the moor
Perches cleverly
On the *bashō*.　　　Issa

The banana-plant, with its broad, yielding leaves, is a difficult
thing for a big bird like the crow to land on. The crow too
knows this, and when he alights, he looks round, as if he
thinks he has made a good job of it, with a self-satisfied glint
in his bright, black eyes.

けさ程やこそりと落ちてある一葉　　　　一　茶
Kesa hodo ya　kosori to ochite　aru hitoha

> Just this morning,—
> A single paulownia leaf
> Has gently fallen.　　　　　　Issa

"Just this morning" implies that it is the first leaf that has
fallen this autumn. "A single leaf" usually means the leaf of
a paulownia. "Has gently fallen" shows the leaf on the dewy
ground, but suggests the silence and stealth with which it fell.
This verse is full of autumn, full of silence and stillness, yet
with a morning freshness and newness that is devoid of
melancholy.

桐の木の風にかまはぬ落葉かな　　　　凡　兆
Kiri no ki no　kaze ni kamawanu　ochiba kana

> The leaf of the paulownia,
> With not a breath of wind,
> Falls.　　　　　　　　Bonchō

The inner necessity of the paulownia tree is strong. With
other trees it is the outer necessity, the autumn wind which
causes them to flutter down, but the large leaves of the pau-
lownia, yellowed and crumpled by the frost, fall without a
sound on windless days, when not a breath of air is stirring.

さびしさを問てくれぬか桐一葉　　　　芭　蕉
Sabishisa wo　tōte kurenu ka　kiri hitoha

> A paulownia leaf has fallen;
> Will you not visit
> My loneliness?　　　　　Bashō

Bacon says in his essay *Of Friendship* that the chief use of
friendship among men,

> is the ease and discharge of the fullness and swelling of
> the heart, which passions of all kinds do cause and induce.

We know diseases of stoppings and suffocations are the

most dangerous in the body; and it is not much otherwise with the mind. You may take sarza to open the spleen; flowers of sulphur for the lungs; castoreum for the brain; but no receipt openeth the heart but a true friend to whom you may impart griefs, joys, fears, hopes, suspicions, counsels, and whatsoever lyeth upon the heart to oppress it, in a kind of civil shrift or confession.

Bacon, as always devoid of all poetical and tender feeling, interprets everything at its lowest level. Bashō did not want Ransetsu to come to him for these reasons. He wanted to be with, physically, someone with whom he was always associated in spirit, someone of the same "nationality" as himself, a citizen of the city that is made glad by the river of poetry that flows through it. This "physically" is an important element of poetry because it is the bodily perceptions as such that are the poetical life at its deepest, though not clearest, and it is only by being together when perceiving the same finite infinity that a touch, a breath, a smile will reveal that we are both gazing at the same thing, in communion, not with each other, but with the same single paulownia leaf that falls silently through the autumn air.

毎日は葡萄も喰はず水藥　　　　　　　　子 規
Mainichi wa　budō mo kuwazu　mizu-gusuri

Every day,
Not eating the grapes,—
Drinking medicine.　　　　　Shiki

Shiki's verses on illness are all very simple, and portray the sick man's mind and feelings so directly that even someone who has "never had a day's illness" in his life can enter into the hopes and fears, the long-suffering and disappointment of those who are ill. There are the following, also by Shiki, who was inordinately fond of persimmons:

我が好きの柿を食はれぬ病かな
Waga suki no　kaki wo kuwarenu　yamai kana

The persimmons I love so much,
Can't be eaten:
I'm ill.

Grapes

by Nikkan, 日観, 1127-1279, a Chinese artist
of the Sung Dynasty.

However, when Shiki was well, he became ill from eating what he could not when he was ill. The translation of the following is rather laconic, but so is the original verse:

柿あまた食ひけるよりの病かな
Kaki amata   kuikeru yori no   yamai kana

Ill,
From overeating
Persimmons.

There is a kind of "death-verse" which says, literally, "It should be transmitted (to posterity) that I was a persimmon-eater that loved hokku":

柿くひの發句好と傳ふべし
Kaki kui no   hokku suki to   tsutau beshi

Write me down
As one who loved poetry,
And persimmons.

柿に思ふ奈良の旅籠の下女の顔   子 規
Kaki ni omou   nara no hatago no   gejo no kao

The persimmons make me think
Of the face of a servant
At an inn of Nara.   Shiki

This is a simple example of the association of ideas, but to Shiki, and to the reader of the verse, if he is willing to put himself in the right frame of mind, the face of the servant, not necessarily pretty, but with something alive in it, is so near to the yellow-red persimmon that the proximity is quite shocking. A little more, and we shall be eating a servant's face. The persimmon will be talking and smiling like the leg of mutton and the pudding in *Through the Looking Glass*. In actual fact, the maid-servant at the inn was a particularly charming and lovely young girl, but this does not affect the matter as far as the reader is concerned.

三千の俳句を閲し柿二つ　　　　　　　　子　規
Sanzen no   haiku wo kemishi   kaki futatsu

Examining
Three thousand haiku:
Two persimmons.　　　　　　　　Shiki

With no more than the above words we should be obliged to
draw very freely upon our fancy to understand the connection,
but fortunately Kyoshi has described the matter quite minutely.
Shiki was extremely painstaking and conscientious in his selec-
tion of haiku. Even when ill in bed, those haiku sent to news-
papers and magazines for his criticism were all the more
scrupulously read and judged. By his bedside was a big box
in which all the haiku sent to him were kept. Though Shiki
was weak in health, suffering from consumption, he was ex-
tremely fond of eating, and above all things he loved persim-
mons, which as is well known are not particularly digestible.
In this verse then, Shiki has promised himself two persimmons
when he has finished perusing what looks like about three
thousand haiku. They are a kind of reward, which spurs him
on to finish his labour. The feverish poet lies in bed poring
over the verses of nincompoops and poetasters, and ever and
anon glances at the two persimmons which wait there to be
eaten or not.

柿喰へば鐘が鳴るなり法隆寺　　　　　　子　規
Kaki kueba   kane ga naru nari   hō-ryūji

Eating persimmons;
The bell sounds,
Of Hōryūji Temple.　　　　　　　Shiki

Hōryūji Temple was founded in 607 A.D. at Nara by Prince
Shōtoku. The oldest temple in Japan, it contains wonderful
treasures of art. Shiki was sitting in a tea-house in Nara,
eating his favourite fruit, when suddenly the great temple bell
of Hōryūji sounded. Eating and listening, the two elements of
human life, material and spiritual, prose and poetry, practical
life and religion,—these are so far apart when we think about
them, but sitting in the tea-house eating persimmons and

listening to the voice of religion, there is felt to be no disparity.
The past and the present, the heard and the tasted are one.

里ふりて柿の木持たぬ家もなし   芭 蕉
Sato furite   kaki no ki motanu   ie mo nashi

The village is old;
No house
But has its persimmon tree.   Bashō

This was composed at the house of a man named Bōsui.
The age of the village, the old cottages, the age of the per-
simmon trees, with their twisted, rheumatic branches, every-
thing seems to belong to the past more than the present. The
old trees have a feeling of calmness which man did not give
and man cannot take away.

しぶいとこ母がくひけり山のかき   一 茶
Shibui toko   haha ga kuikeri   yama no kaki

Wild persimmons,
The mother eating
The bitter parts.   Issa

This is the love that moves the stars, and is easier to see it
in this "impure" form than in the love of Buddha or Christ,
where it often appears, at this distance of time and with the
modern improvements, somewhat abstract and inaccessible.

落る日のくゞりて染るそばの茎   蕪 村
Otsuru hi no   kugurite somuru   soba no kuki

The setting sun
Creeps through the stalks of buckwheat,
Dyeing them.   Buson

This is as near a purely pictorial representation of nature as
can be attained to. There is nothing solemn or sad in the last
rays of the sun, only a stillness in which the red light reddens

the red stalks of the buckwheat, passing through them hori-
zontally. In the following verse, however, also by Buson, the
human element, only alluded to, changes the picture:

道のべに手よりこぼれてそばの花
Michinobe ni   te yori koborete   soba no hana

At the side of the road,
Flowers of buckwheat,
Spilled from someone's hand.

When the buckwheat seeds were being transferred from the
sack to the basket, some dropped by the wayside and have now
flowered there. There is in this verse the pleasant surprise at
finding the beautiful flowers here at the side of the road, with
a feeling of time added, the faint presence of those who dropped
the seeds in this place, the faithfulness of nature, the nature
of the seeds and the rain and dew and earth.

桟やいのちをからむ蔦かつら　　　　　　　芭　蕉
Kakehashi ya   inochi wo karamu   tsuta katsura

The hanging bridge:
Creeping vines
Entwine our life.　　　　　　　　　　Bashō

Bashō, with his disciple Etsujin, was travelling towards Sara-
shina to see the autumn moon there. His journey is described
in detail in the *Diary of Travel through Sarashina*, 更科紀行.
The above verse was composed when crossing the famous
hanging bridge of Kiso, 木曾, after walking along the precipitous
road leading to it. The vines spoken of are growing along the
bridge over the deep ravine. They have entrusted their lives
to the bridge just as Bashō and Etsujin are doing. If we go
beyond this and talk or think of human life and its precarious-
ness, we are falling out of the suchness of things into thinking
and talking about it.

我が聲の風になりけり菌狩   子 規
Waga koe no   kaze ni nari keri   kinokogari

My voice
Becomes the wind;
Mushroom-hunting.   Shiki

The first two lines are clear; the experience is common to
every man who has spoken or called out in a strong wind. But
what is the connection, the poetical connection, between this
and the mushroom-gathering? If there is no intrinsic, unana-
lysable relation between voice and breeze and mushrooms, there
is no poetry. If we can explain all the relation away, it is not
poetry; if we do not feel, with our poetical instinct, some deep,
inexpressible but definite poetical connection between them, it
may be our own failure to enter into the poet's experience, or
it may be that there is no real experience behind the verse at
all, and we can replace one or more of the elements by some
other, quite different element, without altering the value, that
is, the lack of value of the verse. The poetic nexus lies in
the mind of the mushroom hunter. He finds an unusually fine
mushroom; there are such a large number in this particular
spot. He straightens his back and calls to his companions,
who however do not hear or do not attend to him. His voice
fades out into the air as it passes in gusts over the dead and
dying leaves, along the side of the autumn mountains. The
mushroom is in his hand and yet it is not there. Together
with himself, with his voice, with all things it becomes an air,
a floating echo that passes into the timeless, placeless realm
where nothing is, where all things have their real being, and
the poetic soul is satisfied and content.

秋風の吹けども青し栗のいが   芭 蕉
Aki-kaze no   fukedomo aoshi   kuri no iga

The autumn wind is blowing,
But the chestnut burs
Are green.   Bashō

The power of nature is seen in the bright greenness of what
should be by now yellow and dying. It may be too that Bashō

felt some harmony between the prickly spines of the burs and the chilly autumn wind. Compare the following, by a modern poet, Meisetsu:

凩や磯にとび散る青松葉
Kogarashi ya   iso ni tobi-chiru   ao-matsuba

>The cold winter blast;
>On the shore,
>>Green pine-needles flying about.

The twisted pine-trees stand on the seashore, and beneath them and on the sand, green pine-needles are scattering and whirling. The cold, the greenness of the pine-needles, the sand, the strength and fitfulness of the wind that is seen in the twitching needles on the ground and the willy-nilly dancing of those still in the air,—all is as it should be. Nature is an enemy even to itself, but we faintly perceive a harmony in this, though our spirits are too weak to do other than see it as in a glass darkly.

落栗や蟲の啼き止む草の中   蒲　梢
Ochi-guri ya   mushi no nakiyamu   kusa no naka

>A chestnut falls:
>The insects cease their crying,
>>Among the grasses.   Boshō

All is chance, all is fate; cause and effect works invariably, and to the intellectual eye there is no hiatus, no dark area other than that caused by ignorance. The chestnut falls, and the insects stop singing. But the poetical eye does not see this at all. The chestnut falls because it wants to fall, because the poet wants it to fall. The insects are silent because it s their nature and the poet's nature to be silent at such a moment. Man gives to inevitability the nature of will, not only the will to power, but the will to be and to behold. So this falling of the chestnut and the sudden quiet of the chirping insects is felt not in the mind or the heart but in the pit of the stomach. It is so,—and being so, fraught with a meaning that the intellect could never conceive.

Squirrel on a Chestnut-tree

by Oguri Sōkyū, 小栗宗休, said to be a grandson
of Oguri Sōtan, 小栗宗丹, 1398–1464.

拾はれぬ栗の見事よ大きさよ　　　　　　　　　一　茶
Hirowarenu　kuri no migoto yo　ōkisa yo

> What a huge one, how splendid it was,—
> The chestnut
> I couldn't get at!　　　　　　　　　　　Issa

This is the opposite of "sour grapes." It is this (from the Buddhist point of view reprehensible) attachment to things that makes a man a man, not a Buddha. Yet it has something divine, something poetical in it, that we feel in the above verse. It comes from the manhood of God and the Godhood of man that is symbolized in the Incarnation,—all this being seen, not in the abstract, not in the words or thoughts, but in the regret for not being able to reach a particularly fine chestnut.

There is a verse by a modern poet, Eugene Field, in which the rhyme and verbosity spoil the poetry and render it mere senryu:

> I never lost a little fish—yes
> I am free to say,
> It always was the biggest fish
> I caught that got away.

There is another example in *Through the Looking Glass*:

> And it certainly did seem a little provoking ("almost as if it happened on purpose," she thought that, though she managed to pick plenty of beautiful rushes as the boat glided by, there was always a more lovely one that she couldn't reach.
>
> "The prettiest are always farther," she said at last.

ゆで栗や胡坐上手な小さい子　　　　　　　　　一　茶
Yude-guri ya　agura jōzu na　chiisai ko

> Boiled chestnuts;
> A tiny boy
> Squatting cleverly.　　　　　　　　　　　Issa

Sitting on the floor with legs crossed tailor-wise is one of the two beautiful ways of sitting, and the little boy is doing it as only Buddhas of iron and bronze can, with poise, with ease. He is, however, quite unconscious of this, and is busily peeling and eating boiled chestnuts. He is like the cat on the mantlepiece, more beautiful than any of the vases and pictures round him.

木立くらく何の實落つる水の音　　　　子　規
Kodachi kuraku　nan no mi otsuru　mizu no oto

In the dark forest,
A berry drops:
The sound of the water.　　　Shiki

We may compare the mysterious simplicity of this with the wonder and beauty of another verse by Shiki:

鳥鳴いて赤き木實をこぼしけり
Tori naite　akaki konomi wo　koboshi keri

A bird sang,
Knocking down
A red berry.

This verse belongs to the fairy-tale world of childhood and romance. The former is analogous to the verse written by Enju, 延壽, 904–975, when he became enlightened on hearing a bundle of wood drop to the ground:

撲落非他物、縱橫不是塵。
山河並大地、全露法王身。

Something dropped; it is just this.
Nowhere is there any impediment.
Mountains, rivers, and the great earth,—
All manifest forth the Body of Buddha.

梨むくや甘き雫の刃をたるゝ　　　　子　規
Nashi muku ya　amaki shizuku no　ha wo taruru

Peeling a pear,
Sweet drops trickle down
The knife.　　　Shiki

This is a very good haiku, but it might be difficult to prove this to someone brought up entirely on classical western poetry. It brings out the nature of a pear,[1] the nature of a knife, the relation between the two, and this is the real function of poetry, —to hold the mirror up to nature in such a way that we perceive its workings. Haiku is "such a way."

絲瓜咲いて痰のつまりし佛かな　　　　子　規
Hechima saite　tan no tsumarishi　hotoke kana

A snake-gourd is blooming;
Clogged with phlegm,
A dying man.　　　　　　　　　　　　　Shiki

This is the first of three death poems which Shiki wrote on his death-bed. Just at this time, the 19th of September, 1902, a snake-gourd was in bloom. The juice of this plant is used for stopping the formation of phlegm, and this is the painful relation between him and the flowers. The last line is literally "a Buddha," which means "soon to become a Buddha," that is, a dead man.

盗みくふ林檎に腹をいためけり　　　　子　規
Nusumi-kū　ringo ni hara wo　itamekeri

The stolen apples
Which I ate,
Gave me a stomach-ache.　　　　　　　Shiki

The humour of this is obvious, but what is not obvious is the peculiarity of the association of the stomach-ache and the stealing in our feelings. There is a kind of primitive fear that arises in us when the pain is somehow referred to the moral delinquency. It is some atavistic element in our composition (and this is biologically speaking, the origin and foundation of our poetic and religious life), which causes an emotion of (superstitious) awe and consternation.

[1] This a Japanese pear, shaped like an apple, hard but very juicy and sweet.

稲かつて野菊おとろふ小道哉 　　　　子 規
Ine katte   nogiku otorou   komichi kana

The rice having been reaped,
The wild camomiles weaken and dwindle,
Along the path. 　　　　Shiki

The *nogiku* has a stalk and leaves like the chrysanthemum, but shorter. In autumn it forms a pale purple flower with short, simple petals. It is rather childish in appearance, as is shown in the following verse by Gekkyo:

折とれば茎三寸の野菊かな
Oritoreba   kuki sanzun no   nogiku kana

Plucking it,
The camomile has a stem
Of three inches.

While the rice was still standing, the camomiles were erect and bold, but now the rice is cut and the mud shows round the stubble, they droop, fall this way and that, and present a bedraggled appearance quite different from their erstwhile pertness and charm.

白菊にしばしたゆたふはさみかな 　　　　蕪 村
Shiragiku ni   shibashi tayutou   hasami kana

Before the white chrysanthemum,
The scissors hesitate,
A moment. 　　　　Buson

This hesitation, that comes out somehow or other from something unhesitating, is the life that trembles between law and freedom, spirit and matter. It is that which gives value to the flower, whether it is cut down in its prime or not. This pre-hesitation is paralleled by the post-hesitation, portrayed in the following, by the same author:

牡丹切て氣の衰ひしゆふべ哉
Botan kitte   ki no otoroishi   yūbe kana

Having cut the peony,
I felt dejected,
That evening.

The following verse by a modern poet, Kyoshi Takahama, gives the objective side of the matter, although apparently hyperbolical in its expression:

牡丹切つて庭にものなくなりにけり
Botan kitte   niwa ni mono naku   nari ni keri

Having cut the peony,
Nothing was left
In the garden.

No meaning remained after the peony was gone, and where there is no meaning, there is no existence, there is nothing. The garden became a mere emptiness.

ものいはず客と亭主と白菊と
Mono iwazu   kyaku to teishu to   shiragiku to

蓼太

They spoke no word,
The host, the guest,
And the white chrysanthemum.

Ryōta

This white flower was whiter and more beautiful than the flower Buddha held up before the congregation of monks, or that which Christ pointed out to his disciples,—because it was silent. It uttered no aesthetic or spiritual truths; it did not preach Christianity or Buddhism or Zen; it was just its own silent self. And this silence was infectious. Host and guest found that they too had nothing to say.

Let my deep silence speak for me
More than for them their sweetest notes.[1]

見盡した目は白菊に戻りけり
Mitsukushita   me wa shiragiku ni   modori keri

一笑

My eyes, having seen all,
Came back to
The white chrysanthemums.

Isshō

[1] Davies, of the nightingales.

Christ says,

> If thine eye is single, thy whole body is full of light.

When the eye, not the mind, judges, it may be trusted implicitly, but it needs a great deal of genius or determination to distinguish what the eye sees and what the mind adds or takes away. Blake says precisely the opposite to all this; we are right,

> When we see not with but through the eye.

It would be pleasant to say that Blake states the opposite and means exactly the same, but this would not be true. In some sense, Blake was an escapist:

> The land of dreams is better far,
> Above the light of the morning star.

However profound and spiritual these dreams may have been, there was the danger (into which he fell) of being engrossed in the reality inside to the exclusion of that same reality which is outside. The Japanese poet of artist seems by nature immune from such mistakes. Buson, another artist-poet, has Isshō's pure pleasure in colour:

白菊やかゝる目出度色はなくて
Shiragiku ya   kakaru medetaki   iro wa nakute

> White chrysanthemums!
> Where is there a colour
> So happy, so gracious?

黄菊白菊其の外の名はなくもがな   嵐 雪
Kigiku shiragiku   sono hoka no na wa   naku mo gana

> White chrysanthemums,
> Yellow chrysanthemums,—
> Would there were no other names! Ransetsu

From ancient times the thing and its name, God and His name, were considered as in some way identical. The name being known, the thing itself is apprehended in its final essence. The beauty of the white and the yellow chrysanthemums is so overpowering that any other colour is a desecration, a base imitation of them. But desiring that there should be no other *names* than these lifts them into the realm of which it is said,

The name that can be named is not an eternal name.

Nansen, 748–834 A.D., combines this thought of Laotse with the Mahayana idea that with the advent of the Buddha we have unenlightenment; with names the nameless is lost:

南泉云、 空劫之時無一切名字佛纔出世來、
便有名字所以取相。 若有名字、 皆属限量。 (南泉録)

Nansen said, "In the Age of Void, there were no names or words. As soon as a Buddha appeared in the world, names and words came into being, and we became attached to the forms of things. With names and words, all things partake of the finite."

One of Ransetsu's many meanings is: "If we must have names and things with names, let them be few." There is combined here in a remarkable way a linguistic and material asceticism.

白菊やあたりもともに麗はしき　　　　　樗　良
Shiragiku ya　atari mo tomo ni　uruwashiki

White chrysanthemums;
All around them is now
Full of grace and beauty.　　　　Chora

When one thing is seen as meaningful, all things acquire significance:

One touch of nature makes the whole world kin.

This is, superficially speaking, a matter of the association of ideas, and a question of what mood we are in at the moment, but in a deeper sense, since things are as we see them when we see them as they are, our perception of beauty and significance, from whatever indirect or fortuitous cause, creates the meaning and value that is there already. Thus, in the same nonsensical way, only by loving things do we realize their lovability and loveliness.

人形をきざむ小店や菊の花　　　　　　子 規
Ningyō wo　kizamu komise ya　kiku no hana

A small shop,
Carving dolls;
Chrysanthemum flowers.　　　　　Shiki

In this small shop, or workshop, the master and his appren-
tices are engrossed in their carving of dolls. In front of the
shop are growing some chrysanthemums. They are harmonious
with the fine work on the dolls.

菊の香や奈良には古き佛達　　　　　　芭 蕉
Kiku no ka ya　nara ni wa furuki　hotoke-tachi

At Nara;
The smell of chrysanthemums,
The ancient images of Buddha.　　Bashō

The connection between the smell of chrysanthemums and
the ancient Buddhas is subtle and profound. It is utterly
different from that of the Buddhas with the smell of incense,
neither does it resemble Milton's

Storied windows richly dight,
Casting a dim religious light.

Worthy of note, however, is the dignity of sound of the verse,
suiting the graceful, silent voice of both chrysanthemums and
Buddhas. Bashō felt keenly the relation between sight and
odour. We may take as an example:

山吹や宇治の焙爐の匂ふ時
Yamabuki ya　uji no hōro no　niou toki

The yellow-rose blossoms,
When tea-ovens at Uji
Are fragrant.

We may further compare and contrast the following verse by
Kyoshi, where the past and the present are mingled:

蘭 の 香 も 法 隆 寺 に は 今 め か し
Ran no ka mo   hōryūji ni wa   ima mekashi

At Hōryūji,
The scent of the orchids
Is fresh and modern.

The scent of the flowers and the beauty of the wall-paintings
are in harmony; the age of the temple brings out the newness
and freshness of the orchids.   There is a verse by Shiki in
which the harmony is seen between the Buddhist statues and
something quite different:

六 月 の 海 見 ゆ る な り 寺 の 像
Rokugatsu no   umi miyuru nari   tera no zō

The June sea
Seen afar:
Temple statues of Buddha.

In the following, by Sōseki, the harmony is felt between the
flowers and the beautiful character of a dead lady:

あ り た け や 菊 な げ い れ よ 棺 の 中
Aritake ya   kiku nageire yo   kan no naka

All the chrysanthemums you have—
Throw them upon
This coffin!

This was written on the death of Ōtsuka Naoko, a close friend
of Natsume Sōseki. It may be compared in volume of emotional
tone, in finality of utterance, to Bashō's verse on the death of
Isshō.[1] We may compare also a couplet of Silesius, the seven-
teenth century German mystic:

Die Rose, welche hier dein aussres Auge sieht,
Die hat von Ewigkeit in Gott also geblüht.

[1] See Vol. III, page 950.

ともすれば菊の香寒し病みあがり   乙 二
Tomo sureba   kiku no ka samushi   yamiagari

That is what happens:
Recovering from illness,
The chrysanthemums smell cold.   Otsuji[1]

This has the prescript 老躯, "My old body." The poet goes
out into the garden for the first time after his recovery. The
chrysanthemums are beautiful; their scent is that of late autumn
itself. But he begins to shiver. He is growing old, and with
old age, the consequent and inevitable weakening. The chry-
santhemums themselves smell cold, smell of winter, of death.

まけ菊をひとり見直す夕かな   一 茶
Makegiku wo   hitori minaosu   yūbe kana

That evening,
Looking again at the chrysanthemums
That lost.   Issa

The Japanese *mi-naosu* means to look at a thing once more
after one's opinion or feeling has for some reason or other
undergone a change.

There has been a chrysanthemum competition somewhere,
and one of the losers stands in his garden looking at the flower
he has brought back. After seeing the other chrysanthemums
at the show, his own now appears quite different from what
it did that morning. Buson has a verse very similar in content:

行春や選者をうらむ歌の主
Yuku haru ya   senja wo uramu   uta no nushi

Spring is passing;
The composer of the waka
Hates the selector.

Issa expresses the elation of the winner **as he comes back**
home, in the following verse:

[1] Also read Otsuni.

勝 た 菊 大 名 小 路 通 り け り
Katta kiku　daimyō-kōji　tōrikeri

> The winning chrysanthemum
> Passed along
> The daimyō-road.

There are some lines in the *Purgatorio* also, strongly resembling Issa's poem, though of a lower occupation:

> Quando si parte il giuoco della zara,
> Colui che perde si riman dolente
> Ripetendo le volte, e tristo impara;
> Con l' altro se ne va tutta la gente.[1]

When the game of dice breaks up,
He who lost remains sorrowing,
Repeating the throws, and sadly learns;
All the people go off with the other man.

年 々 に 菊 に 思 は ん 思 は れ ん　　　　子 規
Nen nen ni　kiku ni omowan　omowaren

> Every year
> Thinking of the chrysanthemums,
> Being thought of by them.　　　Shiki

We remember things, and they remember us. We wait for the flowers, they await our coming. In other words, things are not merely passive; it is not simply that I sit on the chair, and the chair is sat on by me, but the chair supports me, and I am supported by the chair. There is something active in things that goes beyond the difference of animate and inanimate, willing and involuntary.

菊 作 り 汝 は 菊 の 奴 か な　　　　蕪 村
Kiku-tsukuri　nanji wa kiku no　yakko kana

> Chrysanthemum-grower,
> You are the slave
> Of chrysanthemums!　　　Buson

[1] VI. 1–4.

This verse seems rather short, as if expressing Buson's sense of exasperation. The chrysanthemum addict might retort that the poet is the slave of poetry, and there would be some justice in this, but the aim of the poetic life, or rather the condition of it, is freedom. People with hobbies and -isms, those who twist life to some set of principles or to some object, find themselves twisted and imprisoned within that which they thought to cage. The poetry of the above verse, if any, is in the anger at the misuse of life and beauty. What should be a flower becomes a bond, what should make us smile gives us wrinkles. Instead of following nature, we try to force it. The first shall be last, and the last first. But this is best taken, perhaps, as the poet (or the man cultivating the flowers) speaking to himself. From early morning till late at night he is tending the chrysanthemums, with never a moment free of them. In the evening he sees them through the twilight; the first thing in the morning, before he does anything else, he goes out into the garden and gazes down on them. He feels that man was made for chrysanthemums, not they for him. And which is it in truth? If you think that the sabbath was made for man, then we must say "Man was made for the sabbath." The truth is of course that neither was made for either, and both for each. The poet realizes this in his own feelings, and though he laughs at himself, has a secret satisfaction at the self-forgetfulness with which he tends the plants. There is a pre-Buson verse by Shukuzan, 蕭山:

けふ菊の奴僕となりし手入かな
Kyō kiku no   doboku to narishi   teire kana

Today, trimming, pruning,
I have become
The slave of chrysanthemums.

There is a verse by Issa where the fanatical devotion to the cultivation of chrysanthemums is brought out in a much better because indirect way:

入道の大鉢巻で菊の花
Nyūdō no   ōhachimaki de   kiku no hana

A shaven head,
A towel round it, at an angle,—
Chrysanthemum flowers!

The man, a lay priest, or more probably, an ordinary man with a newly-shaven head, has tied a band round his head to concentrate his energies on looking after the chrysanthemums. His way of wearing this band shows his zeal.

欄干に昇るや菊の影法師   許 六
Rankan ni   noboru ya kiku no   kagebōshi

Onto the balustrade,
Rise up the shadows
    Of the chrysanthemums.   Kyoroku

It is a moon-lit evening of autumn, and beneath the eaves chrysanthemums are blooming. Their shadows fall on the balustrade of the verandah. In the phrase "rise up," we feel something that belongs to art rather than nature, and this is because Kyoroku has taken the verse almost bodily from Ōanseki, 王安石, d. 1086 A.D.

春色悩人眠不得、
月移花影上欄干。

The scenery of spring troubles us, and we cannot sleep;
The moon moves the shadows of the chrysanthemums, and
    they rise up the balustrade.

痩せながらわりなき菊の莟かな   芭 蕉
Yase nagara wari naki kiku no   tsubomi kana

The chrysanthemum
Is thin and weak,
    But has its fated bud.   Bashō

The original is rather different from the translation. Bashō actually says: "Thin as it is, the admirable chrysanthemum bud!"

What Bashō sees here is not merely the chrysanthemum on its too slender stem, or the small bud that surmounts it, but the *inner necessity*, destiny working, life as it is lived, existence as it is being fulfilled. Yet Bashō does not see an abstraction, a cosmic law, or universal principle, but this particular chry-

santhemum with its puny bud and scanty leaves. Issa expresses
this feeling more directly, more colloquially:

庵 の 梅 よ ん ど こ ろ な く 咲 き に 鼻
Io no ume   yondokoro naku   saki ni keri

> The plum-tree of my hut;
> It couldn't be helped,
> It bloomed.

Compare also the following by Taigi, born thirteen years
after the death of Bashō:

痩 せ た る を か な し む 蘭 の 苔 み け り
Yasetaru wo   kanashimu ran no   tsubomi keri

> How pitiful it was,
> This thin weak orchid,—
> But it has budded!

The power and the weakness of nature are seen at one glance
of the eye.

小 便 の 香 も 通 ひ け り 菊 の 花　　　　　　一　茶
Shōben no   ka mo kayoi keri   kiku no hana

> Chrysanthemum flowers;
> And wafted along also,
> The smell of urine.　　　　　　　　　Issa

The critic who thinks that the third line mentions something
unsuitable to poetry had better remember what his own bladder
is half-full of,—and then forget it again. The urinal from
which the smell comes is a small tub let in the ground not
far from the house. The precious liquid is used on the garden
or neighbouring field. Men, after all, are cannibals whether
they like it or not. Which is the "poetical" smell, and why?
Which is the "useful" smell, and why? These problems should
not arise as a result of reading the poem. They are raised so
that the "choosing" faculty of the mind may be somewhat
blunted, in order that we may realize with a much deeper
faculty, the faculty for the perception of reality, that the two
things are, one nice, the other nasty, but both Good.

手燭して色失へる黄菊かな   蕪 村
Teshoku shite   iro ushinaeru   kigiku kana

The yellow chrysanthemums
Lose their colour
In the light of the hand-lantern.   Buson

The strange fact that artificial light takes away the colours
of things is scientifically explainable, but is none the less a
wonderful thing, and the poetic mind will always wonder at
it, especially if, as in the case of Buson, it is strongly inter-
ested in colours and forms. Other verses that show how keenly
and deeply Buson felt the meaning of colour as such, are the
following:

茶の花や白にも黄にもおぼつかな
Cha no hana ya   shiro ni mo ki ni mo   obotsukana

Tea-flowers;
Are they white?
Are they yellow?

野路の梅白くも赤くもあらぬかな
Noji no ume   shiroku mo akaku mo   aranu kana

The path through the fields;
The plum flowers are hardly white,
Nor are they red.

若葉して水白く麥黄みたり
Wakaba shite   mizu shiroku mugi   kibamitari

Among the green leaves,
Water is white,
The barley yellowing.

夕顔や黄に咲いたるもあるべかり
Yūgao ya   ki ni saitaru mo   arubekari

Evening-glories,—
There should be one
With a yellow flower.

山吹の卯の花の後や花いばら
Yamabuki no   u no hana no ato ya   hana-ibara

After the mountain rose
And the flower of the *u*,
The wild rose.

Winter Landscape

by Sesshū, 雪舟, 1420–1506.

冬
WINTER

Winter is the season of cold; not only the cold that animals also feel, and the consciousness of it which exacerbates the feeling of it in human beings, but that cold whose deep inner meaning we realize only at moments of vision, often when connected with fear and loneliness, or with apparently unrelated qualities of things.

In the Solar Calendar, the end of the year does not coincide with any natural change, but in the old Lunar Calendar it marks the beginning of spring in Japan. The winter moon and the cold rain at the end of autumn have special meanings in this season. Snow in winter corresponds in its range of significance and variety of treatment to the cherry-blossoms of spring, the *hototogisu* in summer, the moon of autumn. Fields and mountains, when trees are leafless and thickets are a wild tangle of browns and greys, have a poetic meaning that the green of the other seasons does not know. In Japan the grass all dies and turns colour, making winter more of a time of death than in England. The pine-trees stand apart, as it were, from the seasons. The religious haiku are nearly all concerned with the processional chanting of the *nembutsu* during the period of greatest cold. Plovers, owls, eagles, various water-fowl and fish are the only animals treated, and of trees and flowers, it is fallen leaves that give us the best poems.

時　候 **THE SEASON**

初冬や二つ子に箸とらせける　　　　　　暁　臺
Hatsufuyu ya　futatsugo ni hashi　torasekeru

> The beginning of winter;
> Two years old,
> I showed her how to hold chop-sticks.

Gyōdai

If we put emphasis on the second and third lines we get a
charming and touching picture, the father, or perhaps the
grandfather, teaching the little girl how to hold *hashi* in her
tiny hand, one stick tight and the other wiggling up and down
on top.　But if we emphasize the first line, by putting it last,
we rise into a more universal realm: the feeling of the short-
ening days, the death of the year, the relaxation of energy,—
all these brought out by the sweetness of the domestic scene.

物干の影に測りて冬至かな　　　　　　　子　規
Monohoshi no　kage ni hakarite　tōji kana

> I surmise
> From the shadow of the clothes-pole,
> It is the depth of winter.

Shiki

This is translated as if the original were *Monohoshizao*, 物
干竿, but actually it means the two posts and the bamboo pole
that runs across them, the whole thing.　*Tōji* is the middle of
the 11th month according to the Lunar Calendar, about the
22nd or 23rd of December by the Solar Calendar, when the
days are shortest and the nights longest, in other words, the
winter solstice.

Shiki has done in the above poem what Keats did in the
beginning of *The Eve of St Agnes*; he has made us feel the
cold as it is felt in other things:

> The owl, for all his feathers, was a-cold;
> The hare limped trembling through the frozen grass.

There is a similar, but less explicit verse by Issa:

朝寒や垣の茶筅の影法師
Asazamu ya   kaki no chazaru no   kagebōshi

The morning is chill;
The shadow of the tea-basket
On the fence.

禪寺の松の落葉や神無月   凡　兆
Zendera no   matsu no ochiba ya   kannazuki

Fallen pine-needles
In a Zen temple;
The god-less month.   Bonchō

The "god-less month" is October, when the gods all over
Japan leave their shrines and assemble at Izumo. The merit
of this verse consists in the harmony between the time, the
place, and the things. The Zen temple gives a plain, tasteless
flavour of ascetic simplicity, accentuated by the season and the
brown pine-needles scattered on the dry sandy ground. (See
also pages 1235–36.)

つめたさに箒捨てけり松の下   太　祇
Tsumetasa ni   hōki sutekeri   matsu no shita

So bitter cold it was,
I left the bamboo broom
Under the pine-tree.   Taigi

Tsumetasa has here its original meaning of 爪痛さ, "fingernail-
pain," implying extreme cold.

The poet went out into his garden one winter morning to
sweep up the leaves that had fallen, but it was so cold, and
the bamboo handle so painful to the touch, he left it under the
pine-tree and turned to go into the house again. The broom
stands there, shiny, pale yellow against the rough black bark
of the pine-tree.

身に添ふや前の主の寒さ迄   一 茶
Mi ni sou ya   mae no aruji no   samusa made

    The previous owner:
I know it all,—
    Down to the very cold he felt.   Issa

When a man, especially a poor man, lives in a house, he leaves indelible marks behind him of all the troubles and vexations he passes through. The nail with a piece of string dangling from it (for the mosquito net), the writing on the door-post (for rice), the oil spilled from the lamp, children's drawings on the wall, all the hundred and one signs of the struggle for existence of the previous family which Issa is repeating with his own household,—this is summarized and concentrated in the physical cold which Issa now feels as the former tenant felt it.

Another verse by Issa which has the same thought of things speaking to man but which actually belongs to the season of autumn:

小便所ここと馬よぶ夜寒かな
Shōbenjo   koko to uma yobu   yosamu kana

    "The latrine is over here,"
Says the horse;
    Cold at night.

This has prescript "At being bewildered on waking." Issa woke at night, and, intending to go to the lavatory, stood up, but was utterly unable to get his bearings. Standing there trying to remember where the door was, the autumn cold strikes chill at this moment of indecision. Suddenly the horse in the stable (a part of the house, and next to the lavatory), makes a noise, snuffling or shaking himself or pawing the ground. Issa realizes where he is and recalls the strange feeling and the cold that accompanied it. This haiku is somewhat senryū-like, but the emphasis is on the cold.

大寒や八月欲しき松の月   一 茶
Taikan ya   hachigatsu hoshiki   matsu no tsuki

> The Period of Great Cold:
> I would it were the Eighth Month,—
> The moon in the pine-tree.   Issa

Taikan, 大寒, starts thirty days after *tōji*. Between *tōji* and the beginning of *taikan*, there is *shōkan*, 小寒. This verse is not very deep in meaning. It corresponds to what Coleridge says in *Dejection*:

> Yon crescent moon, as fixed as if it grew
> In its own cloudless, starless lake of blue;
> I see them all so excellently fair,
> I see, not feel, how beautiful they are!

It has its origin, however, not in the failing of the genial spirits, but in simple physical cold. The beauty of moon and pine are there, whatever our own feelings may be, but it is difficult to stand and gaze at them, letting the mind dissolve into their beauty, when the body is occupied with its own discomfort.

何となく冬夜隣を聞かれけり   其 角
Nan to naku   juyuyo tonari wo   kikarekeri

> A winter night;
> Without any reason,
> I listen to my neighbour.   Kikaku

By extreme cold, not only the hearing faculties are made keener, but the whole body is strung up to receive outside impressions. Kikaku lies in bed listening to the little thuds and scufflings, the murmurs, and above all the still more unaccountable silences next door. It is the *nantonaku*, "without any reason," which is the point of the poem, that indefinable, vague feeling of necessity, of destiny, that makes the listening and what is heard of inexplicable significance. Nevertheless, we cannot take this verse in as deep a way as that of Bashō, Vol. III, page 896; Kikaku's is more psychological, it belongs to winter rather than autumn There is a certain numbing of the feelings by intellectuality.

井 の も と へ 薄 刃 を 落 す 寒 さ か な   蕪 村
I no moto e   usuba wo otosu   samusa kana

A thin-bladed kitchen knife
Dropped at the edge of the well,—
The cold!   Buson

The tinkle on the stone is hard and metallic and chilly.
Another example from Buson is:

鋸 の 音 貧 し さ よ 夜 半 の 冬
Nokogiri no   oto mazushisa yo   yowa no fuyu

The sound of the saw
Is poverty-stricken,
This winter midnight.

Here, it is the grating sound that exacerbates the feeling of
cold, but besides this, the saw sounds as if it comes from some
poor workman forced to work far into the winter night while
others are warm in bed.

葱 白 く 洗 ひ た て た る さ む さ 哉   芭 蕉
Negishiroku   araitatetaru   samusa kana

The leeks
Newly washed white,—
How cold it is!   Bashō

Even in summer the leeks would look cool, but in winter,
after having been washed, they look like snowy icicles: This
verse is not objective, as if written:

Washed,
How chill
The white leeks!

It is not subjective, as if written:

The white leeks
Washed,
How cold I am!

Bashō feels himself to be a white leek, newly washed, and stood
there next to the others. But he does not say anything so
absurd as this, nor does he think it.

易水にねぶか流るゝ寒かな　　　　蕪 村
Ekisui ni　nebuka nagaruru　samusa kana

A leek,
Floating down the Ekisui,—
Ah, the cold!　　　　　　　　　　Buson

Keika, 荊軻, of the kingdom of En, 燕, who intended to kill
King Shi, 始, of the kingdom of Shin, 秦, 222–206 B.C., parted
from Prince Tan, 丹, of En, at this river in North China. (He
failed, and was himself killed). Keika composed the following
verse at this time:

風蕭々易水寒、壯士一去兮不復還。
The wind is bleak, the Ekisui cold;
The warrior, once he departs, never returns.

In the *Tōshisen*, there is a poem by Rakuhinō, 駱賓王, called
Parting at the Ekisui, 易水送別:

此 地 別 燕 丹、壯 士 髮 衝 冠。
昔 時 人 已 没、今 日 水 猶 寒。
At this place, Keika parted from Prince Tan of En;
The warrior's hair bristled under his hat.
This man of olden times died long ago,—
But still today the waters are cold.

Buson has taken this long, cold leek and put it in a place a
thousand miles away, and at a time of two thousand years ago.
What a long way to go to express the apparently simple sensa-
tions of whiteness and cold!

Usually Buson adopts the opposite method, of bringing the
past into the present, for example:

白梅や墨芳しき鴻臚館
Shiraume ya　sumi kambashiki　kōrokan

The white plum-blossoms;
In the Kōrokan
The Chinese ink is fragrant.[1]

---

[1] See Vol, II. page 574.

皿を踏む鼠の音のさむさ哉   蕪　村
Sara wo fumu   nezumi no oto no   samusa kana

The sound
Of a rat on a plate,—
How cold it is!   Buson

The sound of a rat's claws as it runs over a plate or dish is
what strikes Buson, though he lays the obvious emphasis on
the coldness he himself feels, a coldness at once symbolized
and intensified by the sound. But it is the peculiar and unique
quality of the sound, identified in some mysterious way with
the sensation of cold, which is here apprehended, and not ex-
pressed but pointed to.   The following, by Taigi, belongs to
autumn:

水瓶へ鼠の落ちし夜寒かな
Mizugame e   nezumi no ochishi   yosamu kana

A rat
Fell into a water-jar:
How cold the night!

This verse is a combination of the sensation of cold, the sound
of the water, the creepiness of the rat, the darkness of the
night.   There is nothing pleasant or beautiful or sentimental;
there is a painfully deep meaning of the life of animate and
inanimate nature.

冬ざれの小村を行けば犬吠ゆる   子　規
Fuyuzare no   komura wo yukeba   inu hoyuru

The desolation of winter;
Passing through a small hamlet,
A dog barks.   Shiki

Trees are bare of leaves, the streams run with a cold glitter,
doors are shut, smoke rises from the chimneys, everything is
silent.   Suddenly a dog that has been half-asleep in a sheltered
spot begins to bark.   The whole scene, the wintry aspect is
bitten into the mind by the barking of the dog.   Or we may
put the whole thing in a profounder, more poetical, and less
psychological way.   The barking of the dog, which can mean

anything and everything, expresses at this moment the whole of winter in a small village. At one and the same time we see the character and habits of the village dog, and, as if accidentally, one of the infinite aspects of winter, one of its natural signs.

寒き夜や海に落ち込む瀧の音 曲翠

Samuki yo ya   umi ni ochikomu   taki no oto

The sound of a waterfall
Falling down into the sea;
The winter night is cold.

Kyokusui

The grandeur of nature, the pitifulness of man are admirably united in this poem, without pomposity on the one hand or sentimentality on the other. The poet's coldness is attributed to the waterfall and the sea, but in compensation, the chilly water falls ceaselessly into the cold ocean of his heart.

十に足らぬ子を寺へやる寒さ哉 子規

Tō ni taranu   ko wo tera e yaru   samusa kana

A child under ten,
Taken to be given to the temple;
Bitter cold!

Shiki

One cold winter day a child of eight of nine is being taken by his parents to a temple where he will become a priest. The parents are too poor to keep him. The uncertainty of his life, and the treatment he will receive, the irresolution of his mother and father, the dark hall of the temple,—all are felt in the cold.

次の間の灯で膳につく寒さ哉 一茶

Tsugi no ma no   hi de zen ni tsuku   samusa kana

By the light of the next room,
I sit before my small food-table;
Ah, the cold!

Issa

Issa is too poor a guest for the inn to provide him with a
light for himself. He sits down in front of his humble meal,
eating by the light of the room next to his.

We cannot say there is nothing of self-pity in this verse, yet
the self that is pitied is seen so clearly, so truly, so uncoloured
by the pity, that the wretchedness is all the deeper. The cold,
again, is felt by Issa, but it is a coldness of all cold people, of
mankind, of the universe, though in no sense impersonal.
Herein lies Issa's genius, to be able to talk of himself, as
Wordsworth did, remaining untouched by the self-consuming
emotion.

郷里松山の子賣遊び

鼻垂れの子が賣れ殘る寒さ哉　　　　　　子　規
Hanatare no　ko ga urenokoru　samusa kana

The snotty child
Is left "unsold";
How cold it is!　　　　　　Shiki

The prescript says: "A child-selling game in my native place,
Matsuyama." In this game, usually for girls, one of two equal
teams chooses the most charming child of the other team and
tries to get her by heads or tails. This goes on until the least
attractive child is left "unsold."

The not very pretty child, running at the nose, is left till
last. He stands there stupidly, his hands in his sleeves, unhappy
and unlovely, and the cold seems more painful when our eyes
rest unwillingly upon him.

齒豁に筆の氷を嚙む夜哉　　　　　　蕪　村
Ha arawa ni　fude no kōri wo　kamu yo kana

Night;
Biting the frozen brush
With a remaining tooth.　　　　　　Buson

As he sits there thinking what to write next, the tip of the
brush becomes hard and frozen. He puts it in his mouth and

寒空や
たゝ暁のみねの松

Pine-tree

Verse and picture by
Gyōdai, 曉臺, 1732–93.

Samuzora ya
tada akatsuki no   mine no matsu

In the cold sky of dawn

Only a single pine-tree

On the peak.

with one of his few remaining teeth he bites it back to softness. We see his poverty in this, but only indirectly, and quite unsentimentally.

我寝たを首上げて見る寒さかな　　　　來　山
Waga neta wo　kubi agete miru　samusa kana

Raising my head,
I gazed at my recumbent form:
Bitter cold.　　　　　　　　　　　Raizan

This an example of "seeing ourselves as others see us," seeing ourselves as God sees us. There is a poem of Hakurakuten very similar, but without the bodily experience that objectifies, personalizes, temporalizes and thus eternalizes the experience:

早秋獨夜

井梧凉葉動、　隣杵秋聲發。
獨向簷下眠、　覺來半牀月。

IN EARLY AUTUMN, ALONE AT NIGHT

The leaves of the paulownia move in the cool breeze;
The neighbour's fulling-mallet sends out the voice of autumn.
I turn and sleep beneath the eaves;
Waking, the moonlight is half across my couch.

The cold of winter is somewhat different from that of autumn, the former being perhaps more physical, the latter more spiritual. The following examples are all by Shiki, so sensitive to the cold of autumn, to which *yosamu* refers.

やゝ寒み灯による蟲もなかりけり
Yaya samumi　hi ni yoru mushi mo　nakarikeri

It is rather cold;
No insects approach
The lamp.

肌寒や子の可愛さを抱きしめる
Hadasamu ya　ko no kawaisa wo　dakishimeru

The air is chill;
I crush the child to me,
So lovely she is.

次 の 間 の 灯 も 消 え て 夜 寒 哉
Tsugi no ma no   tomoshi mo kiete   yosamu kana

The light in the next room also
Goes out:
The night is cold

蜘 蛛 殺 す 後 の 淋 し き 夜 寒 哉
Kumo korosu   ato no sabishiki   yosamu kana

After killing the spider,
A lonely
Cold night.

母 と 二 人 妹 を ま つ 寒 か な
Haha to futari   imōto wo matsu   samusa kana

Mother and I
Waited for my younger sister;
The night was cold.

牧 師 一 人 信 者 四 五 人 の 夜 寒 か な
Bokushi hitori   shinja shigonin no   yosamu kana

A pastor,
Four or five believers;
A chilly night.

瀬 の 音 の 二 三 度 か は る 夜 寒 か な
Se no oto no   nisando kawaru   yosamu kana

A night of bitter cold;
The sound of the rapids
Changed several times.

我 を 厭 ふ 隣 家 寒 夜 に 鍋 を 鳴 ら す　　　　　蕪 村
Ware wo itou   rinka kanya ni   nabe wo narasu

My neighbours hate me,
Rattling their saucepans
This winter night!　　　　　Buson

The people next door are making something in a saucepan
or cleaning the soot off. The thin wall between the two houses
makes everything audible but leaves room for the imagining of

more and greater delicacies than really so. Buson lies there
on the floor with a thin quilt pulled round him, listening to

Man's inhumanity to man.

The sufferer sees the cold indifference of his fellows as an active
hatred, and so it is, for there is in practice no intermediate
stage between love and hate, causing suffering or preventing
it. Even when we do nothing at all, even when we rattle our
own saucepans, our neighbours take it, rightly enough, as
cruelty to themselves.

The excess of syllables in the first and third parts of this
verse, and the repetition of the sounds *o*, *n*, *ka*, *na*, respectively,
augment the feeling of oppression and suggest the sound of
the saucepan being stirred.

我が骨の蒲團にさわる霜夜かな   蕪 村
Waga hone no   futon ni sawaru   shimoyo kana

My bones
Feel the quilts;
A frosty night.   Buson

Japan is not a cold country, comparatively speaking, but the
number of haiku on cold and winter is very great. The Japanese
never had and never seemed to desire any means of being
comfortably warm in winter. Rich and poor alike shivered
from the end of autumn until the middle of spring. Especially
the poets, (who seem to have been indigent on the whole),
more sensitive to the cold than ordinary people, spent many a
night of grinding wretchedness trying to sleep in spite of cold
feet and thin shanks. The way in which Buson says "My
bones feel the quilts" instead of "The quilts touched my bones"
shows the activity of the supersensitiveness.

大名の通つた跡の寒さかな   子 規
Daimyō no   tōtta ato no   samusa kana

A *daimyō* passed:
Afterwards,
The cold!   Shiki

When a feudal lord passed along the road, people had to kneel by the wayside and perform obeisance, not lifting their heads until he had gone by. During the excitement and stimulus of his passage, the cold is unnoticed and forgotten, but afterwards, with the reaction, it comes with redoubled intensity. This, however, is not an expression of a psychological phenomenon, but of the experience of pure cold as such, together with the contrast between the warmly clothed, richly accoutred retinue of the *daimyō*, and the poet's poverty-stricken apparel and blue-pinched face and hands.

There is a distant connection between the above verse and the following by the same author:

狼の糞見て寒し白根越
Ōkami no kuso mite samushi shiranegoshi

Crossing Mount Shirane,
After seeing a wolf's dung,—
How cold it was!

人聲の夜半を過ぐる寒さ哉　　　　野 坡
Hitogoe no yahan wo suguru samusa kana

Voices of people
Pass at midnight:
The cold!　　　　　　　　　　Yaha

Thoreau says in his *Journals*, 1851:

A traveller! I love his title. A traveller is to be reverenced as such. His profession is the best symbol of our life. Going from——toward——; it is the history of every one of us. I am interested in those that travel in the night.

In Yaha's verse there is the additional fact of the connection between the voices and the sensation of cold. The voices themselves have the quality of coldness and night in them.

あたゝかに冬の日なたの寒さかな　　　鬼 貫
Atataka ni　fuyu no hinata no　samusa kana

This winter day,
It is warm in the sun,—
　　　But cold!　　　　　　　　　　　Onitsura

This perception of the relativity of the interpretation of sensory experience is on the border-line between psychology and poetry. The humour of it just pushes it over into poetry. What it lacks is depth, and depth as Spengler points out is the word which really expresses what distinguishes one work of art from another. It is the amount of life in a thing which gives it this depth, this value. Between the poetic and the non-poetic there is a great gulf fixed, narrow, but infinitely deep. Sometimes we hesitate, as we do between beautiful growing crystals and the sea-slug, but there is no doubt in the end which is alive and which never was.

門口に來て凍るなり三井の鐘　　　一 茶
Kadoguchi ni　kite kōru nari　mii no kane

Reaching the gate,
The bell of Mii Temple
　　　Freezes.　　　　　　　　　　　Issa

Mii-dera, also known as Onjō-ji, 圓城寺, many times burnt down and rebuilt, dates from 858 A.D., and is famous in history and legend. When Issa reached the gate of the house, the great bell sounded through the evening air. The flow of sound seemed to solidify in the freezing air around. There is a kind of tactual perception of sound or perhaps a sensation perceived by another sense, or several senses combined. But the poetry of this verse is not here; it is in the humanization of the sensations of cold and sound, that is to say, the sound of the bell and the icy air reach the full stature of a man, they attain their Buddhahood in Issa as he stands a moment at the gate.

ひき目に　見てさへ　寒いそぶりかな　おれが姿にいふ人も一茶

Self-portrait
by Issa

Even considered
In the most favourable light,
He looks cold.

(The one speaking of my figure is also Issa.)

ひいき目に見てさへ寒いそぶり哉   一 茶
Hiikime ni   mite sae samui   soburi kana

> Even considered
> In the most favourable light,
> He looks cold.   Issa

This is written concerning a picture of himself. We have
five other versions of this verse, showing how Issa wrestled
with his material, spiritual and verbal:

うしろから見ても寒げな天窓哉
Ushiro kara   mite mo samuge na   atama kana

> Even seen from behind,
> His head
> Looks cold.

ひいき目に見てさへ寒き天窓哉
Hiikime ni   mite sae samuki   atama kana

> Looked at most favourably,
> It is a cold
> Head.

ひいき目に見てさへも不形な天窓哉
Hiikime ni   mite sae mo bunari na   atama kana

> Looked at most favourably,
> It is a formless
> Head.

ひいき目に見てさへ寒し影法師
Hiikime ni   mite sae samushi   kagebōshi

> Looked at most favourably,
> It is a cold
> Shadow.

ひいき目に見てさへ寒きそぶり哉
Hiikime ni   mite sae samuki   soburi kana

> Looked at most favourably,
> It is a cold
> Attitude.

This last one is the same as the original verse, but translated
more literally. We can see Issa's humorous mouth and critical
eye, as he looks at himself in the picture.

櫓の聲波を打つて腸氷る夜や涙　　　　芭　蕉
Ro no koe   nami wo utte harawata kōru   yo ya namida

A bowel-freezing night of tears:
The sound of the oar
Striking the wave.　　　　Bashō

This verse was written when Bashō was living alone in his
hut at Fukagawa, 深川冬夜の感, and expresses his feelings one
winter night while shivering in bed and listening to some
passing boat. It is unusually irregular, 4, 11, 5. The poem is
rather in the Chinese style. Compare the following of Haku-
rakuten:

把君詩卷燈前讀、　詩盡燈殘天未明。
眼痛滅燈猶暗坐、　逆風吹浪打船聲。

I take up a roll of your poems and read them beside the
lamp;
Finishing them, the lamp is low, day not yet dawned.
The lamp goes out; with sore eyes, still I sit in the dark,
And listen to waves that the contrary wind drives against
the boat.

There are moments when we are simply organs of suffering;
grief and pain alone are our portion; in our own person we
bear the agony of humanity, meaningless, fruitless, unrelieved
misery. The sound of the oar in the rowlocks, the sound of
the wave on the oar is as bitter as death. Even in retrospect
there is no compensation, no relativity; life and hope have no
place here; it is something absolute. Issa has his own way of
experiencing the same thing:

一人と帳面につく夜寒かな
Ichinin to   chōmen ni tsuku   yosamu kana

"I'm alone," I said.
He wrote it down in the register;
How chilly the autumn night!

Issa goes into a very poor kind of inn for a night's lodging.
The clerk glances at him, sizes him up at once, asks his name
and native place; then, though knowing perhaps that Issa is
alone, asks with the cold indifference of routine, "How many
in your party?" Issa with that feeling of irritation that we all

have at being asked obvious questions, answers, "I'm alone."
At that moment, the annoyance, the cold, and that other
meaning of "alone" comes over him in a single moment of
grinding wretchedness.

冬の夜や針失ふて恐ろしき　　　　　　　梅室
Fuyu no yo ya　hari ushinōte　osoroshiki

A winter evening:
The needle has disappeared,—
How dreadful!　　　　　　　　　　　　Baishitsu

The woman has been sitting alone, doing needlework in a
large cold room by a flickering lamp. She pauses, lays down
her work, and her thoughts wander down the past, her child-
hood, girlhood, marriage. With a sigh, she puts down her hand
for the needle,—and it is no longer there! Can some demon
have snatched it away? Has she been bewitched? Again and
again she searches the same places for the needle, but it is
nowhere to be seen. The cold seems to grow more intense as
her fears increase.

This is a comparatively late verse (Baishitsu died in 1852),
but it represents the thought of Old Japan, when as in Europe
also, superstition was rampant. In every age and every country
we all have that feeling of the irrationality, the indetermin-
ability, the *fearful* nature of things.

Compare a verse by Buson, and another by Taigi:

盗人の屋根に消へ行く夜寒かな
Nusubito no　yane ni kieyuku　yosamu kana

The thief disappeared
Over the roofs,—
A cold autumn night!

盗人に鐘つく寺や冬木立
Nusubito ni　kane tsuku tera ya　fuyukodachi

The temple bell is ringing
On account of a robber:
The winter grove.

霜がれや鍋のすみかく小傾城　　　　一　茶
Shimogare ya　nabe no sumi kaku　kokeisei

The winter season;
A young harlot
Scraping the soot from a saucepan.　Issa

The frozen ground and wilted grasses, the dishevelled and
tawdry finery of the woman, the harsh scratching sound and
uncouth filthy shape of the saucepan,—all these have a harmony
of ugliness that lifts them into the realm of the significant.
And the youth of the woman strikes a note of wasted and
discordant beauty that deepens the harmonious pathos of the
whole.

乾鮭も空也の瘦も寒の内　　　　芭　蕉
Karazake mo　kūya no yase mo　kan no uchi

Dried salmon,
And Kūya's emaciation also,
During the coldest season.　Bashō

Saint Kūya, 902–972, lived a wandering life, beginning the
Kamakura democratic form of Buddhism already in the Heian
Period, building bridges and roads, digging wells, and doing a
great many other works of public service. There is a well-
known statue of him exhaling the *nembutsu.*

Bashō is reported by Tohō[1] to have said concerning this poem:

心の味を云ひとらんと數日腹を絞るなり。　三冊子

To express the flavour of the inner mind, you must
agonize during many days.

This *kokoro no ajiwai*, "the flavour of the mind," is very impor-
tant. Shikō, 支考, in the *Kokonhaikaikakai*, speaks of Bashō's
"physiognomic judgement," 觀相, and "mutual reflection," 互照,
in regard to the dried salmon and Kūya. We may say also
that it is Bashō's poetic spirit, but it would be better with Nose
Tomoji, 能勢朝次,[2] to understand that it implies a sinking into
the form of a thing sufficiently deeply to catch instinctively

[1] 土芳, 1657–1730, disciple of Bashō.
[2] In 芭蕉俳論評釈。

the life-flavour, にほひ, of it. In this case it is some common essential element of dried salmon and the Buddhist Saint. To express the matter straight-forwardly (perhaps too much so for such a delicate matter), it is the simultaneous perception of the dried-fishiness of Kūya, and the Buddhahood of the dead salmon. To express this in words requires indeed that one "agonize for many days."

ゆく年や職人町の夜の音　　　　午　心
Yuku toshi ya   shokunin machi no   yoru no oto

The year is departing:
A street of artizans,—
All the sounds tonight!　　　　Goshin

It is the last night of the year. All the tinsmiths and tatami-makers, carpenters and basket-makers, weavers and printers are working up to a climax of various noises of hammering and sawing and rattling and cutting. The poet sits listening to them and hears these uncouth, discordant noises for what they are, as full of meaning and therefore as poetical as the song of birds or the ripple of a stream over the pebbles. Not only are the sounds clearer than usual in the cold air, but the poet is predisposed to hear what he hears.

行年や親に白髪を隠しけり　　　　越　人
Yuku toshi ya   oya ni shiraga wo   kakushikeri

The departing year;
I hid my grey hairs
From my father.　　　　Etsujin

There is here the pathos of filial affection. All love has something pathetic in it. But beyond this, there is some deep irony in the hiding of age from the aged.

The saint, the sage and the poet express in their lives the reality of human nature. But do not the hypocrite, the fool, and the egotist also express something equally essential in human nature, omitted by these? Still more the delicate sub-terfuges, the subtle evasions of love that in their very denial of love (by lack of frankness and trust) yet proclaim and magnify it.

ふる里や臍の緒に泣く年の暮   芭 蕉
Furusato ya   hozo no o ni naku   toshi no kure

My native place;
Weeping over the umbilical cord,
At the end of the year.   Bashō

It was the custom in Japan, and still is in many places, for
the mother to keep the umbilical cord of the child, and when
Bashō went back to his native place, long after the death of
his parents, he found this wrapped up in paper, with his name
and the date of his birth written on it. Bashō made travel his
home, but yet, and perhaps all the more, his feelings towards
his father and mother and his old house were painfully deep.
It is only those who realize the impermanency of things that
can know the meaning of passionate attachment to things and
persons and places.

叱らるゝ人うらやましとしの暮   一 茶
Shikararuru   hito urayamashi   toshi no kure

I am envious
Of him who is being scolded:
The end of the year.   Issa

At the end of the year, relatives are reunited, parents and
children feel their relationship more warmly and deeply.   In
such an atmosphere, Issa overhears a father or mother grumbl-
ing at a child.   Guilt on the one side, anger on the other,—
there seems little room for envy, but Issa, an orphan, envies
the child his power to be reprimanded, that is, his having a
father or mother.

ともかくもあなた任せの年の暮   一 茶
Tomokaku mo   anata makase no   toshi no kure

Even so, even so,
Submissive before Yonder,—
The end of the year.   Issa

This was written on the 29th of December, 1819, appearing at the end of Issa's *Oragaharu*, with the following long prescript, in which he expresses his religious attitude. In part, it represents what Shinran was reported to have said in the *Tanishō*, 歎異抄; in part it is a criticism of the members of the Shin Sect to which Issa belonged. A rather free translation of what Issa says follows:

> Those people who put all their strength into Other-Power, and relying completely on it, say, "Faith in Other-Power, faith in Other-Power," bound with the bonds of Self-Power, fall with a crash into the Hell of Self-Power. Then they request Amida to cover the filthy dirt of their own unenlightenedness with gold foil. Though they pretend to be imbued with the Buddhist spirit, they are really the embodiment of Self-Power. They may ask, "What condition of mind would fit your conception of things?" The answer is: There is nothing especially difficult; only get rid of all the nonsense about Self-Power and Other-Power, letting it float away to Chikura Sea. The Great Thing of the next world, is simply to throw yourself before the Nyorai and beseech that you may be sent to Paradise or Hell according to his good pleasure. Having decided the matter in this way, we say *namuamidabutsu*; and we must not darken the eyes of others with the lustful nets of the long-legged spider, or like the world-o'er-passing wild goose have any inclination thievishly to draw others' water into our own field.
>
> At such a time, why should you say the Nembutsu in a feigned voice? Without being asked, the Buddha will keep his word. This is the true peace of mind.

The *anata* which is translated "Yonder" is the Japanese word commonly used to mean "you," literally, "on that side." This word brings out the difference between Jōdo, the Pure Land Sect, and Zen, which lies not so much in the distinction of Other-Power and Self-Power as in the manner in which the oneness of these two is realized. In Jōdo we simply submit (with emphasis on the "simply") to the Other-Power; we realize that we were, from the first, nothing of ourselves, and when we have no will of our own, God's will is done in and through us. The danger here, as pointed out in Issa's prescript, is that

in submitting to the Other-Power, people think they are sub-
mitting *something*, that *they* are submitting something. That
is, the danger is in the division of self and other.

In Zen, this division of the world into self and other, this
and that, good and bad, enlightened and unenlightened,—the
destruction of this distinction is the great aim. And the farther
we go into Jōdo and Zen, the less the difference between them
becomes. If we compare, for example, Issa, a believer of Jōdo,
and Bashō, a student of Zen, we shall be struck with the fact
that it is Issa whose self colours every verse he wrote, and
Bashō whose self melts away at the touch of the slightest thing,
a pebble or a spray. The "even so, even so" is the fox that
gnaws at Issa's entrails, grief and remorse for the past, a
divided mind in the present, hopes and fears for the future.

But the meaning of the verse, submission and renunciation,
are in accord with the season, the winter of the mind, the end
of Issa's year.

年くれぬ笠着て草鞋はきながら　　　　芭　蕉
Toshi kurenu　kasa kite waraj　hakinagara

The year draws to its close:
I am still wearing
My *kasa* and straw sandals.　　　　Bashō

At the beginning of *Oku no Hosomichi*[1] Bashō says:

月日は百代の過客にして、行かふ年もまた旅人なり。

Months and Days are travellers through countless ages;
travellers too are the passing Years.

It was this fundamentally Buddhist idea of the ephemeral nature
of all things that gave to Bashō his deep insight into their
value. Other people are at home enjoying the reunion of their
families and friends. Bashō is on a journey,—but this is the
true state of all men. The difference between one man and
another is a matter of the degree to which they realize this fact.

---

[1] Written and rewritten between 1689 and 1694.

芭蕉去てその後いまだ年暮ず　　　　蕪 村

Bashō satte　sono nochi imada　toshi kurezu

Since Bashō left the world,
Not yet has
"The year drawn to its close."　　　Buson

Bashō gave the words "the year has drawn to its close" a
deep meaning that it never had before. While he was alive he
used the words in this profound way, but since his death there
has been no one to do the same, that is, the year has not
drawn to its close since he departed from this world. This
seems a simple verse but there is depth of emotion, reverence
for the teacher, and the deep philosophy of the Mahayana
behind it. Buson perhaps remembered a line from the beginning
of *Sotoba Komachi*, the most profound and touching of all Nō
plays:

それ前佛は既に去り、後佛はいまだ世に出です。

The Buddha who was before is gone; the Buddha that
shall be, not yet has come into the world.

There is a passage which may serve as a prescript. Buson
writes, quoting Bashō's verse on page 1158:

名利の街にはしり、貪欲の海におぼれて、かぎり
ある身をくるしむ。わきて、くれゆくとしの夜のあ
りさまなどは、いふべくもあらず、いとうたてきに、
人の門たゝきありきて、ことことしくのゝしり、あ
しをそらにしてのゝしりもてゆくなど、あさましき
わざなれ、さとておろかなる身はいかにして塵區を
のがれん。
　としくれぬ笠着てわらじはきながら
片隅によりて此句を沈吟し侍れば心もすみわたりて、
かゝる身にあはと、いと尊く我ための摩訶止觀とも
いふべし。蕉翁去て蕉翁なし、とし又去や又來るや。

Rushing along in the road to fame and riches, drowning
in the sea of desire, people torture their ephemeral selves.
Especially on New Year's Eve their behaviour is unspeak-
able. Despicably walking about knocking at doors, treating
everyone with contempt unnecessarily, insanely vulgar be-

haviour, and so on, is not decent. Even so, we foolish mortals can hardly escape from this world of dust and sin.

> The year draws to its close:
> I am still wearing
> My *kasa* and straw sandals.

Reading this poem quietly in a corner of the room, my mind becomes clear; were I living Bashō's life, how good it would be! The verse is uplifting to me, and it may be called a Great Rest-and-Enlightenment as far as I am concerned. Bashō once gone, we have no master to teach us, whether the year begins or ends.

わんといへさあいへ犬もとし忘れ   一 茶
Wan to ie sā ie inu mo toshiwasure

> "Bark! come on now, bark!"
> The dog also speeds the year,
> With the rest of the party.   Issa

Toshiwasure is the meeting of friends or relations to eat and drink and forget all the troubles of the past year, in other words a New Year's Eve party. Bashō has a verse that might well have been written by Issa:

年忘三人寄つて喧嘩かな
Toshiwasure sannin yotte kenka kana

> Three men meeting
> For a New Year's Eve party,
> And quarreling.

In Issa's verse, the family are all together, enjoying themselves in their humble way, and the children are trying to get the dog to bark for something "on trust." The dog jerks his head and wishes to bark but is not yet quite worked up to it. It is this moment of the dog's inability to express himself that Issa has caught, with his "*sā, ie!*"

お仲間に猫も坐とるや年忘れ 一 茶
Onakama ni neko mo za toru ya toshiwasure

As one of us,
The cat is seated here;
The parting year. Issa

The mildness of Issa, his power to be pleased and content with little, his lack of distinction between human and nonhuman animals, his "politeness" to all and everything that is itself and sincere, his living in the eternal present which is also the fast-fleeting time,—all these are manifest in the artless simplicity that he attained to with so much effort and practice.

踏づ蹴つ跡も見ずして年ぞ行く 仙 鶴
Funzu ketsu ato mo mizu shite toshi zo yuku

Kicking and spurning,
With not a look behind,
Off goes the year! Senkaku

Time and tide wait for no man. Sometimes, in what are wrongly called moments of weakness, we perceive that God cares nothing for us, Nature is heartless and mechanical:

And that inverted Bowl they call the sky,
Whereunder crawling coop'd we live and die,
Lift not your hands to *It* for help—for It
As impotently moves as you or I.

But when we have taken this agonising truth alive into our hearts, we understand for the first time that

Underneath are the everlasting arms.

夜歩きや年の名殘の雪が降る 舍 羅
Yoaruki ya toshi no nagori no yuki ga furu

Walking in the night;
Snow is falling,
A farewell to the year. Shara

There is always something wistful in the fall of snow, but especially at night, and most of all at the end of the year. Its silence, the way in which it appears from nowhere, and seems to disappear immediately, has something of pathos in it, and the poet walking in the darkness through which snow-flakes are falling feels them to be a farewell to the old year which is about to end.

隠れ家や歯のない聲で福は内　　　　　　　　一　茶
Kakurega ya　ha no nai koe de　fuku wa uchi

From a hermitage,
A toothless voice crying,
　　"Blessings inside!"　　　　　　　　　　Issa

At the time of *Setsubun*, the eve of the Spring Equinox, people scatter beans in the house, calling out "Devils outside! Blessings inside!" The above verse portrays the weakness and pathos of human nature. The old man, not many more years of life left to him, is still praying for external happiness, asking that he may be spared the bludgeonings of fate. Where are

　　The years that bring the philosophic mind,

where is the saint that should be living in this quiet hermitage? This may well be Issa himself.

いざや寝ん元日は又あすの事　　　　　　　蕪　村
Iza ya nen　ganjitsu wa mata　asu no koto

　　Come now!　I will sleep;
New Year's Day
　　　　Is a thing of the morrow.　　　　Buson

This verse goes beyond the words of Christ,

　　Take no thought for the morrow,

and includes tomorrow's joys.

　　We look before and after,
　　And pine for what is not,

and this is part of our human nature, to some extent inescapable, but it is our littleness. The poetical is the victorious life, of which the life of Christ is the shining example. With him too, as men, we say

If it be possible, let this cup pass from me,

but the final word is that of the poet; whatever he sees or hears or suffers, all that happens, the falling as well as the blooming of the flowers, sleeping tonight and waking to the first day of the new year; it is

Not my will, but Thine be done.

年とらぬ積りなりしが鐘の鳴る   助 葷
Toshi toranu   tsumori narishi ga   kane no naru

I intended
Never to grow old,—
But the temple bell sounds!   Jokun

What a universal emotion is expressed in the first two lines! Making our peace with age is part of our acceptance of death. The bell speeding the old year comes sounding across the fields. We are a year older whether we will it or not.

天　文　SKY AND ELEMENTS

三日月はそるぞ寒はさえかへる　　　　　　一　茶
Mikazuki wa　soru zo samusa wa　saekaeru

> The crescent moon
> Is warped and bent:
> Keen is the cold.　　　　　　　　　　　Issa

The translation misses the onomatopoeia of the original. There is nothing in the verse to suggest it, but we can hardly avoid connecting the cold with the shape of the moon.

連もなく野に捨てられし冬の月　　　　　　露　石
Tsure mo naku　no ni suterareshi　fuyu no tsuki

> Companionless,
> Thrown away on the moor,
> The winter moon.　　　　　　　　　　Roseki

The poet has seen an aspect of the moon that Shelley also portrays in *To the Moon*:

> Art thou pale for weariness
> Of climbing heaven, and gazing on the earth,
> Wandering companionless
> Among the stars that have a different birth?

It is the separateness of things that we see here; they are joyless, unwanted, useless.

A verse by Meisetsu:

木枯や空にころがる月一つ
Kogarashi ya　sora ni korogaru　tsuki hitotsu

> In the withering blast,
> A single moon
> Rolls through the sky.

This has simplicity, grandeur, and perfect objectivity. The adjective "rolling" unites the moon and the winter blast with a Shelleyan violence of movement. We may compare it with a very different, a lyrical and weaker treatment of the same subject in a waka by Azumamaro, 1668–1736:

嵐吹く音もおよばぬ雲の上は
いかに静けく月のすむらむ

> The tempest roars,—
> But above the clouds,
> Where the din
> Cannot reach her,
> Dwells the moon serene.

寒月や我ひとり行く橋の音　　　　　太　祇
Kangetsu ya ware hitori yuku hashi no oto

> I walk over it alone,
> In the cold moonlight:
> The sound of the bridge.　　　　Taigi

Taigi is walking on *geta*. It is not the crunching sound of shoes, as in Buson's verse, page 1167, but the hard-soft wooden sound that has a sympathetic tone with that of the wooden bridge. The cold, the round silver moon, the loneliness,—all are contained within "the sound of the bridge." A verse by Shiki with the same consciousness of self and the outer world:

木の影や我が影動く冬の月
Ki no kage ya waga kage ugoku fuyu no tsuki

> The shadow of the trees;
> My shadow is moving,
> In the winter moonlight.

寒月や僧に行き逢ふ橋の上　　　　　蕪　村
Kangetsu ya sō ni yukiau hashi no ue

> Meeting a monk
> On the bridge:
> The winter moon.　　　　Buson

The black-robed monk in the bright moonlight, the crunching of the *geta* on the frozen road in the silence,—all these things have an exacerbating effect on one another. The fact also that

the man is a monk has a deepening effect upon the meaning of
the verse, in an altogether inexplicable way. His inscrutability
of countenance, the feeling that he belongs in part to a different
world from ours,—this gives him a ghostly appearance that
belongs especially to the moon of a winter night.

月雪の中や命の捨てどころ   其 角
Tsuki yuki no   naka ya inochi no   sutedokoro

The moon-lit snow
It where life
Is to be thrown away.   Kikaku

This was written for the night of the 14th of December, 1701,
when the Forty Seven Rōnins attacked their enemy Kira Yoshi-
naka, under Ōishi Yoshio. In the snow and the moon, their
purity and quietness, the poet sees the calm and disinterested
action of the samurai. Kikaku, 1660–1707, was a contemporary
of those concerned.

寒月に立つや仁王のからつ脛   一 茶
Kangetsu ni   tatsu ya niō no   karassune

The Deva kings standing there,
The icy moonlight
On their bare legs.   Issa

There is always a roof over each of the two Niō that guard
the entrance to the temple gate, and the cold, slanting rays of
the moon fall on their sinewy legs, which express, themselves
also, something of the coldness of the night. *Karassune* is the
point of this haiku. It emphasizes and isolates the legs of the
giant figures, as if only they can be seen, the rest of the figure,
the clenched fists and scowling, threatening faces, being hidden
in the shadow.

犬を打つ石のさてなし冬の月   太　祇
Inu wo utsu   ishi no sate nashi   fuyu no tsuki

> Not a single stone
> To throw at the dog:
> The winter moon.   Taigi

A real religious poem. The circumstances of the poem are
thus well described by Mr. Miyamori in *An Anthology of Haiku*:

> The poet was walking home along the road by night.
> A dog barked at him. He wanted to throw a stone at it.
> So he looked all round for a stone on the road bathed in
> an icy bright winter moon; but to his mortification, he
> could not find one.

If you wish to know where the religion is in this, think of the
lines in *Expostulation and Reply*:

> Nor less I deem that there are powers
> Which of themselves our minds impress.

"Of themselves." Man's extremity (just that moment of ego-
lessness, when mental and physical action is suspended) is God's
opportunity,—something, Something, some Power, slides imper-
ceptibly into the mind in the form of cold moonlight.

> Think you, mid all this mighty sum
> Of things forever speaking,
> That nothing of itself will come,
> But we must still be seeking?

A similar verse by Jōsō:

のら猫のかけ出す軒や冬の月
Noraneko no   kakedasu noki ya   fuyu no tsuki

> A stray cat
> Running off under the eaves,—
> The winter moon!

寒月や小石のさはる沓の底   蕪　村
Kangetsu ya   koishi no sawaru   kutsu no soko

> In the icy moonlight,
> Small stones
> Crunch underfoot.   Buson

This poem represents a poetic experience similar to that of Taigi's verse given on page 1165, but goes deeper. Here also, the feel of the small stones under the feet shod with leather, the sound of them, is in mysterious accord with the light of the moon and the wintry chill of the air. How is this? Is it purely fanciful? Is it only subjective? Is it a coincidence of visual, tactual, and auditory sensations which, because of some primitive undifferentiated core of sensitivity, cause us to suppose a transcendental unity of the objects which give rise to those sensations? It may well be so, but further, it may be that this elemental core is the microcosm, the objects part of the macrocosm, and these two be an interpenetrated one. The experience itself, though actually internal, is an experience of external unity.

寒月や石塔の影松のかげ   子 規
Kangetsu ya   sekitō no kage   matsu no kage

Winter moonlight;
The shadow of the stone pagoda,
The shadow of the pine-tree.   Shiki

There is no moon or pine-tree or grave-stone here, only the icy moonlight on the frozen ground, with the edge-clear outline of the pagoda and tree in the shadow.

寒月に木を割る寺の男かな   蕪 村
Kangetsu ni   ki wo waru tera no   otoko kana

The old man of the temple,
Splitting wood
In the winter moonlight.   Buson

The temple is in the shade, the chilly moon shining over the roof onto the man-of-all-work who is late with his firewood. The axe flashes up and down in the light of the moon. The crash of wood sounds clear in the silent night.

寒月や門なき寺の天高し   蕪　村
Kangetsu ya   mon naki tera no   ten takashi

The winter moon:
A temple without a gate,—
How high the sky!   Buson

Every temple has a great gate at the entrance to the grounds.
For some reason or other this particular temple has none, and
when the poet comes out of the temple building and finds his
view completely unobstructed, the sky is unexpectedly vast and
lofty, with a small moon rolling through the clouds   The
following are by Kikaku and Taigi:

此の木戸や鎖のさされて冬の月
Kono kido ya   kusari no sasarete   fuyu no tsuki

This small gate,—
It is bolted:
The winter moon!

駕を出て寒月高し己が門
Kago wo dete   kangetsu takashi   ono ga mon

Getting out of the palanquin,
Over my gate the winter moon
Is high in the sky.

網代木の揃はぬ影を月夜かな   白　雄
Ajirogi no   sorowanu kage wo   tsukiyo kana

A moonlit night:
The sticks of the wicker fish-trap,—
Their shadows are uneven.   Shirao

In rivers and ponds, a kind of fish trap is made of slender
stakes bound together to make a sort of matting. One part is
left open, and when sufficient fish enter, it is shut and the fish
caught. The tops of the sticks are uneven, and their shadows
on the placid surface of the water exaggerate this irregularity.
The poet sees this unevenness; it catches his eye, his mind, it
will not let him go. What is this deep meaning in imperfection,
in asymmetry, in discord, in sin and death?

屋根の上に火事見る人や冬の月   子　規
Yane no ue ni   kaji miru hito ya   fuyu no tsuki

> Upon the roof,
> People looking at a fire:
> The winter moon.   Shiki

Japanese roofs are low, and not steep, in old Japan almost
touching in the cities. There is a fire not far off, and spectators
are on the roofs, getting as good a view as possible. Above
them in an inky sky the wintry moon is shining.

雪よりも寒し白髪に冬の月   丈　草
Yuki yori mo   samushi shiraga ni   fuyu no tsuki

> Colder even than snow,
> The winter moon
> On white hairs.   Jōsō

To the *samurai*, for whom poetry and duty are one, dishonour
is worse than physical death. To King Lear, the unthankfulness
of his daughters is more painful than cold air.

> Blow, blow, thou winter wind!
> Thou art not so unkind
> As man's ingratitude.

These feelings are spoken of physically because felt so. The
white light of the wintry moon upon the head of the old man
intensifies the feeling of the irrevocable advance of time of
which his white hairs are the token. The moonlight too shines
more chill above the white hairs of old age, for the icy and
the merciless enhance and reinforce each other.

背の高き法師にあひぬ冬の月   梅　室
Se no takaki   hōshi ni ainu   fuyu no tsuki

> I met and passed
> A tall Buddhist priest,
> Under the winter moon.   Baishitsu

The interesting point here is the relation of tallness to the moon. The gaunt, pale-faced monk clad in black robes seems to belong to winter, night, and the moonlight.

冬の月川風岩をけづるかな   樗良
Fuyu no tsuki   kawakaze iwa wo   kezuru kana

Under the winter moon,
The river wind
    Sharpens the rocks.   Chora

If the wind may be said to have any effect at all upon the rocks, it blunts them; it does not sharpen them. But Chora is not pretending it does. He is saying something else, something that cannot be said in words. Not that the words themselves are lacking. It is something that a man may experience so that he knows what the poet might have said, were it not for the fact that the saying of it would have robbed it of the life which of its nature can never be solidified into words. The unsaidness is the express attestation of the unsayableness that is part of the essential nature of poetry.

Poetry has an onomatopoeic character, an affinity to nonsense verses, in which certain concatenations of words, an apparently fortuitous juxtaposition of certain sounds raises in the depths of the mind meaning-echoes that go back down into the past, grow into the distant future, in a way that like life itself, defies analysis. So in the above poem, (omitting the purely sound elements which can never be reproduced in translation) the words winter, moon, river, wind, sharpens, rocks, produce in the (poetic) mind an effect out of all proportion to dictionary definitions of them, and quite regardless of their logical and intellectual relations. The poet is pointing to something in his mind which corresponds exactly with what is happening outside it. The "wind" in his mind "sharpens" the "rocks" in it.

山鳥の寝かねる聲に月寒し   其角
Yamadori no   nekaneru koe ni   tsuki samushi

At the voice of the copper pheasant,
That cannot sleep,
    The moon is chill.   Kikaku

初時雨
自在の
竹に吹かゝれ

Hatsushigure
jizai no take ni　fukikakare

The first winter shower;
The bamboo of the kettle-hanger
Is blown to and fro.

(For kettle-hanger, invisible in this
picture, see frontispiece, p. 978.)

Entering Chikurisha Hermitage

Verse and picture by Seira, 青蘿,
(1739-91)

The sharp voice of the sleepless bird, the pale, clear-cut moon, and the bitter, silent cold intensify one another. There is in the world outside a unity of these three things that corresponds to the single poetico-physical feeling of the poet.

旅人と我が名呼ばれむ初時雨　　　芭　蕉
Tabibito to   waga na yobaren   hatsushigure

The first winter rain,
And my name shall be called,
"Traveller." Bashō

In October, 1689, Bashō set out from Edo on a journey to his native place in Iga, and in his *Oi no Kobumi* says:

神無月の初空定のなきけしき身は風葉の
行末なき心地して

In the Month-when-the-gods-are-absent (October), the sky when I set out was uncertain, myself a leaf blown by the wind, unmindful whither.

The above haiku then follows. It shows Bashō setting out in a drizzle, soon wet through from the knees downward, alone, yet not lonely, not knowing where he would lay his head that evening, if at all; but in everything, he

Turns his necessity to glorious gain.

化けさうな傘かす寺の時雨かな　　　蕪　村
Bakesō na   kasa kasu tera no   shigure kana

It may transform itself,
This umbrella lent by a temple,
In the winter rain. Buson

Rain begins to fall, and Buson goes to an old temple nearby and asks for the loan of an umbrella. The monk gives him one, so old that it is hardly worth while returning. As he leaves the temple in the gathering darkness, the rain falling steadily and monotonously, Buson feels that this aged umbrella may suddenly transform itself into a fox or a witch or goblin.

The old monk, the old temple, the rain, the tattered umbrella, the evening, the thoughts of ghosts and apparitions are all blended together with a power and compactness in the original which even a literal translation cannot emulate. "Rain of a temple lending a bewitched umbrella" is nearer the Japanese, but omits the "may be" element of "looks as though it may be going to transform itself" expressed by "bakesō."

生きて世に寝覺嬉しき時雨かな   召 波
Ikite yo ni   nezame ureshiki   shigure kana

To wake, alive, in this world,
What happiness!
Winter rain.   Shōha

Happiness is from within. Though winter rain is almost a symbol of dreariness, the poet finds the cold rain no hindrance to joy:

Only to be,
Made quiet his breast.

悲しさや時雨に染まる墓の文字   浪 化
Kanashisa ya   shigure ni somaru   haka no moji

The winter rain dyes
The letters on the grave-stone:
Sadness.   Rōka

The grave-stone is covered with green lichen, and as the cold rain falls on it and trickles down over the name of the dead person carved on it, it begins to turn almost black. The sadness of the poet is what enables him to "see" this fact, that is, to attend to it so that its meaning reflected from his mind sinks back again into his heart.

新庭や石も落ちつく初時雨   酒 堂
Shinniwa ya   ishi mo ochitsuku   hatsushigure

In the newly-made garden,
The stones have settled down in harmony;
The first winter shower.   Shadō

"Ochitsuku" has both the physical meaning of the stones subsiding into their place, and the aesthetic meaning of their becoming an artistic unity with the rest of the garden. The rain that begins to fall adds the final touch of nature which makes this world kin.

In the wilderness of nature, man has made a garden, by impressing upon the mechanical disorder of natural things the activity of mind. But we must not make the mistake of supposing that things are simply passive in this relation. The material itself both assists and opposes. From the point of view of art, Nature suffers most from a superabundance, an excess, a plethora of material. One or two stones here and there, a pine-tree, an evergreen bush, a small, half-seen pool of water, —this is enough. But when upon this the life-giving rain falls, especially for the first time after the garden is finished, we feel rightly that Nature is herself confirming the deeds of man. Thoreau says,[1]

> Thus all things pass directly out of the hands of the architect into the hands of Nature, to be perfected.

幾人かしぐれかけぬく勢田の橋   丈 草
Ikutari ka   shigure-kakenuku   seta no hashi

How many people in the winter shower,
Running across to the other end
Of the long bridge of Seta!   Jōsō

A sudden shower has come on, and people on the long bridge begin to run through the slanting rain with umbrellas and *kasa* tilted in all directions. In this verse we feel through the length of the bridge the nature of the shower. The scene is without colour, and in this is superior to the ukiyoe which portrays it. Another verse like an ukiyoe, by Masahide, 正秀, d. 1723, which shows man not subdued by but rather defiant of the rain:

鑓持や猶振たつるしぐれ哉
Yarimochi ya   nao furitatsuru   shigure kana

The javelin bearers
Still brandish them
In the winter rain.

[1] *A Week on the Concord.*

On the daimyō procession rain has begun to fall, but they still raise and lower their spears and continue their accompanying rhythmical cries.

傘におしもどさるゝしぐれ哉   紫青女
Karakasa ni   oshimodosaruru   shigure kana

As I walk in the winter rain,
The umbrella
Presses me back.   Shisei-jo

Is it the umbrella, or the wind that presses me back? Or is it something else entirely?

I felt you push, I heard you call,
I could not see yourself at all.[1]

In this realm of mystery that the reason endeavours in vain to diminish, to penetrate and conquer, the soul wanders freely, feeds on pure joy and knows no sadness,—and yet it is only being pushed back in the cold rain by an umbrella.

凩の地にもおとさぬ時雨かな   去來
Kogarashi no   chi ni mo otosanu   shigure kana

The gale will not let
The cold winter rain
Fall to the ground.   Kyorai

This is a verse portraying something we have all seen, a wind so strong that the naturally perpendicular rain seems to become horizontal, or even to rise rather than fall.

いそがしや沖の時雨の眞帆片帆   去來
Isogashi ya   oki no shigure no   maho kataho

How busy they are
Out at sea in the rain,
Full sails, close-hauled sails!   Kyorai

[1] Stevenson, *The Wind.*

The "busyness" is in the poet's mind as he stands watching. The reader's mind, if Kyorai can succeed in making it "busy," perceives the value, the poetic significance, but can never explain it. All pictures are the same; the picture, the picturesqueness is nothing, unless we share in the activity or rest that is pictured there.

釣人の情のこはさよ夕しぐれ   蕪 村
Tsuribito no   jō no kowasa yo   yūshigure

The angler,—
His dreadful intensity,
In the evening rain!   Buson

What is there about the fishing that causes the man to sit there stiff, cold, hungry, wet-through, for fish that may never bite, for fish that could be bought for a paltry sum at the fishmonger's? It is not merely blood-lust, the desire to get something for nothing, brute obstinacy, the so-called sport, that is, the chances of the game, though all these enter into it. It is man against nature, the struggle of Jacob with the angel, the desire of the moth for the star, something as blind, as fatal, as fearful as life itself.

屋根葺の海をふりむく時雨かな   丈 草
Yanefuki no   umi wo furimuku   shigure kana

Rain begins to fall:
The thatcher turns
And looks at the sea.   Jōsō

The thatcher is engrossed in his work; the rain begins to fall and he raises his head and looks towards the sea that whitens in the distance.

This is explained as the thatcher being in a state of *muga*, 無我, egolessness, and then coming back to himself when he feels drops of rain, and hanging his now suspended mind onto the sea. The only mistake in this interpretation is the "coming back to himself." His state of mind as he gazes at the sea is not ego-centric.

竹林に時雨吹き込む夕かな　　　　　　青々
Chikurin ni   shigure fukikomu   yūbe kana

Rain blows
Into the bamboo forest;
Evening.　　　　　　　　　　　　　Seisei

This may seem perhaps an over-simple verse, but after all,
if "one thing is enough," we have two here. There is nothing
more beautiful in the world than bamboos in the windy rain,
but that is not the point of the verse. The rain comes slanting
into the forest through the green stems of the bamboos into
the twilight beyond. As is dark, the bright rain-drops are seen
rather clearly.

池の星又はらはらと時雨哉　　　　　　曾良
Ike no hoshi   mata hara hara to   shigure kana

The stars on the pond;
Again the winter shower
Ruffles the water.　　　　　　　　　　Sora

The point of this verse is in the word "again." The cold
stars are brightly reflected in the cold dark water. Then wind
and rain sweep the surface, and they disappear. This happens
several times, with that wonderful regularity, that unchanging
strangeness and depth of meaning that belongs only to the
simplest things of life.

半江の斜日片雲の時雨かな　　　　　　蕪村
Hankō no   shajitsu henun no   shigure kana

Sunbeams slant onto one side of the river;
From a floating cloud
Cold rain falls.　　　　　　　　　　　Buson

It is a pleasure to read a poem that is purely objective, partly
because it is in the Chinese, classical style without the possibility
of any subjective overtones. It is the world as it is, as it would
be without man. And yet we know that the drive and direction
of this "slanting" and "falling," the weight of this "mass" of

cloud all have their origin in the lively power of the mind that perceives them, all are

but the painted vicissitudes of the soul.

牛つんで渡る小舟や夕しぐれ　　　　　子　規
Ushi tsunde　wataru kobune ya　yūshigure

With a bull on board,
The ferry boat,
Through the winter rain. Shiki

Across the river passes very slowly a flat-bottomed boat with a few country people, and a bull. Rain is falling steadily and human beings and animal alike,

If I might lend their life a voice,
Seem to bear rather than rejoice.[1]

But Shiki only wishes to paint a picture in black and white.

楠の根を静に濡らす時雨哉　　　　　蕪　村
Kusu no ne wo　shizuka ni nurasu　shigure kana

The drizzling winter rain
Quietly soaks
The roots of the camphor-tree. Buson

Under the great tree rain does not fall, but down the trunk trickle lines of water that darken the bole and roots and disappear in the ground. There is a certain loneliness, sadness here, but it is something inherent in the things themselves, a heaviness that belongs to brute matter, to darkness, to old age, something that the bright seraphim never know. Contrast this with the subjectivity and moral-drawing of Shelley's lines:

Rough wind that moanest loud
Grief too sad for song;
Wild wind, when sullen cloud
Knells all the night long;

[1] Matthew Arnold, *Resignation.*

Sad storm whose tears are vain,
Bare woods whose branches stain,
Deep caves and dreary main,—
Wail for the world's wrong!

しぐるゝや田のあらかぶの黒む程　　　　芭 蕉
Shigururu ya　ta no arakabu no　kuromu hodo

It has rained enough
To turn the stubble in the field
Black.　　　　　　　　　Bashō

If one has seen this, both in reality and in ukiyoe wood-prints,
the poetic meaning, as a picture of life, is obvious.

しぐるるや角まじへゐる野べの牛　　　　蘭 更
Shigururu ya　tsuno majieiru　nobe no ushi

Cold winter rain;
Mingling their horns,
The oxen of the moor.　　　　Rankō

There is something in this herd of cattle with the rain falling
on them, their horns all pointing upwards, which reminds one
of Monet's picture of Umbrellas.

笠もなき我を時雨るか何となんと　　　　芭 蕉
Kasa mo naki　ware wo shigureru ka　nan to nan to

To be rained upon by the winter rain,
And with no *kasa*,—
Well, well!　　　　　　　Bashō

The meek shall inherit the earth. God is not a respecter of
persons. He maketh his rain to fall upon the just and upon
the unjust. Man has dignity before men, but none before
Nature. To describe the above verse as a religious poem may
well seem to some an absurdity, and yet it is such. There is
no ecstasy, no lofty flights of the imagination; it is life lived

at its common level, the will of God accepted and cheerfully fulfilled.

鶏の聲にしぐるゝ牛屋かな   芭 蕉
Niwatori no   koe ni shigururu   ushiya kana

Winter rain
Falls on the cow-shed;
A cock crows.   Bashō

The harmony between these three things—the cold rain slanting down, the huge black cow-shed with its high steep roof, the shrill, falsely triumphant cry of the cock—is partly in the rise and fall of the cock's voice that blends with the rise of the roof and the fall of the rain; partly in the shrillness of the cry with the chilly drops that fall.

夕時雨蟇ひそみ音に愁ふかな   蕪 村
Yūshigure   gama hisomi ne ni   ureu kana

Cold winter rain;
In the subdued voice of the toad,
Grief and woe.   Buson

Rain is falling on the dead leaves. The deep voice of the toad has grown weaker as winter begins, and expresses the sadness and pathos of the ending of life and warmth.

しぐるゝや我も古人の夜に似たる   蕪 村
Shigururu ya   ware mo kojin no   yo ni nitaru

The evenings of the ancients
Were like mine,
This evening of cold rain.   Buson

Compare this to the following, by Southey, from *The Scholar*:

My days among the dead are past;
Around me I behold,
Where'er these casual eyes are cast,

The mighty minds of old;
My never-failing friends are they,
With whom I converse day by day.

The Japanese poet listens to the sound of the rain, the English poet looks at the volumes that rise in serried ranks around him. The one attains to unity with men of past times through nature in its simplest form, the other through books, through men. But both realize a deep truth, that we look not with our own eyes, but with the eyes of the great men of the past. We hear not with our own ears, but with those of long dead poets.

The heroic Heart, the seeing Eye of the first times, still feels and sees in us of the latest.

There may be in Buson's verse a reference to Bashō's:

世にふるも更に宗祇のやどり哉
Yo ni furu mo   sara ni sōgi no   yadori kana

It rains o'er all the earth;
Still more upon the dwelling-place
Of Sōgi.

This again comes from the verse of Sōgi, 1420–1502:

世にふるは更にしぐれのやどり哉
Yo ni furu wa   sara ni shigure no   yadori kana

It rains o'er all the earth,
Still more it falls
On this my dwelling-place.

Even this seems to depend on a waka by Nijōin Sanuki in the *Shinkokinshū*, first compiled in 1205:

世にふるは苦しきものを槙の家に
安くも過くるむら時雨哉

Painful it is indeed,
Passing through the world;
But in a hovel like this,
I live on in peace and quiet,
Winter rain falling.

目前を昔に見する時雨かな					蕪　村
Mokuzen wo   mukashi ni misuru   shigure kana

The winter rain
Shows what is before our eyes,
As though it were long ago.					Buson

We expect this verse to run, "The winter rain shows us the past, before our very eyes." By a kind of trick of words Buson has blurred the present and the past, the looker and what is looked at. He has done here rather artificially what it is the aim of all poetry to do, to confuse while keeping distinct, to enable us to lose ourselves in mutual interpenetration and yet preserve the identity and uniqueness of the thing itself.

時雨るゝや鼠のわたる琴の上					蕪　村
Shigururu ya   nezumi no wataru   koto no ue

Winter rain;
A mouse runs
Over the *koto*.[1]					Buson

The poet or someone else has been playing the harp and at last leaves it on the tatami. Standing on the verandah, he gazes out at the rain which has fallen all day. It grows darker and darker. Suddenly, the *koto* gives out a slight sound; a mouse must have scuttled across it. Contrast this with the following by Rankō:

五月雨や鼠の廻る古葛籠
Samidare ya   nezumi no mawaru   furu tsuzura

The May rains;
A mouse is running round
The old wicker basket.

In this verse it is the old wicker basket that, because of the mouse's activities, has become alive and meaningful. The rain is merely a setting. In Buson's poem it is not the *koto* or the mouse that is significant, but the rain which is expressed through these two apparently unrelated things.

Another verse of Buson's, already given, where coldness, a

[1] A kind of harp, about six feet long, played horizontally.

mouse, (which in many cases if not all, must be a rat), and a
certain sound all express the same thing:

皿を踏鼠の音のさむさかな
Sara wo fumu   nezumi no oto no   samusa kana

> The sound of a mouse
> Treading on a plate
> Is cold.

The association of mice with coldness is common in Buson:

鐵をはむ鼠の牙の音寒し
Tetsu wo hamu   nezumi no kiba no   oto samushi

> The sound of the teeth
> Of a rat biting iron
> Is cold.

寺寒く樒はみこぼす鼠かな
Tera samuku   shikimi hamikobosu   nezumi kana

> In the cold temple,
> The sound of a mouse
> Nibbling a chinese anise.

野分して鼠のわたる潦
Nowaki shite   nezumi no wataru   niwatazumi

> A mouse
> Crossing a puddle
> In the autumn tempest.

小夜時雨隣へはいる傘の音　　　　　嵐 蘭
Sayo shigure   tonari e hairu   kasa no oto

> On an umbrella, a patter of raindrops,
> But it enters next door;
> The evening darkens.　　　　　Ranran

The poet is sitting alone in the house, reading desultorily,
and though he does not realise it, lonely. It is raining outside.
The sound of raindrops suddenly becomes louder. It is the
patter on an approaching umbrella. Will the person come here?
The sound passes by and seems to enter the neighbour's.

Silence is scattered like a broken glass.
The minutes prick their ears and run about,
Then one by one subside again and pass
Sedately in, monotonously out.
You bend your head and wipe away a tear.
Solitude walks one heavy step more near.[1]

何人の寝ぬ灯ぞ小夜時雨   蓼 太
Nanibito no   nenu tomoshibi zo   sayo shigure

> Who is it that is awake,
> The lamp still burning?
> Cold rain at midnight.   Ryōta

As is so often the case, the order of the parts of the haiku
is of the greatest importance.   If this verse had been written,
as it could easily have been,

小夜時雨何人の寝ぬ灯ぞ
Sayo shigure   nanibito no nenu   tomoshibi zo

> Cold rain at midnight:
> Who is it that is awake,
> The lamp still burning?

the emphasis would be and remain on the light burning in the
lonely hut on the distant mountain-side.   The rain would be
only part of the scenery, a mere season-word in the poem.
In the actual verse however, the melancholy of that one star
of light in the dark outside enables him to hear for the first
time the rain that has been falling since dusk.

初霜や飯の湯あまき朝日和   樗 良
Hatsushimo ya   meshi no yu amaki   asabiyori

> The first frost:
> Fine morning weather,—
> How the rice-water tastes!   Chora

The weather has got suddenly colder. This morning, frost

[1] *Solitude*, by Harold Monroe.

lies white under a blue sky. The water in which the rice has been boiled, tasteless for a long time, is now delicious to sip.

Where is the poetry in this? The poet felt there was something significant in it. The rice-water tastes different from before. Is there some change in himself or in the rice-water? The answer is yes. Scientifically speaking, he has changed. Poetically speaking, what he eats is changed for this morning he is tasting the blue sky and the white hoar-frost.

赤き實一つこぼれぬ霜の庭　　　　子　規
Akaki mi　hitotsu koborenu　shimo no niwa

A red berry
Spilled
On the hoar-frost of the garden.　　Shiki

This red berry must be that of a nanten or nandin, but the (deliberate) lack of the name makes the verse a pure picture, instead of a representation of life. It is a spot of red upon white. Yet it is still hoar-frost, not mere whiteness; it is a berry, not a piece of red paper. Noteworthy is the 4, 7, 5. The shortness of the first 4 syllables brings out the round, hard clarity of the red berry on the white frost.

淋しさの底ぬけて降る霙かな　　　　丈　草
Sabishisa no　soko nukete furu　mizore kana

Sleet falling:
Fathomless, infinite,
Loneliness.　　Jōsō

Soko nukete, literally, "the bottom falling out," is a Zen expression (applied to sudden enlightenment) very much more concrete and less sentimental than "fathomless, infinite."

A leaden sky, bare branches above, dead leaves underfoot, not a sound anywhere. Then there comes falling, not rain, which has the promise of growth, its many-sounding music, and the charm of its round bright drops; not the snow which unites all things as it beautifies them; but wet cold sleet, with neither life nor hope in it. It needs a God-like mind to rejoice

in it, and this is what the poet has given us in this verse, and
enabled us also to do.

古池に草履沈みてみぞれかな   蕪　村
Furuike ni   zōri shizumite   mizore kana

The old pond;
A straw sandal sunk to the bottom,
Sleet falling.   Buson

We cannot help thinking of Bashō's verse, Volume II, page
540, when we read the first line of this poem. Perhaps the
simplest thing to say is that one represents spring with all its
power and possibility; the other winter, the death of all things.

初雪や水仙の葉のたはむまで   芭　蕉
Hatsuyuki ya   suisen no ha no   tawamu made

The first snow:
The leaves of the daffodils
Are just bending.   Bashō

The delicacy of the observation is not less than that of Nature
itself. A few flakes of snow, and the mind of the poet bends
with the long, slender leaves. There is a similar but rather
less simple verse by Buson:

春雨や小磯の小貝ぬるゝほど
Harusame ya   koiso no kogai   nururu hodo

Spring rain,
Enough to wet the little shells
On the small beach.

Note how Buson makes everything as small as possible. Shiki
has a verse which is almost a parody of Bashō's:

夕立や蛙の面に三粒ほど
Yūdachi ya   kaeru no tsura ni   mitsubu hodo

A summer shower;
About three drops
On the frog's face.

初雪やかけかゝりたる橋の上   芭 蕉
Hatsuyuki ya   kake kakaritaru   hashi no ue

The first snow of the year,
On the bridge
They are making.   Bashō

This was composed when Bashō was living at Fukagawa; the bridge was half-finished. The poetical point of this is of an extreme delicacy. It concerns the bringing together of the first soft, white snow and the new white wood of the bridge over which no traveller has yet passed. The virginity of both is brought out by their juxtaposition.

初雪や海をへだてゝ何處の山   子 規
Hatsuyuki ya   umi wo hedatete   doko no yama

The first snow;
Beyond the sea,
What mountains are they?   Shiki

The snow falls for the first time, and as the poet gazes over the sea, he sees, as if a'so for the first time, distant mountains capped with white snow shining in the morning sunshine. The snow can say too, "Behold, I make all things new!"

天も地もなしに雪の降りしきり   芭 臣
Ten mo chi mo   nashi ni yuki no   furishikiri

There is neither heaven nor earth,
Only snow
Falling incessantly.   Hashin

Thomson has expressed this, though in more words:

Earth's universal face, deep hid and chill,
Is one wide dazzling waste, that buries wide
The works of man.

Jōsō has a very similar verse:

野も山も雪に取られてなにもなし
No mo yama mo　yuki ni torarete　nani mo nashi

Fields and mountains,—
The snow ·has taken them all,
Nothing remains.

金殿の灯火細し夜の雪　　　　　子　規
Kinden no　tomoshibi hososhi　yoru no yuki

The lights of the palace
Are narrowed,
This night of snow.　　　　　Shiki

On ordinary nights, the lamps of the palace blaze out into
the darkness, but after the fall of snow, everywhere is lighter
than usual, and when the lamps are lit, they appear smaller
and dimmer by contrast. This is poetry from the degree of
delicacy and fineness of the perceptions of the poet.

古池の鴛鴦に雪降る夕かな　　　　　子　規
Furuike no　oshidori ni yuki furu　yūbe kana

Evening snow falling,
A pair of mandarin ducks
On an ancient lake.　　　　　Shiki

There is a remarkable harmony here. The age of the lake
has a deep affinity with the snow, which though it may be new
in time is old in its seasonal meaning. The mandarin ducks
also are somewhat artificial and more· picturesque, less alive
than other birds.

鶏の寝て居るうちの深雪哉　　　　　奇　淵
Niwatori no　nete iru uchi no　miyuki kana

While the fowls
Were asleep,—
A heavy fall of snow.　　　　　Kien

The interest of this verse lies in the fact that the poet has written it from the point of view of the fowls, not his own. And implied is a picture that could never be painted, the fowls sitting on their perches in the dark hen-roost, eyes shut, oblivious of everything, while outside, in equal darkness invisible snow is silently falling; deeper and deeper it lies on the roof and the ground.

刈殘す芒の株の雪高し   子 規
Karinokosu   susuki no kabu no   yuki takashi

On the stubs
Left after cutting the pampas grass,
The snow is high.   Shiki

This is a scene which everyone has seen in the Japanese countryside in winter. The pampas grass seeds, and it is cut down, and when the snow falls, accumulated snow makes a heap where the stubble of the pampas grass stood. This verse is simply a picture of a familiar scene, and its poetical virtue lies to a large extent in the very fact of choosing it out. It is an example of

And you must love him ere to you
He will seem worthy of your love.

樂書の壁をあはれむ今朝の雪   蕪 村
Rakugaki no   kabe wo awaremu   kesa no yuki

The scribbling on the wall,—
It looks pitiful,
This morn of snow.   Buson

The pictures and writing that children have done on the white wall with charcoal have been there for a long time, but as a result of the fall of snow in the night the wall is brightly illuminated by the reflection of the snow in the morning sunlight. The snow has shown up human nature in its triviality, its stupidity, its vulgarity, its worthlessness. But the poet feels worth and value in this very absence of it. In the same way, "wonder" will not account for poetry; it is the "ordinary-wonderfulness" of things which we want, and it has.

馬をさへながむる雪のあしたかな　　芭 蕉
Uma wo sae nagamuru yuki no ashita kana

We gaze
Even at horses,
This morn of snow!　　Bashō

Goethe says, as before quoted: "Ein wenig Regen, ein wenig Sonne, und es wird jeden Frühling wieder grun." It is the same with winter. A little coldness in the upper air, and the whole world is renewed. Everything is dazzling white, sounds and sights completely changed. The poor pack-horses that our eyes avoided from pity or indifference are now objects of interest again.

ながながと川一筋や雪の原　　凡 兆
Naga-naga to kawa hitosuji ya yuki no hara

One long line of river
Winds across
The snowy moor.　　Bonchō

The mind fluctuates between two desires, a desire for novelty and a desire for repetition. It yearns for both variety and uniformity, the Manifold and the Unity. This is true of the mind's everyday workings and its highest flights. We see it in works of art and in science. If two incomparables may be compared, we must say that the pleasure of recognition goes deeper than that of surprise, and the true spirit of wonder is at what Emerson calls "the Ever-blessed One." The river is this, and the snowy moor is this. A modern verse, by Meisetsu, is also a beautiful picture in black and white:

女一人僧一人雪の渡しかな
Onna hitori sō hitori yuki no watashi kana

A woman and a monk,
Ferried across
Through the falling snow.

Fishing alone by a Winter River

by Barin, 馬麟, son of Baen, 馬遠, of the Sung Dynasty.

The boat glides across the black water, the white snow falls down over the whole picture, and there is a repetition of this spatial motive of horizontal and vertical movement in the spiritual realm. The monk and the woman, though in the boat together, are moving in different directions. This poem is a picture, but the significance of the form is deepened by the correspondence and consequent intensifying power of the meaning of the objects composing the picture.

日頃にくき烏も雪のあしたかな   芭 蕉
Higoro nikuki   karasu mo yuki no   ashita kana

How beautiful
The usually hateful crow,
This morn of snow!   Bashō

"Hateful" is a very strong word and it is probably applied by Bashō to the greedy, mischievous, impudently cynical, maliciously inquisitive, Iago-like character of the bird. But one touch of nature makes all things kin.

野に山にうごく物なし雪の朝   千代尼
No ni yama ni   ugoku mono nashi   yuki no asa

On moor and mountain
Nothing stirs,
This morn of snow.   Chiyo-ni

This verse has a simplicity that is supremely fitting to the subject. Snow has a simplifying effect equivalent to that of the greatest artists. All unnecessary detail is obliterated, all unnecessary motion obscured.

君火をたけよき物見せん雪丸げ   芭 蕉
Kimi hi wo take   yoki mono misen   yukimaroge

You light the fire,
And I'll show you something nice,—
A huge ball of snow!   Bashō

This is hardly poetry, but shows Bashō's overflowing gentleness and hospitality in a life of abject poverty, his sole worldly possessions being a few books and writing materials. At this time Bashō was living at Fukagawa. Sora, the disciple who accompanied him on the first part of his journey to Michinoku, provided him with a one-roomed hut, food, and firewood. One morning when Sora arrived at the hut, Bashō had been playing with the snow, rolling it into a great ball. The picture we get here is well done in the following haiku by Ōemaru:

雪丸げ大きうなつてしまひけり
Yukimaroge   ōkiu natte   shimaikeri

The snowball
Finally grew
Immense.

One can see the exhausted toilers standing there with red hands and glowing faces, gazing on their handiwork, now too heavy to roll another inch. Compare also the following by Yaezakura:

雪まろげはやも力の及ばざる
Yukimaroge   haya mo chikara no   oyobazaru

How soon
The snowball
Got beyond our strength!

The snow falls down without weight or strength and we begin to roll a ball of it. It gets bigger and bigger, until, *quite suddenly*, we find we cannot move it, it is too large and heavy. The poetic point is not of course the contrast between the snow and the snowball. It is in the contrast between our strength and the weight of the ball. It is in the suddenly perceived relation between spirit and matter. We forget when we talk in fine phrases of love conquering death, of eternal beauty, of the power of the mind, that after all it is matter that has the final word,—and this is what we perceive when the snowball will not budge.

衽なりに吹込む雪や枕もと　　　　　　　一　茶

Okumi nari ni　fukikomu yuki ya　makura moto

In the form of an *okumi,*
The snow sifts in
At my pillow.　　　　　　　　　　　　Issa

This verse has the prescript "Issa in a state of illness," 一茶
病中のていたらく. The seams of the door and the space between
the plaster and posts of the wall allow the snow to blow in.
The fine particles gradually collect on the floor in a fan-shaped
form which Issa has described as like an *okumi,* the gradually
widening insertion or inset that lies along a kimono from the
"collar" downwards. As Issa lies there, he watches the snow
form into this simple pattern, and with the same "simple"
mind, describes it. It is in this simplicity of mind that the
poetry of this verse consists.

さくさくとわら食ふ馬やよるの雪　　　旧　国

Saku-saku to　wara kū uma ya　voru no yuki

Crunch, crunch,—
The horse munching straw;
An evening of snow.　　　　　　　　Furukuni

The relation between the sound of the horse eating the
chopped straw and the silence of the fall of the snow is a
strange and deep one. How far off they are from each other,
and yet the very contrast between them, each intensifying the
other, makes us feel them both as "portions of eternity too
great for the eye (and ear) of man."

眞直な小便穴や門の雪　　　　　　　　一　茶

Massugu na　shōben ana ya　kado no yuki

The straight hole
Made by pissing
In the snow outside the door.　　　　Issa

The lavatory is outside the house, separate from it, and the
snow has already fallen to the depth of two or three feet. Issa

just opens the door and makes water into the deep snow. A round, straight hole is left in the snow, slightly discoloured, and it somehow makes an impression on him which is no different from that which is always the sign of the working of poetry, its secret life within him. He writes his verse, not in spite of, not because of the peculiarity of the subject, but simply because (and the "simply" has an important meaning here) it insisted on its being expressed. A good haiku is to be distinguished from a poor one by the *depth* of the impression it makes on the reader; there is no other standard, though we are on our guard against artificiality, sentimentality, exaggeration, intellectuality, excessive strain, cynicism, and some other unnamed enemies of poetry.

たたずめば猶降る雪の夜道かな　　　　　几　董
Tatazumeba　nao furu yuki no　yomichi kana

Standing still
In the evening road,
The snow fell more insistently.　　Kitō

When we are walking along a snowy road at night, we are busy with our own locomotion, but when we stand still, the snow seems to fall more rapidly, and we can hear its soft swiftness.

いざ行かむ雪見にころぶ處まで　　　　芭　蕉
Iza yukan　yukimi ni korobu　tokoro made

Now then!
Let's go snow-viewing,—
Till we tumble down!　　Bashō

This has the same vehemence of spirit as Christ's

Unto seventy times seven!

upon a subject of similar gentleness.

犬どもがよけてくれけり雪の道   一　茶
Inudomo ga   yokete kurekeri   yuki no michi

The dogs
Kindly get of the way,
In the snowy road.   Issa

There is only a single track in the middle of the road, where
the snow has been trodden down enough to walk. Not being
sure of their reception, dogs that come in the opposite direction
move aside to allow someone to pass, and then come back and
run along the narrow path again. Here is a whole world of
feeling, of the lives of human beings who suffer their poor
relations to dwell amongst them for profit, material and senti-
mental; and of dogs, who have enough intelligence to know
who are the lords of creation.

二人見し雪は今年も降りけるか   芭　蕉
Futari mishi   yuki wa kotoshi mo   furikeru ka

The snow we saw come down,—
Has it fallen,
This year too?   Bashō

This has the prescript: "Sent to Etsujin, thinking of our
sleeping together in poverty last year," 去年の侘寝を思ひ出して
越人に贈る. This verse has several meanings. It asks whether
there is any change of heart, any alteration of mind both
towards the snow and towards himself. It also suggests that
the snow last year and that of this year are no different. Time
and eternity, the personal and impersonal are blended in this
simple verse.

風の雪イむ我を降りめぐる   樗　良
Kaze no yuki   tatazumu ware wo   furimeguru

The windy snow
Falling and blowing around me
As I stand here.   Chora

What a world of unspoken, unspeakable poetic life is revealed

Winter Mountains

Attributed to Kōzenki, 高然暉, a Chinese painter unknown in China, said by Sōami (d. 1525) to belong to the Yuan Dynasty, 1279–1368.

in this verse, as surely as shrieks and cries attest agony of soul, as unmistakably as the cold corpse shows that the spirit has returned to God who gave it. And how is this done? With a paucity of material, surpassed perhaps in life, but not in art. In fact, it is the simple elimination of the unessential that brings out what was there all the time,

> As perchance, carvers do not faces make,
> But that away, which hid them there, do take.[1]

降雪の野に死なば我も雪佛　　　　　　長　翠
Furu yuki no　no ni shinaba ware mo　yukibotoke

> Should I perish
> On this snowy moor, I also
> Shall become a snow-Buddha. Chōsui

A snow-Buddha is a snow-man, in Japan usually an effigy of Daruma. The poet says that if he freezes to death on this vast plain on which the snow is falling, he will become a Buddha. This verse is partly humorous, but partly serious. He has grasped his fate with a strong hand, and in so far as he does this, he has attained Buddhahood.

一人づゝ降隠れ行く雪見かな　　　　可都里
Hitori zutsu　furikakureyuku　yukimi kana

> Snow-viewing,
> One by one they disappear
> In the falling snow. Katsuri

They have gone, as spectators, to look at the snow and the scenery it has recreated, but the snow is not thus passive. The snow falls upon them, as one by one, in single file, they walk along the narrowed path. The snow which they are going to gaze at swallows each one up into its silence and white darkness.

---

[1] Donne, *The Crosse.*

我雪と思へば軽し笠の上   其 角
Waga yuki to   omoeba karushi   kasa no ue

When I think it is my snow
On my hat,
It seems light.   Kikaku

There is a short story by Chekov about a stray dog. A
crowd collects and decides to get rid of the nasty creature,
when someone says it belongs to the local Police Inspector.
Immediately they all begin to praise the beauty and sagacity
of dogs in general and this dog in particular, when another
man says no, it only looks like the Police Inspector's dog, and
public opinion at once veers round, and all the Vicars of Bray
decide that it is a blot on the landscape and a disgrace to the
town, and so on and so on.

> The mind is its own place, and in itself
> Can make a heaven of hell, a hell of heaven.

This explanation is of the following popular form of Kikaku's
verse:

我がものと思へば軽し笠の雪
Waga mono to   omoeba karushi   kasa no yuki

When I think it is mine,
The snow on the umbrella
Is light.

Shiki rightly says that it must be 我が雪と思えば, "When I
think it is my snow."

As a haiku, the poetry lies in the intimate feeling of owner-
ship by the poet of the snow which is on his own umbrella,
but the verse lends itself to generalization so easily that it
cannot be called a good one.

應々と言へど叩くや雪の門   去 來
Ō ō to   iedo tataku ya   yuki no mon

"Yes! Yes!" I cried,
But someone still knocked
On the snow-mantled gate.   Kyorai

One cold snowy night the poet was sitting by the brazier when someone began knocking at the outer gate. He hurriedly got up and went outside, calling out, "All right! I am coming!" but for some reason or other the person outside continued to knock.

The point of the poem lies in the poet's lack of knowledge as to why the person outside did not stop knocking. And this mysterious knocking is in some way connected with the snow that has piled up on the roof of the gate and blown halfway up the door itself. This too, the identity of meaning of the thick layer of snow and the dull, continuous, blind knocking, is a mystery. Compare Kyoroku's quieter verse on page 1241.

傘の幾つ過ぎゆく雪の暮　　　　北　枝
Karakasa no　ikutsu sugiyuku　yuki no kure

> Many umbrellas
> Are passing by,
> This eve of snow.　　　　Hokushi

The art of haiku is not to make poetry, or even to see and record poetical things and events as they chance to appear and occur, but rather to seize the inner essence of any commonplace, everyday occurrence, to touch that inner nerve of life, of existence, that runs through the dullest and most unmeaning fact.

Snow has been falling all day. The flakes are large. Through the dusk people pass, their walk soundless, their origin and destination unknown, their form and sex indistinguishable, hardly more than moving umbrellas, snow above, beneath and all around them. The snow and the umbrellas hide the unessential elements, thus revealing—what?

我が子なら供にはやらじ夜の雪　　　　羽紅尼
Waga ko nara　tomo niwa yaraji　yoru no yuki

> Were he my child,
> He should not accompany you,
> This night of snow!　　　　Ukō-ni

This is a very well-known verse, and expresses the tenderness of a "woman's care" that overflows to children not her own, but some critics consider this to have no value at all as haiku. It needs, however, a tougher mind than mine to reject it, and it seems one of those rare exceptions where morality and poetry are indistinguishable. In any case, it is unreasonable to refuse the verse simply because it expresses a union of feeling between the woman and a boy, not her own, who was to accompany her husband through the snowy night with a lantern,—and does not deal with crickets or cherry-blossoms. Where it is lacking, is in the fact that the snow is only a stage-property; it is simply cotton-wool, paper snow, like that of *Uncle Tom's Cabin.* There is a similar verse, probably later than the former,[1] by Kanri:

> 雪の日やあれも人の子樽拾ひ
> *Yuki no hi ya　are mo hito no ko　taruhiroi*

> A day of snow;
> He also is somebody's son,
> That empty-barrel collector.

It may not be poetry, but it is good democracy.

> 大雪となりけり關のとざし時 蕪村
> *Ōyuki to　nari keri seki no　tozashidoki*

> A heavy snow-fall,
> They are just about to close
> The great gate of the barrier.　Buson

The poet has been plodding along the road towards the barrier. The snow is deep and is still falling. It is growing dark, and the soldiers are just going to shut the barrier gate. As he hurries towards it, it looms up higher than usual with many feet of snow upon it.

The lofty barrier with its ponderous gates has some deep affinity with the snow in the gathering darkness. It is something more than the mere feeling of physical weight.

---

[1] Ukō-ni was the wife of Bonchō, d. 1714, and the elder sister of Kyorai, b. 1651. Kanri died 1732.

十一騎面もふらぬ吹雪かな   子 規
Jūikki   omote mo furanu   fubuki kana

> Eleven knights
> Ride through the whirling snow
> Without turning their heads.   Shiki

These eleven horsemen ride through the blizzard, the wind
blowing around them, but none of them turns his head to avoid
the wind or look round. Besides the intensity of storm and
riders, there is the straight lines of the eleven, and the swirling,
criss-cross lines of the snowflakes.

宿かせと刀投出す吹雪かな   蕪 村
Yado kase to   katana nagedasu   fubuki kana

> Coming in from the whirling snow,—
> "A lodging for the night!"
> And he throws down his sword.   Buson

It is not necessary to limit this man to a member of the
samurai class, though for the picture it may be better so. The
door is suddenly opened, the snow and wind come in, and with
it an exhausted traveller who has at last reached this hut as
night is beginning to fall. He throws down his sword on the
tatami and gasps his request, almost a demand, for a night's
lodging here. "Throwing down the sword" expresses perfectly
his state of mind and body, his extremity of feeling. The
onomatopoeia is noteworthy. The sounds of d, t, g and k
predominate.

宿かさぬ火影や雪の家つづき   蕪 村
Yado kasanu   hokage ya yuki no   ietsuzuki

> Denied a lodging,—
> The lights from a row of houses
> In the snow.   Buson

On a journey, the poet reached a village when dusk had
already fallen, and was refused a night's lodging,—not altogether
unexpectedly, for solitary travellers late at night were not

welcomed. Buson retreats from the house, and looks back at
it and the houses that stand beside it. The lights from within
shine over the snow under the dark sky. He gazes at this
scene for a moment, not objectively, as without human meaning;
not as "man's inhumanity to man," but as life, as existence,
as poetry, in which the poet and the scene are undivided.
When they are seen as two things, we get the always solemn
words of Marcus Aurelius:

> Let aught external, that so chooses, befall those parts
> which can feel the effects of its incidence. They may
> complain if they will. But I myself have taken no hurt,
> so long as I refrain from pronouncing what has chanced
> an evil. And this abstention is within my power.

行燈の煤けぞ寒き雪の暮　　　　　越　人
Andon no　susuke zo samuki　yuki no kure

　　The night-light is smoke-stained,
Snow falls chill
　　Through the dusk.　　　　　　　Etsujin

An *andon* is a kind of night-light made of wood and paper.
In Etsujin's life-time (he was a pupil of Bashō) they were usually
small oil lamps emitting more smoke than light. The whole
thing would soon become sooty, and it is this sootiness which
is the central point of the poem. The cold night, the gloom,
snow falling with its almost soundless sounds, the melancholy
of it all in a straw-thatched hut that leaks here and there,—it
is summed up in the soot that begrimes the paper and wood
of the lamp. This is as cold to the mind as the snow outside.

からかさの一つ過行く雪の暮　　　野　坡
Karakasa no　hitotsu sugiyuku　yuki no kure

　　An umbrella—one alone—
Passes by:
　　An evening of snow.　　　　　Yaha

It is a never-ending source of intellectual wonder that the

more we decrease the quantity of material, the number of
things, the deeper the meaning becomes. For poetry it is
hardly necessary to be able to count above one. This single
umbrella, nothing else seen, moving through the snowy dusk,
—as we gaze at it passing by, the mind moving with the
umbrella and with no more thought and emotion than it, we
know the meaning of the umbrella and him who holds it, and
That which holds all things as they pass by. But this is what
we say to anyone who asks what we are looking out at. This
is not the realm of our experience, not the movement of things
which we share, but only the chattering of words around it.
The same experience is seen in the following by Bonchō; it
belongs to autumn:

桐の木の風にかまはぬ落葉かな
Kiri no ki no   kaze ni kamawanu   ochiba kana

Regardless of wind,
A leaf of the paulownia
Falls.

鵯のそれきり啼かず雪の暮   亜 浪
Hiyodori no   sorekiri nakazu   yuki no kure

A bulbul cried,
And cried no more:
Snow fell through the dusk.   Arō

After the bulbul[1] cries, "Pee-a, pee-a," there is silence; it
grows darker, and the snow seems to fall more swiftly.

時々や霰となつて風強し   子 規
Tokidoki ya   arare to natte   kaze tsuyoshi

Now and again
It turns to hail;
The wind is strong.   Shiki

[1] The Brown-eared Bulbul. Its body is bluish grey, the cheeks red-
dish brown. It has a habit of flying from branch to branch, calling
"pee-a, pee-a." "It also likes berries, and sometimes it ventures to
come to the garden to eat the fruit of "nandin" and of other trees
that bear berries." The above verse is a modern one.

This is a scene in which the vagueness is the beauty of it, vagueness of scene that is left undescribed, vagueness of time. There is nothing but wind and gusts of rain and hail, but in them we feel the power of nature in its destructively constructive forms. In the following verse, also by Shiki, there is an addition of place, of the human element, of loneliness, given by the empty boat:

捨舟の中にたばしる霰かな
Sutebune no　naka ni tabashiru　arare kana

> In the abandoned boat,
> The hail
> Bounces about.

In the ordinary way the hail bounces only at one angle, but the inside of the boat is curved and the hail dances about in every direction. There is also a connection between the wanton, free-for-all antics of the hail, and the boat left there without owner or boatman. The hail is thrown away into the thrown-away boat.

呼かへす鮒賣見えぬあられかな　　　　　凡 兆
Yobikaesu　funauri mienu　arare kana

> Going out to call back the crucian-seller,
> He was not to be seen;
> Hail began to fall.　　　　　Bonchō

This verse needs no explanation, but literally it is: "Calling back the crucian-seller, not visible, hail."

Such a state of mind, an extremity which is God's opportunity, is perhaps the commonest poetic experience of so-called unpoetic people. Poets and psychologists attend to such things, for they are accustomed to notice how a dilemma, a lack of outlet for action causes the mind to become abnormally receptive. They are quick to remark upon the peculiar meaning of some trivial or habitual occurrence. The hail would never have been attended to were it not for the non-plussed condition caused by the disappearance of the fishmonger when he was expected to return.

いかめしき音やあられの檜笠   芭 蕉
Ikameshiki   oto ya arare no   hinokigasa

How sternly majestic,
The sound of the hail
On my *hinokigasa*.   Bashō

The rattle of the hail-stones, like arrows on armour, gives a
feeling of the nature of both the *kasa*, a kind of umbrella-hat
made of strips of cypress wood, and the hail. In another verse
by Bashō we see the same thing with hail and rocks:

石山の石にたばしる霰かな
Ishiyama no   ishi ni tabashiru   arare kana

The hail-stones
Glance off the rocks
Of the Stony Mountain.

A modern poet, Kyoshi, adds human emotion to the mere
sounds, reminding us of Wordsworth as a boy:

盗んだる案山子の笠に雨急なり
Nusundaru   kakashi no kasa ni   ame kyū nari

How heavy the rain
On the *kasa* I stole
From the scarecrow!

Thoreau says in *Walden, Higher Laws*:

Our whole life is startlingly moral. There is never an
instant's truce between virtue and vice.

Even to steal from a scarecrow makes us uneasy, and renders
us more sensitive to impressions. So the rain that falls on the
kasa that he has "appropriated" fairly thunders in his ears.

山風や霰吹き込む馬の耳   大 魯
Yama-kaze ya   arare fukikomu   uma no mimi

The mountain blast!
The hail is driven
Into the horse's ear.   Tairo

This verse expresses the power and omnipotence of nature

in a homely and humorous way. We see clearly the small pellets of ice, and the coarse hairs in the ear of the horse.

甲板に霰の音のくらさ哉   子 規
Kampan ni   arare no oto no   kurasa kana

On the deck
The sound of the hail
Is dark.   Shiki

On hearing the hail, the idea of an overcast sky is instantly presented to the mind, so that the sound seems dark as ice looks cold. But in addition to this, the hollow, pattering sound of the hail on the deck above sounds dark in itself.

いざ子供はしり歩かん玉あられ   芭 蕉
Iza kodomo   hashiriarukan   tamaarare

Look, children,
Hail-stones!
Let's rush out!   Bashō

This may be compared with some of Wordsworth's minor poetry, where superficial readers can see but little. It is little, but that little is something precious. The poet felt that "twinge" at the moment, even when he failed to express it, even though there was a still-birth, and the appropriate language was not generated by the experience. What is peculiarly beautiful about Bashō's verse is the fact that Bashō's ejaculation, "Let's rush out," expresses the hail far more than it does Bashō's attitude towards the hail. It gives us the very nature of the hail itself, in its swift, bouncing, rushing mobility.

一さんに飛で火に入るあられかな   一 茶
Issan ni   tonde hi ni iru   arare kana

Hail,
Flying into the fire
As fast as its legs can carry it.   Issa

The faithfulness of things, their will to live which is united
to an equal will to die, the constructive and destructive both
working to the utmost limit, begins to be deformed in the
higher animals and is hopelessly perverted in men. The (ap-
parent) power to choose that human beings have makes them
heat the fire hotter, into which they fall as fast as the rest of
things, as swiftly as the hail-stones. Issa is also perhaps think-
ing of the moths of summer that flutter round the lamps,
attracted yet afraid.

山寺の硯に早し初氷   蕪　村
Yamadera no   suzuri ni hayashi   hatsugōri

In the ink-stone
Of the mountain temple,
The first ice is early.   Buson

The night before, he was writing, and when he gets up he
finds the ink frozen. The season is too early for this to happen
in ordinary places. In the ice that has formed in the well of
the ink-slab, Buson sees the remoteness and height of the
temple where he is staying.

瓶わるる夜の氷のねざめかな   芭　蕉
Kame waruru   yoru no kōri no   nezame kana

I woke up suddenly,
With the ice of a night
When the water-pot burst.   Bashō

The form of the expression in Japanese shows us that what
Bashō experienced was an aural perception of the "Buddha
nature" of ice. He "woke up" to what ice was.

森の中に池あり氷あつき哉   子　規
Mori no naka ni   ike ari kōri   atsuki kana

A pool,
Deep in the forest;
The ice is thick.   Shiki

In this simple verse, in the mere thickness, the extra thickness of the ice, a whole world is revealed. The depth of the forest, its remoteness from human habitation, the pale sunlight that leaks through the highest boughs of the trees, the late morning, the early evening,—all are contained in this one phrase, "The ice is thick."

It is thick because the sun hardly penetrates to the surface of the pond, but this explanation, however true, is not the living, poetical truth. In the mere thickness of the ice we see the power of nature, the stern inevitability of things.

ともし火に氷れる筆を焦しけり   大 魯
Tomoshibi ni   kōreru fude wo   kogashikeri

> I burnt
> The frozen brush
> In the lamp-flame.   Tairo

The night was so cold that when the poet opened his brush and ink-box, and made ink with the ink-stick, he found that the brush was frozen. He tried to thaw it in the flame of the lamp, but through his carelessness, the brush was burnt, or rather, singed. The whole verse, and the final picture, the poet sitting looking at the spoiled brush, the silence outside and inside, the intense cold, the feeble light of the wick floating in oil,—this is all an expression of loneliness, inevitable, and of no ulterior meaning.

氷る燈の油うかがふ鼠かな   蕪 村
Kōru hi no   abura ukagau   nezumi kana

> A rat approaches
> The freezing oil
> Of the lamp.   Buson

There are certain subjects, such as scarecrows, mice, fallen leaves, chrysanthemums, upon which all poets write well. There must be some deep relation between human beings and these things. The light of the lamp flickers, gutters, goes out; the oil begins to solidify in the cold. A rat approaches the lamp, its nose twitching, its jerky movements betraying its fearful eagerness. The extinguished, silent lamp, the motionless yet palpitating rat,—"these have a deep meaning, but when we wish to express it, the words suddenly fail us."[1]

何故に長みじかある氷柱ぞや　　　　鬼　貫

Nani yue ni　naga-mijika aru　tsurara zoya

Why
Are some icicles long,
Some short?　　　　　　　　　　　　　Onitsura

We are poets and sages in so far as we do not ask such questions, or rather, asking them we expect no answer, and do not desire one. To keep things in this state of wonder and suspense, to want without desire, to love deeply without attachment,—this is the real part of all our living. Then the different lengths of the icicles, the different heights of wooden palings, the difference between the sun and the moon, these things are of perpetual and never-ending surprise, for

長者長法身　短者短法身　（禪林句集）

A long thing is the Long Body of Buddha;
A short thing is the Short Body of Buddha.

野佛の鼻のさきからつららかな　　　一　茶

Nobotoke no　hana no saki kara　tsurara kana

The Buddha on the moor;
From the end of his nose
Hangs an icicle.　　　　　　　　　　　Issa

We see here the difference between Christianity and Buddhism, or rather, between the English and the Japanese, in their concept of nature, of religion, and of the uses (and necessities) of humour.

[1] See Tōenmei's poem, given in *Zen in English Literature*, page 61.

こ が ら し や 岩 に 裂行 水 の 聲 　　　　　 蕪 村

Kogarashi ya　iwa ni sakeyuku　mizu no koe

The winter storm,
The voice of the rushing water,
Torn by the rocks.

Buson

The phrase 裂行, might be translated literally "tearing," that is, the "tearing" is literal, for the water swiftly flowing is torn in two by the rocks which stick out above the water. However, this verse is entirely aural, as Meisetsu observes with his penetrating brevity: "This has its poetical import entirely for the ear," 是は耳ばかりの趣なり.

木枯 や 竹 に 隠れ て し づ ま り ぬ 　　　　 芭 蕉

Kogarashi ya　take ni kakurete　shizumarinu

The winter tempest
Hid itself in the bamboos,
And grew still.

Bashō

A great gust of wind comes roaring towards the bamboo grove; the bamboos sway and toss, the leaves quiver and rustle, then everything is still and silent again, all that force and sound swallowed up completely.

こ が ら し や 頬腫 痛 む 人 の 顔 　　　　　 芭 蕉

Kogarashi ya　hōbare itamu　hito no kao

The tempest is blowing:
Someone's painfully
Swollen face.

Bashō

The harmony here is one of grotesqueness; the swollen, disfigured, grimacing face, and the blustering, insolent, uncouth wind have a peculiar relation to each other that defies intellectual analysis.

It is interesting to compare this to another verse of Bashō's, in which he uses a boil to bring out the delicacy and femininity of the willow-tree:

はれ物にさはる柳のしなへかな
Haremono ni   sawaru yanagi no   shinae kana

    As if touching a tumour,
    The drooping branches
    Of the willow.

Spinoza says,

Whenever, then, anything in nature seems to us ridiculous, absurd, or evil, it is because we have but a partial knowledge of things, and are in the main ignorant of the order and coherence of nature as a whole, and because we want everything to be arranged according to the dictates of our own reason; although in fact, what our reason pronounces bad is not bad as regards the order and laws of universal nature, but only as regards the laws of our own nature taken separately.[1]

凩や小石のこける板庇   蕪 村
Kogarashi ya   koishi no kokeru   itabisashi

    The cold blast;
    Small stones rattling
    On the planks of the pent-roof.   Buson

In this verse there is no talk about seeing the world in a grain of sand; it is actually heard in the small stones rattling over the pent-house roof. And in the dry harsh timbre, we feel the same meaning as in the sound of the wind, the bleakness and deathliness of winter. Another excellent verse with a slightly different meaning,—the sting and bitterness of winter, is the following:

凩や鐘に小石を吹きあてる
Kogarashi ya   kane ni koishi wo   fukiateru

    The winter tempest
    Blows small stones
    Onto the temple bell.

Other verses in which Buson has used stones to express the

[1] *Tractatus Politicus*, Ch. 2.

nature of the winter wind:

凩や野河の石を踏みわたる
Kogarashi ya   nogawa no ishi wo   fumiwataru

> The winter tempest;
> Crossing over the stones
> Of the river on the moor.

凩や畠の小石目に見ゆる
Kogarashi ya   hatake no koishi   me ni miyuru

> The winter tempest;
> The small stones of the field
> Are clearly seen.

He has used stones also to show the peculiar quality of the winter moor, the cold wind being taken for granted:

てらてらと石に日の照る枯野かな
Teratera to   ishi ni hi no teru   kareno kana

> Brightly the sun
> Shines on the stones
> Of the withered moor.

石に詩を題して過ぐる枯野かな
Ishi ni shi wo   daishite suguru   kareno kana

> Writing a poem about a stone,
> And passing on,—
> The withered moor!

蕭條として石に日の入る枯野かな
Shōjō to shite   ishi ni hi no iru   kareno kana

> Dreary and desolate,
> The sun sinks behind the stones
> On the withered moor.

息杖に石の火を見る枯野かな
Ikizue ni   ishi no hi wo miru   kareno kana

> Sparks on a stone
> From the palanquin-bearer's staff,—
> Over the withered moor.

木枯の果はありけり海の音   言 水
Kogarashi no   hate wa arikeri   umi no oto

　　The winter blast
　　Has its final end
　　In the sound of the sea.   Gonsui

All day long the wind has been raging. Towards evening
the wind drops, and the roaring of the waves is heard in the
distance. There is a very obvious connection between the
blowing of the tempest and the clamour of the sea-shore, be-
tween the subsidence of the sound of the wind and the rising
of that of the water. This is Emerson's "systole and diastole of
nature." But we must also say, with Blake:

　　The roaring of lions, the howling of wolves, the raging
　　of the stormy sea, and the destructive sword, are portions
　　of eternity too great for the eye of man.

There is also a feeling of the unceasing work of nature, as in
Keats' sonnet:

　　It keeps eternal whisperings around
　　Desolate shores, and with its mighty swell
　　Gluts twice ten thousand caverns.

冬枯や世は一色に風の音   芭 蕉
Fuyugare ya   yo wa hito iro ni   kaze no oto

　　Winter desolation:
　　In a world of one colour
　　The sound of the wind.   Bashō

The grass is brown, and branches bare,

　　The sedge has wither'd from the lake,
　　And no birds sing.

Winter has taken away the colours from the earth; the only
sound is that of the wind, of no tone-colour, a wind that tells,
in its harshness, of withered leaves, dry sticks and sharp stones,
waste and empty places.

うら枯や馬も餅くふうつの山　　　　　　其 角
Uragare ya　uma mo mochi kū　utsu no yama

On Mount Utsu
All is withered and desolate:
The horse also eats the *mochi*.　　　Kikaku

Mt. Utsu, 宇津山, refers to a mountain pass in Suruga no Kuni,[1] 駿河の國, where there was the customary teahouse for the refreshment of travellers, with the equally customary special delicacy of the district.

All touches of nature make the whole world kin. Somebody gives the horse a rice-cake. The horse puts his ears forward, takes the cake with his thick lips, and begins to munch it. The sacrament of eating together is performed, all are companions. Eat and be eaten is the law of life. But what is this "touch of nature" in a world where everything is natural?

こがらしやひたとつまづく戻り馬　　　　蕪 村
Kogarashi ya　hita to tsumazuku　modori uma

A wintry wind:
The horse suddenly stumbles
As it comes back home.　　　Buson

Evening is falling, a cold, gusty wind blows along the road. An old horse, thin and bony, hastens its step as it nears the village. Suddenly it stumbles over a stone in the uneven ground. And this pathos has something to do with the meaning of the poem. Sometimes, in some circumstances, in some moods, the breaking of a plate, of even a pencil point, some accidental occurrence causes us to feel in a moment all the tragedy of life, its uselessness, its constant danger, the precariousness of happiness, the enmity of Nature, the anger of God, the ultimate annihilation of the universe. The verse above is born of one of these moments. If we speak of the tired horse, its thinness and hunger, still a long way to go,—this is morality; it may be sentimentality, but it is not poetry. The real "pathos" of the horse is seen when it is in its dark stable, eating its evening meal, its luminous eyes half-shut. It is the eagerness, the hopes

[1] Shizuoka.

which are tragic, not despair or desperation. It is the gratitude of men that leaves us mourning. But the sudden stumbling of the horse has its poetic meaning in this verse by virtue of its mysterious relation with the violent wind that is blowing its mane and tail. When the horse stumbles, some feeling far above pity and fear is aroused, which nevertheless springs from them and cannot exist without them. The stumble causes us a deep, painful joy,—which is, itself, the poetic life.

木枯に岩吹きとがる杉間かな   芭 蕉
Kogarashi ni iwa fukitogaru   sugima kana

The rocks among the cryptomerias
Are sharpened
By the withering blast.   Bashō

The scene is of the sharp rocks lying beneath the pointed cryptomerias, and the piercing wind that blows among them. The coldness of the wind and the jagged edges of the rocks are in a deep harmony that is expressed as causal in character. Compare Chora's (later) verse on page 1171.

木がらしやからよびされし按摩坊   一 茶
Kogarashi ya   karayobi sareshi   ammabō

In the winter blast,
The *amma*
Is called in vain.   Issa

The winter wind sweeps away the voice of someone calling to the *amma*, or masseur, and the blind man walks on, blowing his plaintive whistle of two notes. This picture of futility Issa perfected after three trials:

寒月やむだ呼びされし座頭坊
Kangetsu ya   mudayobi sareshi   zatōbō

Under the winter moon,
A fruitless cry
For the blind man.

夜按摩やむだ呼びされて降る時雨
Yoamma ya   mudayobi sarete   furu shigure

> The masseur at night
> Is vainly called,
> Cold rain falling.

夜時雨やから呼びされし按摩坊
Yoshigure ya   karayobi sareshi   ammabō

> Cold rain at night;
> The useless cry
> For the masseur.

These examples will show how easy haiku are not, when a poet experiences something that demands expression, yet seems also to defy it.

地　理　**FIELDS AND MOUNTAINS**

鳥飛んで荷馬驚く枯野哉　　　　　　　　　　子　規
Tori tonde   niuma odoroku   kareno kana

A bird flies up,—
The pack-horse shies,—
The withered moor!　　　　　　　　　　　Shiki

The bird is not particularized; it is not necessary, and better
so. The horse is a pack-horse because it is old and thin and
in harmony with the scenery; and because such a decrepit
creature being startled is more striking. The central point of
the verse is the withered moor, its silence and lifelessness,
brought out by this unexpected sign of life. The driver also
is startled in his turn. A pianissimo version of this contrast,
by Kanrō:

庭鳥の遠く遊べる枯野かな
Niwatori no   tōku asoberu   kareno kana

Chickens pecking about
In the distance,
On the withered moor.

片道は日のくれになる枯野かな　　　　　　木　導
Katamichi wa   hinokure ni naru   kareno kana

On the way back home,
Evening has fallen
Across this withered moor.　　　　　　　Mokudō

The poetical life of this is very still and quiet. It needs
quite an effort to suppress oneself sufficiently to enter into the
poet's state of mind. He is coming back from doing some
affair that was neither overwhelmingly successful, nor a failure.
A poem of Hakurakuten of a similar tone-feeling:

渭　村　雨　歸

渭水寒漸落、　離離蒲稗苗。
閑傍沙邊立、　看人刈葦苕。

Snowy Landscape

by Ryōkai, 梁楷; flourished in the
first half of the 13th century.

近水風景冷、　晴明猶寂寥。
復茲夕陰起、　野思重蕭條。
蕭條獨歸路、　暮雨湿村橋。

RETURNING TO THE VILLAGE OF I,
IN THE RAIN

The waters of the River I had fallen with the cold;
On the bank, reeds and deccan-grass were rank.
I walked along by the sand-banks, and stood there in quietness,
Watching a man cutting bulrushes.
By the water, the scene was cold and bleak;
The clear light seemed to add to the desolation.
But when the shadows of night began to fall,
The plain was yet more dreary.
As I walked back in loneliness,
Falling rain was staining the bridge to the village.

馬の尾にいばらのかかる枯野かな　　　　蕪 村
Uma no o ni　ibara no kakaru　kareno kana

The horse's tail
Caught in the bramble
On the withered moor.　　　　　Buson

It is a scene of desolation, withered grasses, dead leaves,
sticks and stones, frozen pieces of earth. But there is life here
too. The long tail of the horse has caught on the thorns of a
bramble by the side of the path. The life is not that of the
horse and the bramble as animal and plant. It is that of the
nature of the long strands of hair, the sharp thorns, and the
potential relation between them that is suddenly actualized in
a chance, yet pre-destined, yet free event. It is a picture, but
a picture whose meaning eludes all analysis because it means
no more and no less than itself.

手を出さず物荷ひゆく冬野かな   來 山
Te wo dasazu   mono ninaiyuku   fuyuno kana

Carrying a load,
Both hands in his sleeves,
Over the winter moor.   Raizan

The point of this verse is the second line. There is some-
thing in the handlessness of the picture, or rather of the
imagined experience, which strikes the poet. Sometimes it would
be good to have no hands; they are useless encumbrances that
have to be kept warm by tucking them in our sleeves or pockets.
But the verse is not conscious of anything more than the
feel of the hands in the sleeves as something peculiar, yet
characteristic.

馬叱る聲も枯野のあらしかな   曲 翠
Uma shikaru   koe mo kareno no   arashi kana

The voice shouting at the horse
Is part of the storm
Of the withered moor.   Kyokusui

The voice of the people is the voice of God. The voice of
man is the voice of nature. The voice of the carter raging at
his horse is the voice of the storm that blows over the wintry
scene.

山を越す人に別れて枯野かな   蕪 村
Yama wo kosu   hito ni wakarete   kareno kana

Parting from him,
He crossed over the mountain:
This withered moor!   Buson

The poet and his friend walk along the winter path, talking
or silent, "revolving many things." Parting, his friend crosses
over the mountain, and the poet goes on alone. The face of
nature is changed, the winter scene joyless and dreary. He
sees only separation and death in it. This may be called a
simple case of the association of ideas, but the barrenness and

deadness of the winter moor that are seen subjectively, are also
objectively there. It is only when we are subjectively in accord
with some aspect of a thing, that we see that aspect, an aspect
which has objective justification. But how are we to distinguish
that objectivity from this subjectivity? Like Villaespesa in
Animae Rerum,

> Y en medio de este obscuro silencio, de esta calma,
> Y no se si es la sombra la que invade mi alma,
> O si es que de mi alma va surgiendo la sombra.

> And during this obscure silence, this calm,
> I know not if it is that the shadow invades my soul,
> Or if it is from my soul that the shadow arises.

This question cannot be answered and should not be asked.
What is wrong is the lack of something, the absence in the
mind of those colours which will enable us to see them in the
object. If our minds are coloured in any particular way, we
can see that (actually existent) quality in anything we behold.
God looks at everything with a mind which is coloured with
every colour, that is, with

> the bright radiance of eternity.

As human beings we can do this to only a limited extent, and
in the above poem it is not attempted. The poet expresses his
experience, not as simply registering a passing mood, but in-
wardly convinced that there is some unfathomable correspond-
ence between the cheerlessness of the wasted winter scene, and
the dejection he feels.

> 提灯の一つ家に入る枯野かな   子 規
> *Chōchin no   hitotsu ya ni iru   kareno kana*

> A lantern
> Entered a house
> On the withered moor.   Shiki

It is night, and in the distance, the light of a lantern is seen
moving along. It enters a small house standing there in the
midst of the cold winds, and all is dark. What this light and
its disappearance into the unknown mean, no one can express,

for all our thoughts and feelings are concentrated on this wavering spot of light, a light that moves of itself and then goes out of itself.

鳥一羽道づれにして枯野かな   千　邪
Tori ichiwa   michizure ni shite   kareno kana

A solitary bird
For my companion
　　Upon the withered moor.   Senna

As he walks along the winter path, the dead grass, the fallen twigs flowing away beneath his lowered eye, a small bird of some unknown kind flits from one point to another beside the path he is treading, as if it finds a faint pleasure in the poet's company.　They are a strange-looking pair, the man and the bird, but there is something in common between them.

大木の雲にそびゆる枯野哉   子　規
Taiboku no   kumo ni sobiyuru   kareno kana

A great tree
The rises up into the clouds,
　　On the withered moor.   Shiki

There is something about an enormous tree that is different in quality from the trees of ordinary size. This particular tree rises up and up like the tree of Jack the Giant-killer, its head lost in the clouds, while all around stretch withered grasses and cold fields.　We ourselves are lifted up out of ourselves and are subdued into the highest boughs and branches silently spreading out their hands in the misty air.

門ばかり殘る冬野の伽藍哉   子　規
Mon bakari   nokoru fuyuno no   garan kana

Only the gate
Of the abbey is left,
　　On the winter moor.   Shiki

As we look at this gate into nothing at all we feel the death of nature, the destruction of the world, the final extinction of human hopes. But the depth of the feeling makes it bearable. It is to experience death and all its meaning that man was born. The scene of desolation on the winter moor, the ancient gate, and the ruins of the temple beyond it, these have a significance that the spring flowers cannot attain to.

ところどころ菜畑遠き枯野哉   子 規
Tokorodokoro   nabatake tōki   kareno kana

Here and there in the distance,
Fields of vegetables
    On the withered moor.   Shiki

These small patches of green on the brown and blighted moor bring out the ruin of nature still more strongly. And the fact that they are seen far-off brings in an element of grief. Distance in space always implies distance in time, and time is the deepest and most mysteriously painful thing in our experience, the more indirectly perceived the more poignant.

里の子の犬引いて行く枯野哉   子 規
Sato no ko no   inu hiite yuku   kareno kana

A boy of the village
Leading a dog
    Over the withered moor.   Shiki

The boy and the dog trudging along the cold, dusty road over the winter moor express each other, fulfil each other in some mysterious way. The little dog unconscious of everything but the smells and sights around him, the boy with some unknown object, pulling the dog along,—these two accentuate the loneliness of the road, the futility of life which must always end in death.

むささびの小鳥食み居る枯野かな　　　蕪　村
Musasabi no   kotori hamioru   kareno kana

The flying-squirrel
Is crunching the small bird
On the withered moor.　　　　　　　　Buson

This example of "Nature red in tooth and claw," is not to be followed by Tennysonian wails of distress or theological sophistries; neither can it be laughed off or ignored. It is as it is, and is, in its way, as good as anything else. The fall of the cherry-blossoms is as necessary, as poetical as their blooming:

一切聲是佛聲、一切色是佛色。

All sounds are the voice of Buddha,
All forms are the forms of Buddha.
Hekiganroku, 79, Criticism.

Santayana[1] says the same thing:

It is right that the world should illustrate the full nature of the infinite, and not merely the particular ideals of man.

There is also a peculiar testimony from Newman in *The Idea of a University*:

And so again, the sight of beasts of prey and other foreign animals, their strangeness, their originality (if I may use the term) of their forms and gestures...throw us out of ourselves into another Creator.

大徳の糞ひりおはす枯野かな　　　　蕪　村
Daitoku no   fun hiriowasu   kareno kana

His Eminence the Abbot
Is shitting
On the withered moor.　　　　　　　Buson

There is a double contrast here, visual and mental: the monk in his multicoloured robes of silk and satin in the monotone of brown of the winter moor; the spiritual loftiness of the priest

---

[1] *Introduction to Spinoza's Ethics.*

and his performing of what is considered the lowliest of all human functions. There is no thought in Buson's mind of the fact that all cats are grey in the dark, or that all functions are human, are divine. Herein lies the Zen of the poem. In Nature, which includes man, there is nothing fair, nothing foul;

> I would warn you that I do not attribute to nature either beauty or deformity, order or confusion. Only in relation to our imagination can things be called beautiful or ugly, well-ordered or confused.[1]

旅人の蜜柑くい行く枯野哉   子 規
Tabibito no   mikan kuiyuku   kareno kana

The traveller walks
Over the withered moor,
    Eating an orange.   Shiki

Oranges of the tangerine type appear in winter, and the solitary traveller walks slowly along the bleak road, peeling and eating one. The sourish taste makes him shiver, and the cold air makes the orange still more sour; one intensifies the other, so that all things imperceptibly draw closer to one another and to him.

松杉や枯野の中の不動堂   子 規
Matsu sugi ya   kareno no naka no   fudōdō

Pine-trees and crytomerias;
A shrine of Fudō
    On the withered moor.   Shiki

Fudō stands within the shrine gnashing his teeth, his eyes glaring out of a crimson face. Around the small shrine are dark, evergreen trees, and beyond them stretch out the frozen fields and bare trees. There is something alive in the midst of the cold waste, under the black trees in the old and silent shrine.

[1] Spinoza, *Epistle* 15.

旅 に 病 ん で 夢 は 枯 野 を か け め ぐ る   芭 蕉
Tabi ni yande   yume wa kareno wo   kakemeguru

Ill on a journey;
My dreams wander
Over a withered moor.   Bashō

This is Bashō's death-verse, written for his pupils, though he
had declared, the evening before, that for the last twenty years
every poem had been his death poem.

Look thy last on all things lovely,
Every hour. Let no night
Seal thy sense in deathly slumber
Till to delight
Thou hast paid thy utmost blessing;
Since that all things thou would praise
Beauty took from those who loved them
In other days.

This poem, Walter de la Mare's *Farewell*, shows what Bashō
meant by saying that all his real poetry was death-verses. And
so this verse of Bashō's is simply his death-verse about life and
death. What he showed them when they gathered round his
bed in the morning has the subdued tones of Christina Rossetti's
Uphill:

Does the road wind uphill all the way?
Yes, to the very end.
Will the day's journey take the whole long day?
From morn to night, my friend.

It has the Buddhistic agnosticism of Clough's lines:

Where lies the land to which the ship would go?
Far, far ahead, is all her seamen know.
And where is the land she travels from? Away,
Far, far behind, is all that they can say.

But Bashō does not look before and after, and pine for what
is not. He does not look back at a well-spent life, nor hope
for future bliss in Paradise. He has the habit of sincerity, for
studia abeunt in mores. For many years he has looked at truth
with her inflexible regard; what does he see at this moment?
He is ill, dying; it is a withered moor through which he now

journeys, and this too, is but a dream.

In Bashō's verse, there is implied also self-reproach, a continuous, daily, hourly thing for idealists. We may compare Issa's verse written when he was forty-nine, as he thought of the way of poetry that he had walked through fair weather and foul:

月花や四十九年のむだ歩行
Tsuki hana ya   shijū ku nen no   muda hokō

> Under moon and flowers,
> Forty nine-years
> Of fruitless wandering.

Compare a verse of Bashō's written the same year:

世を旅に代かく小田の行きもどり
Yo wo tabi ni   shiro kaku oda no   yukimodori

> Journeying through the world,—
> To and fro, to and fro,
> Harrowing the small field.

のら猫の糞して居るや冬の庭 　　　子 規
Noraneko no   fun shite iru ya   fuyu no niwa

> A stray cat
> Excreting
> In the winter garden. 　　　　　Shiki

This an extraordinarily good haiku. The harmony between the three things is perfect. The thin, mangy, unlovely and unloving cat, sitting there in the cat's only ungainly attitude, with its eyes vacantly staring; the cold hard ground and withered grasses and fallen leaves. Nature has its ungraceful and ugly side, which has, however, no less meaning than the comely and beautiful.

冬川にすてたる犬の屍かな 　　　子 規
Fuyukawa ni   sutetaru inu no   kabane kana

> The body of a dog
> Thrown away
> In the winter river. 　　　　　Shiki

This is a sight everyone has seen. Small boys pelt it with stones as it comes floating down, distended with gas, a straw rope round its neck. Women and girls say "Poor thing!" and mean very little; other people avert their eyes and pretend they have seen nothing. But in the river of our minds, drowned dogs are always floating down, their sightless eyes staring at us. These things cannot be overlooked; we and they are all floating in the same river, and from the disintegration and wreckage of their lives and ours, new forms arise, to gladden the hearts of new worlds of men. There is no pathos or sympathy for animals in this verse. The dead body of the dog brings out the nature of a river in its carrying along with it anything that may be thrown in, just as a mirror reflects all things without fear or favour; and the nature of a winter river especially, in its emphasis on death and desolation. There is no love or loveliness, only a narrow current of cold waters between wide banks of stones and gravel. Another verse by Shiki, which shows the life of the river:

冬川の菜屑啄む家鴨かな
Fuyukawa no　nakuzu tsuibamu　ahiru kana

Ducks dabbing
At leaves and stalks of greens
In the winter river.

冬川や家鴨四五羽に足らぬ水　　　　　　　子　規
Fuyukawa ya　ahiru shigowa ni　taranu mizu

The winter river;
Not enough water
For four or five ducks.　　　　　　　　Shiki

There are only a few ducks, but the water of the river is hardly enough for them, and in them we see the dryness of winter. They stand for the winter river, or rather, they express more than the river does. The ducks and the river are on the one hand a picture of desolation and water-poverty, and on the other hand the ducks manifest forth the nature of the river in winter. There is another verse by Shiki of similar import, but where the humour overflows from the small duck onto the life of men:

冬籠盥に馴るる小鴨かな
Fuyugomori   tarai ni naruru   kogamo kana

> Winter seclusion;
> The *kogamo*
> Is used to the tub.

冬川や佛の花の流れ來る   蕪　村
Fuyukawa ya   hotoke no hana no   nagarekuru

> The winter river;
> Down it come floating
> Flowers offered to Buddha.   Buson

This is just a picture, a moving picture, of cold water flowing darkly, and a few flowers, half-submerged, that come floating down. But the *reason* for the significance (not the significance itself) is that these flowers once stood before the image of Buddha and received and shared and communicated the reverence and adoration of the worshippers. Yet they are of no more and no less value now, sodden and limp, floating far away to lie rotting in some back-water. Their no-value, their really "religious" value is just the same, but more easily seen now than before, because they have been given the background of Great Nature, instead of the background of Buddhism.

瀧涸れて木の葉を叩く雫かな   唇　風
Taki karete   ko no ha wo tataku   shizuku kana

> The waterfall drying up,
> Water drips down
> Onto the leaves.   Shimpū

"Drips down onto" is *tataku*, "strikes," in the original, and has its proper onomatopoeic effect.

神 佛 GODS AND BUDDHAS

紛るべき物音絶えて鉢叩 　　　　　　　　樗良
Magirubeki monooto taete hachitataki

The noises that must have mingled with it
Died away:
The sound of bowl-beating remains. Chora

At first the sound of the bowl-beating outside was blended
with the noises of people passing, talking, working, but after
a time these sounds died away and only the bowl-beating of the
devotees was heard.

The twenty third day of the eleventh month according to the
Lunar Calendar is the anniversary of the death of Saint Kūya,
空也上人, 903–972 A.D., who built bridges and dug wells in
various provinces, preaching Buddhism especially in the pro-
vinces of Dewa and Mutsu. From about the thirteenth of
November, for forty eight nights, the priests and devotees go
round beating a kind of drum, chanting the name of Buddha.
In some places they beat a gourd, chanting Buddhist hymns of
the impermanence of things and receiving alms in the gourd
in place of the usual bowl. From this comes the expression
"bowl-beating."

鉢たゝき顔の雫を呑みにけり　　　　　　　來 山
Hachitataki kao no shizuku wo nominikeri

Bowl-beating,
And drinking the drops of rain
From my face Raizan

In the ordinary way we shake or wipe the drops of water
from our faces, but when we are entirely engrossed in what
we are doing, in chanting the sutra and beating the gourd, the
drops of rain or melted snow run into the mouth and we
swallow them naturally, involuntarily. In this involuntariness,
the secret will that is so much more powerful than the waking
and conscious volition, the poet sees a profound meaning. It
is so natural, so little in need of explanation that he cannot
but record it.

夜泣する小家も過ぎぬ鉢叩   蕪 村
Yonaki suru   koie mo suginu   hachitataki

A child weeping at night;
We passed that cottage too,
Bowl-beating.   Buson

The small group of believers passes from house to house
beating their drums and gourds with monotonous and threaten-
ing regularity. From one of the houses, a poor cottage, comes
the sound of the wailing of a child. As they pass by in the
cold and darkness, the throbbing of their drums mingles with
the woeful voice of the infant.

There is a kind of sad resignation about this verse. Some
groan in their infantile anguish, some beat inexorable drums.
It must be so, and we must bear it.

Buson has a verse somewhat similar and yet different:

子を寝させて出行闇や鉢叩
Ko wo nesasete   ideyuku yami ya   hachitataki

Putting the child to sleep,
And going out bowl-beating,—
The darkness!

Kyoroku, who died in 1715, the year of Buson's birth, has a
verse where contrast is the motif; not "the woes that infants
bear," but the bustle of marriage:

嫁入の門も過ぎけり鉢叩
Yomeiri no   kado mo sugikeri   hachitataki

Passing by
A house with a wedding service,—
Bowl-beating.

兄弟が同じ聲なる鉢叩   樗 良
Kyōdai ga   onaji koe naru   hachitataki

Bowl-beating,
The brothers chanting
In the same voice.   Chora

When we read this we have a Dantean vision of all men

praising God, with one heart and mind and soul and voice. But it can never be; and this it is which gives the meaning to the unison. We say,

> Ah love! could thou and I with Fate conspire
> To grasp this sorry Scheme of Things entire,
>   Would we not shatter it to bits—and then
> Remould it nearer to the Heart's Desire!

This pseudo-ideal world towards which we aspire in our moments (and how many they are!) of weakness, at a low ebb of life, this world too has its use, in deepening the value of the real world of blood and tears. How different from the world of the poem is that which Christ prophesies of, where

> the brother shall deliver up the brother to death, and the father the child.

提灯の猶ほあわれなり寒念佛　　　　蕪 村
Chōchin no　nao aware nari　kannembutsu

> The hand-lanterns,—
> Still more pathetic;
> Winter *nembutsu*.　　　　Buson

For thirty days, in the coldest part of the year, believers go round the streets asking for alms, beating a kind of drum and chanting sutras the while. As they come near the house, their unmusical voices sound full of pathos to the poet's ear. Faith is more pathetic than disbelief, goodness than badness;

> Alas, the gratitude of men
> Hath oftener left me mourning.

They move away, their plaintively discordant voices more and more pitiful as they go farther and farther into the distance. At last, their chanting is no more to be heard; only the lanterns they carry show spots of light on the snow.

白雪の中に聲あり寒念佛   蓼 太
Shirayuki no   naka ni koe ari   kannembutsu

> Within the clouds
> There are voices:
> Winter *nembutsu*.   Ryōta

In a verse like this haiku has an unusual élan which we as-
sociate with the poetry of Shelley. There is felt to be something
supernatural in nature. The mountain has the awe of Mount
Sinai.

鳶ひよろゝひゝよろ神の御立げな   一 茶
Tobi hyororo   hiiyoro kami no   otachigena

> The gods are setting forth, it seems;
> *Hyororo hiiyoro*,
> Cry the kites.   Issa

On the 1st of October, all the gods throughout Japan leave
their own shrines to assemble at the Great Shrine of Izumo.
On this day, the kites are circling round in the pale blue sky,
uttering their plaintive cry. This resembles the sound of fifes
and pan-pipes that accompany the Shintō ceremonies.

Are there really heavenly beings that set out on the 1st of
October? Have the kites any connection with the journeying
of the gods? Both these questions have the same answer. If
we say yes, we commit ourselves to superstition and fancifulness.
If we say no, we deny the deepest intuitions of the heart, and
the rights of the poetic imagination. This verse requires the
religious insight that penetrates to the truth underlying all
creeds and dogmas.

留守の間にあれたる神の落葉かな   芭 蕉
Rusu no ma ni   aretaru kami no   ochiba kana

> The god is absent;
> His dead leaves are piling,
> And all is deserted.   Bashō

The god has gone to the gathering at Izumo. On this day,

the whole shrine is unusually lonely and neglected. The fallen leaves lie here and there, and no one seems to care.

The attitude of the Japanese to the gods is worth noting here; it strongly resembles that of the Greeks, but the outlines are softer, lacking the rather hard clarity of the western mythology. In the following verse, Bonchō has included Buddhism into this atmosphere of pre-history and legend:

禪寺に松の落葉や神無月
Zendera ni　matsu no ochiba ya　kannazuki

> In the Zen temple,
> Pine needles are falling;
> The god-less month.

我宿の貧乏神も御供せよ　　　　　　　一　茶
Waga ie no　bimbōgami mo　otomo se yo

> Poverty-stricken
> Gods of my house,—
> Pray accompany them too!　　　Issa

Humble though they be, Issa wishes his own Lares and Penates to go together with the gods of august shrines to Izumo.

Humour and piety are here blended into one religious emotion. To believe deeply yet lightly, fervently but as though hardly at all,—this belongs uniquely to Zen, and Issa here shares in this "national treasure," though he was a believer in Jōdo, as far his theology was concerned. Another verse by Issa has the same spirit:

神々の留守洗濯や今日も雨
Kamigami no　rusu sentaku ya　kyō mo ame

> Doing their washing
> While the gods are absent,—
> Today also is rainy.

もろもろの愚者も月夜の十夜かな   一 茶
Moromoro no   gusha mo tsukiyo no   jūya kana

The Ten Nights:
Various sorts of nitwits,
On a moon-lit evening.   Issa

From the fifteenth to the twenty sixth of October, believers
of the Pure Land Sect gather at temples and recite the Nem-
butsu.

When Issa uses the word idiots, fools, he is including himself
and us as he gazes round at the motley collection of human
beings. Yet however stupid and malicious we may be, the moon
of truth and goodness shines clearly in the sky above us.

手序に煙管みがくやお取越   一 茶
Tetsuide ni   kiseru migaku ya   otorikoshi

While about it,
Polishing the tobacco pipe;
The ceremony in advance.   Issa

The above version is, I think, a perfect example of the impos-
sibility of understanding a literal translation of quite a number
of haiku. The "O-tori-koshi" means the celebration of Shinran
Shōnin's death, 1268 A.D., a month before the actual date. At
this time all the brass utensils of the family altar are taken
out and polished. Somehow or other, because of this, someone
takes the tobacco pipe (made also of brass), and polishes it up.
To make a verse of this simple fact, with its implications of
universal human nature, is a kind of poetical missionary work,
declaring to us that every detail of our lives is meaningful, and
must be done and seen meaningfully. Another verse by Issa,
somewhat similar to the above in its senryū-like character:

ちとたらぬ僕や隣の雪もはく
Chito taranu   boku ya tonari no   yuki mo haku

Simple and honest,
The man-servant
Sweeps away next door's snow too.

野佛の鼻のさきからつららかな   一 茶
Nobotoke no   hana no saki kara   tsurara kana

> The Buddha on the moor;
> From the end of his nose
> Hangs an icicle.   Issa

See also page 1211. Issa is not "debunking" the Buddha; he is just telling the whole truth, not the romantic part only. To the icicle, all men are the same:

> Nature, with equal mind,
> Sees all her sons at play.

人の爲しぐれておはす佛哉   一 茶
Hito no tame   shigurete owasu   hotoke kana

> Standing in the cold rain,
> For others' sake,
> *Hotoke sama*!   Issa

It is raining—winter rain—but Issa does not pass the wayside shrine without bowing his head. The verse expresses his state of mind as he stands there, in this desolate place, with bent head and clasped hands. He feels as one (for one they really are) his own poverty and gratitude, the misery and greatness of man, the suffering and the compassion of Buddha (*Hotoke sama*). And we take all this from Issa as we would from no one else, because we know he is fully aware that it is only a bit of stone before which he feels this profound emotion.

人　事　HUMAN AFFAIRS

煤拂や神も佛も草の上   子　規
Susuharai ya   kami mo hotoke mo   kusa no ue

Spring cleaning,—
Gods and Buddhas
Out on the grass.   Shiki

This "spring-cleaning" or "cleaning the soot off" really takes
place in winter. The family altars, both to the gods and to
Buddha, are dismantled, and the things, images of Buddha,
sacred vessels and so on, are put out somewhat unceremoniously
into the garden. To see them there lying on the grass in the
cold and open air, is to get a new view of the nature of the
gods and Buddha, that is, of the nature of all things, and of
one's own nature.

衰ひや歯に食ひ當てし海苔の砂   芭　蕉
Otoroi ya   ha ni kuiateshi   nori no suna

Failing health and strength;
My teeth grate
On the sand in the seaweed.   Bashō

What is the connection between old age and stones we sud-
denly bite on? When we are young we feel we can eat anything,
pebbles or glass or grit. As we grow old, little things begin
to pain us, to tweak our nerves, to press and strain us. Bashō
sees, not a world of place, but a world of time in a grain of
sand of the seaweed he is eating.

In the following verse, also by Bashō, the poet thinks of old
age as something desirable, because, freed from passion and
egoism, we may see things as they really are, and see the
inner necessity of apparently dreary and meaningless things:

けふばかり人も年よれ初時雨
Kyō bakari   hito mo toshi yore   hatsushigure

The first winter rain;
Today alone,
May others also be old!

米買ひに雪の袋や投頭巾   芭 蕉
Kome kai ni   yuki no fukuro ya   nagezukin

Going to buy rice,
The snow-covered bag
As a kerchief.   Bashō

This an earlier haiku by Bashō, about 1686, as we see by the
word-play of *yuki*, snow, and *yuki*, going. A *nagezukin* was a
four-cornered hood or wimple, the upper part turned over to
the back. We have the scene of Bashō plodding through the
snow, in a sense only a picture, yet a picture of life, and the
point of interest, his head-covering, is where life is being lived,
because a thing is being put to

a use, like sticks and stones, which is above or beside
their design.[1]

炭の火や齢のへるもあの通り   一 茶
Sumi no hi ya   yowai no heru mo   ano tōri

This charcoal fire;
Our years decline
In just this same way.   Issa

Compare and contrast this with Landor's lines:

I warmed both hands before the fire of life;
It sinks, and I am ready to depart.

There is an obvious similarity of thought but a difference of
mood. Landor says, "I have had a good life. In poetry and
in communion with nature, I have lived fully. Life is drawing
to a close, and I leave it without regret." This is the Epicurean
attitude, that of the Stoic philosophers, of Marcus Aurelius.

Issa sits, not before a large fire-place in a dining room, but
over the glowing embers of charcoal in the brazier. Imper-
ceptibly but irrevocably the red hue is paling, heat dying low,
the ashes increasing. Issa draws his thin garments closer round
him and huddles over the fire that is sinking. Life too declines
unnoticed but inevitably. That is its nature, as it is also the

[1] Thoreau, *A Week on the Concord.*

nature of fire. But Issa does not say, and does not think, "I am ready to depart." While life continues, we must be ready to burn. Only when life has already ceased should we be willing not to be.

埋火や夜ふけて門をたたく音   許 六
Umorebi ya   yo fukete mon wo   tataku oto

A banked fire;
It is deep night;
Knocking at the gate.   Kyoroku

The charcoal fire is dead, yet alive; the night is deep, but full of meaning in its silence, a latent meaning that is aroused by a mysterious knocking at the gate.

埋火や終には煮える鍋のもの   蕪 村
Umorebi ya   tsui ni wa nieru   nabe no mono

A banked fire:
Later on, the things in the saucepan
Are boiling.   Buson

Putting the saucepan on a brazier in which the live coals are buried beneath the ashes, the people of the house have forgotten about it and are engaged in something else. Suddenly they are aware of a cloud of steam and a hissing, bubbling sound. The power of nature, our own limited, feeble consciousness, the faithfulness of things, are perceived, "unknowingly" in the fact that the saucepan is boiling.

油こほりともし火細き寝覺哉   芭 蕉
Abura kōri   tomoshibi hosoki   nezame kana

Waking in the night;
The lamp is low,
The oil freezing.   Bashō

Bashō woke up shivering in the middle of the night. The

tiny light, only a wick floating in oil, hardly more than enough to see itself by, is going out. Lifting up the small bottle of oil standing by the side, he tips it but nothing comes out; the oil is frozen. He lies there watching the flickering flame grow smaller and smaller. There is a verse by a modern poet, Kyoshi, which may be given here:

部屋部屋に配る行燈や鹿の聲
Heyabeya ni   kubaru andon ya   shika no koe

Bringing round paper night-lights
For each room,—
The cry of the deer!

At this time (the Meiji Era) in inns at night, there was brought round to each room an *andon*, or paper lantern. The travellers sat and ate or read or slept by their feeble light. The verse was composed just when the servant was bringing round the *andon*. In this pause of faint expectation, and this is the point of comparison between the two verses, the voice of the deer is heard from the mountains outside in the darkness, and desolation and melancholy are seen in the lights coming and come, and heard in the cry of the deer.

裾に置きて心に遠き火桶かな   蕪 村
Suso ni okite   kokoro ni tōki   hioke kana

I put the brazier
By my skirt, but my heart
Was far from it.   Buson

The alliteration of this verse is important. Eight of the eighteen syllables contain the sound of "o," and six the sound of "k". "O" gives the sensation of distance; "k" sharpens the cold feeling round the heart.

番小屋に晝は人なき火鉢哉   子 規
Bangoya ni   hiru wa hito naki   hibachi kana

In the watch-shed, in the day-time,
A brazier;
No one there.   Shiki

Once more we have the fact illustrated that the absence of a thing is more significant than its presence. In the hackneyed phrase, man is conspicuous by his absence. Again, in this verse the cold is not mentioned, but all the more we receive the sensation of it. The watch-shed is empty, and a brazier stands there, empty of fire. This empty hut and mute, insensate *hibachi*, or brazier, are more eloquent than the greatest orator. They tell us more

> Of moral evil and of good
> Than all the sages can.

づぶぬれの大名を見る炬燵かな   一　茶
Zubunure no   daimyō wo miru   kotatsu kana

> Out there, a *daimyō*,
> Drenched to the skin,—
> And I in my *kotatsu*!   Issa

A *kotatsu* is a small, covered-in brazier, over which quilts are spread. The feet and legs are put under these.

This verse is often taken as a kind of proletariat sneer at the aristocracy, but this is far from Issa's meaning. He is simply saying, "That is how things happen sometimes, inevitably." We have the counterpart in *King Henry IV*, Part II, Act III, Scene I, where the sleepless king exclaims,

> How many thousands of my poorest subjects
> Are at this hour asleep! . . .
> Why rather, sleep, liest thou in smoky cribs,
> Upon uneasy pallets stretching thee,
> And hush'd with buzzing night-flies to thy slumber,
> Than in the perfum'd chambers of the great,
> Under the canopies of costly state,
> And lull'd with sound of sweetest melody?

還　還
我　我
舍　舍
梨　梨
來　來

Tanka burning the Wooden Image of Buddha
by Fūgai, 風外, 1779–1847.

還我舍梨來　It is I who am the Sarira.

(the holy substance found when a Buddha's body is burned)

See Suzuki, *Essays in Zen Buddhism*, 1st Series, pp. 316–17.

守り居る炬燵を庵の本尊かな   丈 草
Mamoriiru   kotatsu wo io no   honzon kana

The *kotatsu*
That guards my hermitage,
Is my principal image.   Jōsō

In the winter the *kotatsu*, *hibachi*, stove, or whatever heats
the room, takes on a very different appearance and significance
from what it would have in the summer. Warmth is one of
the few essentials of life. This is what Tanka, 丹霞, 738–824
A.D., a Chinese Zen monk, showed when he took one of the
wooden Buddhist images and made a fire in order to warm
himself. David did a similar thing when he partook of the
sacred shewbread.

This verse has of course a fanciful humour in it, but behind
this and through this there is faintly adumbrated the fact that
the Buddha is not only the tree in the garden, a pound of flax,
a sesame cake, but a *kotatsu*.

物かくに少しは高き炬燵かな   猿 雖
Mono kaku ni   sukoshi wa takaki   kotatsu kana

For writing on,
The *kotatsu*
Is a little too high.   Ensui

It is important to distinguish in this verse the (not very
interesting) prose from the (not very remarkable) poetry. A
kotatsu, when we sit in it, comes up to about the level of the
chest, and that is too high for comfortable writing. But what
was significant to the poet was not this indubitable fact. It
was the feeling of discomfort, something not understood, some-
thing which could be explained but not expressed by the mere
statement of fact, which made itself memorable to the poet
and which he sought to put into in his verse. This verse is a
failure because it has delayed too long, and allowed the rational
faculty to pretend to give the whole matter in a statement of
the excessive height and inconvenience of the *kotatsu* as a
writing table. This haiku might be taken as an example of
"emotion forgotten in tranquillity."

きりぎりす忘れ音に啼く炬燵哉   芭 蕉
Kirigirisu   wasurene ni naku   kotatsu kana

The cricket chirps
In a forgetful way:
This *kotatsu*!

Bashō

Bashō sits alone in the *kotatsu*. From time to time a cricket chirps, as though it had remembered it was still alive, then relapses into silence again. Its melancholy note in the midst of the desolation of winter makes Bashō feel his old age and failing strength more keenly, and he draws the quilts of the *kotatsu* more closely round him. Bashō was at this time about forty six years old. He had four more years to live.

住つかぬ旅のこゝろや置炬燵   芭 蕉
Sumitsukanu   tabi no kokoro ya   okigotatsu

Unsettled,
The mind of a traveller,—
This movable *kotatsu*.

Bashō

At this time Bashō was living with various of his pupils, moving from one to another quite frequently. To the *kotatsu,* which can be put anywhere in the room, he ascribes his own feelings of uncertainty and inconstancy of place, that characteristic which caused him to be always on the move.

十年の苦學毛のなき毛布哉   子 規
Jūnen no   kugaku ke no naki   mōfu kana

Ten years of study in poverty:
A threadbare
Blanket.

Shiki

The pain and poverty of those ten years of study are visible in the absence of wooliness in the blanket. How much can be seen in this blanket! The whole history of those ten years of study under difficulties, the struggle to learn, and make a living at the same time.

飯粒で紙衣のやぶれふたぎけり   蕪 村
Meshitsubu de   kamiko no yabure   futagikeri

Patching a tear
In the *kamiko*,
With a few grains of cooked rice.   Buson

A *kamiko* was a kind of rain-coat, or rather, a thin overcoat
for protection against cold. It was made of paper crumpled
soft and treated with persimmon juice.

We forget sometimes that the most imposing edifices are only
made of mud and branches of trees. We are still clothed in
the skins of animals, living a borrowed life only a few hours
from starvation, or death by exposure. Buson is mending a
miserable kind of garment with a few sticky grains of cooked
rice. In wet weather the tear will certainly open again, but
we do not build houses or wear clothes for eternity, but only
for a season. Shiki says, truly enough:

俳諧の腸見せる紙衣かな
Hakai no   harawata miseru   kamiko kana

A *kamiko*
Shows the bowels
Of haikai.

菊枯れて垣に足袋干す日和哉   子 規
Kiku karete   kaki ni tabi hosu   hiyori kana

Chrysanthemums withering;
Socks drying on the fence;
A fine day.   Shiki

It is cold, but the sun is shining. Flowers are there, but
they are dying. White Japanese tabi are hung on the fence to
dry. All nature, all humanity is there in the cold sunshine.

冬籠その夜に聞くや山の雨　　　　　　　一　茶
Fuyugomori sono yo ni kiku ya   yama no ame

Winter seclusion;
Listening, that evening,
　　To the rain in the mountain.　　　Issa

Winter seclusion, especially in the north of Japan, was a kind
of hibernation. All the necessities of life being collected, each
house underwent a kind of siege, as it were, by winter. Spir-
itually also, there was a kind of rest and digestion of all that
had happened during the year. When the winter seclusion had
begun, the mind not having attained its proper semi-comatose
condition, the senses were unusually sharp and active. This
particular evening, the silence, then the rustling of leaves, then
the steady drumming of the rain, the regular drip-drip of the
eaves,—these things have a meaning that cannot be fully under-
stood except by those who have gone through this "winter
seclusion" in a lonely mountainous place.

The last line shows that the poet has combined the sights
of the day with the sounds of the night. It is not hearing
with the physical ear the rain on the roof or the drippings
from the eaves, but listening with that inward ear to the rain
which falls through the darkness, the trickle of water down
the trunks of the trees, the splash of rain-drops on the dead
leaves below. And he hears those faint sounds of the ancient
earth, that

　　　　　　　　have power to make
　　Our noisy years seem moments in the being
　　Of the eternal silence.

Issa all the more appreciated the meaning of winter seclusion
in one's own home since for many years he was unable to have
it. He writes, in his forty-third year:

五十にして冬籠さへならぬなり
Gojū ni shite   fuyugomori sae   naranu nari

Fifty years old,
But no, never
Winter seclusion.

Another of his verses which describes the monotony, material
and spiritual, of this hibernation of mind and body:

能なしは罪も又なし冬ごもり
Nō nashi wa   tsumi mo mata nashi   fuyugomori

Merit-less,
And guilt-less:
Winter seclusion.

冬籠りまたよりそはん此はしら   芭　蕉
Fuyugomori   mata yorisowan   kono hashira

Winter seclusion;
Again I will lean myself
Against this post.   Bashō

Bashō will once more rest his thin shoulders against this
post; when weary of reading and writing he leans back against
it. There is something about this verse that reminds one of
Wordsworth. Bashō's pleasure in prospect also is "the bliss of
solitude." See the frontispiece, p. 978.

金屏風松の古びや冬籠   芭　蕉
Kinbyōbu   matsu no furubi ya   fuyugomori

Winter seclusion;
On the gold screen,
The pine-tree ages.   Bashō

The pine-tree drawn on the gold background of the folding
screen is an old one, but added to this is the age of the screen
itself. Time is being added to the timeless. In his *Ode on a
Grecian Urn*, Keats claims absolute timelessness for the urn.
In fact, the urn, like all sublunary things, is transitory, but
eternal like all art. Without time there is no eternity; without
timelessness nothing can exist in time. This is what the ever-
lasting pine-tree actualizes as it ages on the gold screen. This
verse may also be taken as an example of what is called *sabi*
both in its semi-literal and in its derived, spiritual meaning.
The screen has *sabi* in that the bright golden colour has been
toned down with age; it has sunk itself into the surroundings,
and they in it, so that it is not now, what it once was, a
separate thing, one of a random collection of objects, but has

a deep and subtle relation of tone and position with the room it stands in. But *sabi* is in the mind as well as in the thing. It is in the mind of Bashō, with its roots in the past, its relations with the Shintō festivals, Chinese philosophy and poetry, the Buddhist ceremonies and doctrines, the Imperial House, the mountains and rivers of his native place, the nights when he lay sleepless with cold, the days spent under the cherry-blossoms, —all this *age*, (that has nothing to do with Bashō's own forty nine years when he composed this verse), is expressed in it.

冬籠心の奥のよしの山　　　　　　　　　蕪　村
Fuyugomori　kokoro no oku no　yoshinoyama

　　　Winter seclusion;
　In the inmost mind,
　　　　The mountains of Yoshino.[1]　　　Buson

This also reminds one of Wordsworth:

　　　For oft, when on my couch I lie
　　　In vacant or in pensive mood,
　　　They flash upon that inward eye
　　　Which is the bliss of solitude;
　　　And then my heart with pleasure fills,
　　　And dances with the daffodils.

At school we were taught to regard this last verse of the *Daffodils* as not merely superfluous but spoiling the objectivity of the rest of the poem. "That inward eye," we were told, is the memory. This is not so. It is the eye of the imagination.

親も斯う見られし山や冬籠　　　　　　　一　茶
Oya mo kō　mirareshi yama ya　fuyugomori

　　　Mountains seen also
　By my father, like this,
　　　　In his winter confinement.　　　Issa

[1] The second and third lines are probably Buson's transposition of 霞 の奥の吉野山, "the misty depths of Mt. Yoshino."

We do not see each other; we see only the same things.
Issa is united with his long-dead father through mountains that
his father used to gaze at during the long, monotonous winter
days at home. Compare the following also by Issa:

なきははや海見るたびに見るたびに
Naki haha ya umi miru tabi ni miru tabi ni

When I see the ocean,
Whenever I see it,
Oh, my mother!

Issa's mother died when he was three years old, but when
he looked over the sea his thoughts always turned to her. The
repetition, *miru tabi ni miru tabi ni*, expresses his unsatisfied
emotions.

ともし火も動かで丸し冬籠   野 坡
Tomoshibi mo ugokade marushi fuyugomori

The flame is motionless,
A rounded sphere
Of winter seclusion.   Yaha

The round flame of the lamp does not move. It burns in-
visibly. The poet also is in a state of spiritual hibernation.
Everything outside and inside is asleep; life is at a standstill,
neither advancing nor receding. The poet's life is contracted
into a span, into the flower-like soul of the steady flame, that
is at the same time his own changing, changeless being.

釋迦に問ふて見たき事あり冬籠   子 規
Shaka ni toute mitaki koto ari fuyugomori

Winter seclusion;
There is something I'd like to ask
Shakamuni.   Shiki

The significance of this verse lies in the fact that what the
poet desired to ask is not stated. He does not state it because,
in reality, if actually put to it, he would not know what to say.

The reason for this is that our real problems are not intellectual
and verbal, but practical and physical.

鳥啼いて水音くるゝあじろかな   蕪 村
Tori naite   mizuoto kururu   ajiro kana

A bird calls;
The sound of the water darkens
Round the fish-trap.   Buson

Bamboo rods bound together like a long net are stuck in lines
along the shallow bed of the river forming a kind of trap for
fish in winter. In the evening, the trapper goes to see the
place and shut up the narrow opening. At this moment some
water-bird screeches, and at the sound the waters darken.

朝晴にぱちぱち炭のきげん哉   一 茶
Asabare ni   pachipachi sumi no   kigen kana

A bright winter morning;
The charcoal is in good spirits,
It goes crackle! crack!   Issa

The word "winter" is not in the original but is to be under-
stood from the reference to charcoal.
It is early morning, cold, but with a clear blue sky; still dark,
and the morning star still bright. The charcoal is being lighted
with sticks and leaves. It crackles suddenly, with a cheerful,
lively, energetic sound.

更る夜や炭もて炭をくだく音   蓼 太
Fukeru yo ya   sumi mote sumi wo   kudaku oto

Night deepens:
The sound of breaking
Charcoal on charcoal.   Ryōta

It is an odd thing, but the best way to break a piece of
charcoal, is to hit it with another piece. The poet is lying

wakeful in a not over-warm bed. There is suddenly the sound, peculiar and characteristic, of someone breaking one piece of charcoal on another. The brittle, tinkling, faintly harsh sound expresses not only the character of the charcoal, but also his own feelings this cold winter night.

手に戻る鷹の眼に入る日哉   大 魯
Te ni modoru   taka no manako ni   iruhi kana

The sun,
In the eye of the falcon
That returned to my hand.   Tairo

There is a poem of Vaughan referring to the cock, of which the first few lines register the same feeling, though the object is related to the Divinity:

Father of Lights!   What sunnie seed
Hast thou confined within this bird?

すくみ行や馬上に氷る影法師   芭 蕉
Sukumiyuku ya   bajō ni kōru   kagebōshi

On horseback;
My shadow
Creeps freezing below.   Bashō

The shadow is here treated (because seen and felt so) as a separate entity, and the poet disappears in his empathy with a feelingless object. But the object is not thereby falsified or sentimentalised. We may compare this higher subjectivity, where the poet and the object are divided only in thought, but not in experience, with the pure objectivity that we find so often in Buson:

てらてらと石に日の照る枯野かな
Teratera to   ishi ni hi no teru   kareno kana

The sun glitters
On the stones
Of the withered moor.

We may compare also the following waka by Saigyō:

何 と な く 汲 む 度 に 澄 む 心 か な
岩 井 の 水 に 影 映 じ つ つ

Somehow or other, whenever I draw water—
My figure reflected
In the waters
Of the spring under the rock—
My heart is cleansed.

This loses in objectivity but gains in mysteriousness. Bashō's verse by comparison is almost flat, two-dimensional in feeling as in space.

御 經 に 似 て ゆ か し さ よ 古 暦   蕪 村
Onkyō ni   nite yukashisa yo   furugoyomi

The old calendar
Fills me with gratitude,
Like a sutra.

           Buson

The ancient Japanese calendar was in the folding, concertina form in which we still find sutras. The appearance, then, is similar. But more important, though implicit, is the feeling of the poet towards both, a religious feeling. The sutra is Buddhist, the calendar a mixture of Buddhism and the degenerate, superstitious forms of the teachings of Rōshi (Laotse) and the Book of Changes, 易經. It contained the very necessary information for farmers according to the Lunar Calendar, lucky and unlucky days, horoscopes, etc. Another verse by Buson on the same subject:

闇 の 夜 に 終 る 暦 の 表 紙 か な
Yami no yo ni   owaru koyomi no   hyōshi kana

In this dark evening,
The cover of the calendar
Coming to an end.

餅搗が隣へ來たといふ子なり   一　茶

Mochitsuki ga   tonari e kita to   iu ko nari

"The rice-cake makers
Have come next door,"
Says the child.   Issa

"Mochi" is made from a special kind of rice, boiled and pounded into a mass. Japanese people all enjoy it very much; it corresponds (in feeling, not in its taste) to Christmas pudding in Europe and America. Pounding the rice is hard work and needs a very large mallet etc., and specialists, so to speak, go from house to house making it. Some are too poor to afford it, and of such is the child who is speaking. He runs in to his mother and tells her that the men who make the mochi have come to the house next door. The mother cannot answer; there is nothing to say. They cannot afford it, and other children must have the happiness forbidden to hers. Even if she says this, it is all the more painful. This kind of thing must also be taken into account when we are considering the causes of social delinquency and of war amongst nations. But Issa is not thinking of this; he only registers the contraction of his heart when he hears the child's words, and looks at its half-expectant face, and the wholly dejected face of the mother.

動 物 **BIRDS AND BEASTS**

蝙蝠のかくれ住みけり破れ傘   蕪 村
Kōmori no   kakure sumikeri   yaburegasa

> The bat
> Lives hidden
> Under the broken umbrella.   Buson

Buson probably saw a bat fly out from under a paper umbrella that had been thrown away near some deserted temple. The umbrella has a life of its own as it moves uneasily in the wind, and there is something about the colour and texture of it that makes it akin to the bat. The affinity between the two things, however, goes deeper than this. They both belong to a realm into which man can only occasionally enter, with a sense of the uncanny, the unknown and the unknowable.

汐汲や千鳥踐して歸る蜑   鬼 貫
Shiokumi ya   chidori nokoshite   kaeru ama

> After carring the salt-water,
> The fisherman goes home,
> Leaving behind the plovers.   Onitsura

Some commentators take the poetical thought of this verse as centreing in the state of mind of the fisherman, or fisher-woman, who has been carrying the salt water all day, and who regrets leaving the plovers alone on the darkening shore. To say that while the fisherman is at home eating his evening meal, the plovers' cry still echoes in his ears, that they are still pecking about on the shore of his mind,—this is true enough. If it were not so, how should we also ever be able to see the poetry, the Fact of the matter? But this is not to say that the poem itself portrays the mind of the fisherman. It is a picture, no more, no less. No more, in that it has no conscious representation of the state of mind of the fisherman. No less, in that it is a picture of the same value and meaning as a Chinese landscape, as Gray's *Elegy*.

磯千鳥足をぬらして遊びけり   蕪　村
Isochidori   ashi wo nurashite   asobikeri

 The plovers of the shore
Played about,
  Wetting their feet.   Buson

 Forgetting for a moment the never-ending search for food
which is the price every creature pays for existence, the plovers
are hopping and flying round each other in some game of which
they alone understand the meaning. They alight in the ebbing
water with a little splash and fly up into the air again, the
water dripping from their legs that hang down ready to alight
again. The poet, though he gazes with pleasure at their airy
gambols, is more intensely moved by the drops of water splashed
up by the birds, the cold wet dripping legs as they swerve up
from the surf. Just as in bowing, the lower the better, so in
haiku, the smaller the better.

消えてもせむ有明月の濱千鳥   樗　良
Kiete mo sen   ariake tsuki no   hamachidori

 The moon at daybreak;
The plovers of the shore
  Vanishing far away.   Chora

 In the western sky the pale moon is sinking over the sea.
With plaintive cries the plovers are swiftly flying into the
distance. Though it is the dawn of a new day, this too is
impermanent. The moon, the crying plovers, the waves,—all
are transitory, evanescent as a dream.

鍋洗ふ水のうねりや鴨一羽   蕪　村
Nabe arau   mizu no uneri ya   kamo ichiwa

 Cleaning a saucepan,—
Ripples on the water:
  A solitary sea-gull.   Buson

 It is early morning. A woman comes down to the creek
and begins to wash a saucepan in the fresh water that flows

noiselessly into the sea. Over the smooth surface of the water spread ripples in ever-widening circles. A sea-gull that sits on the water is very gently rocked by them. There is the same feminine association in the following verse:

水鳥や舟に菜洗ふ女有り
Mizutori ya　fune ni na arau　onna ari

The water-birds;
A woman in a boat,
Washing young greens.

Buson is looking at the water-birds; his eye is then caught by the sight of a woman leaning over the side of a boat, washing some greens. Between the birds and the woman there seems to be only a pictorial relation, but they are joined also by the water, the feminine element.

水鳥や枯木の中に駕二挺　　　　　　蕪 村
Mizutori ya　kareki no naka ni　kago nichō

Water-birds;
Among the withered trees,
Two palanquins.　　　　　　　Buson

On a lonely winter road beneath the leafless trees there stand two empty palanquins. Beside the path there is a marshy pool, on which a few water-birds are seen. The sky is grey and low, but it is too cold to rain.

(Meisetsu thinks that there are people in the palanquins; Shiki says not.)

These two palanquins, where are carriers, where are the passengers? What are the water-birds doing there?

みやしろや庭火に遠きうきね鳥　　　　子 規
Miyashiro ya　niwabi ni tōki　ukinedori

A shrine;
Birds float asleep;
Garden-lights are distant.　　　　Shiki

The Shintō shrine is almost in darkness; on the pool there float a few water-birds, their heads tucked beneath their wings. There is a faint, hardly-to-be-remembered connection between the sanctity of the place and the safety of the birds. But there are also the far-off lights of the gardens. Without them, the verse would be empty of poetry. Darkness is better than light, but it is nothing in itself.

水鳥の胸に嘴置く浮寝かな   吟 江
Mizutori no   mune ni kuchibashi oku   ukine kana

The water-fowl
Lays its beak in its breast,
And sleeps as it floats.   Ginkō

As he gazes at the bird, the poet feels towards it faintly the tender care, the unsleeping faithfulness which the Hebrew poet, because he too felt it, attributed to God:

He will not suffer thy foot to be moved;
He that keepeth thee will not slumber.

The waking-mind of the bird is non-existent. It lives a plant-like life, swaying on the water like a water-weed. The body of the water-fowl "remembers" its levity. The water too is faithful, and cannot deny itself.

水鳥の重たく見えて浮にけり   鬼 貫
Mizutori no   omotaku miete   ukinikeri

The water-bird
Looks heavy,—
But it floats!   Onitsura

Is there anything in this beyond what an intelligent child could see and say? The fact that a child could have written this poem, or at least expressed the idea in it, in no way invalidates it as poetry; quite the contrary. But the question is, is the idea intellectual only, or is it poetical? It is poetical, since, besides being an expression of Wonder, it is also an expression

of Life, the Wonder of Life, its intellectual inexplicability.
Why does the water-bird float? Because it is *alive*.

水鳥やかたちに影の腹合せ   眞 原
Mizutori ya   katachi ni kage no   haraawase

The breast
Of the water-fowl
Meets its reflection.   Mahara

In *Yarrow Unvisited* we have the lines,

The swan on still St. Mary's lake
Floats double, swan and shadow.

Wordsworth sees this, but the Japanese poet sees something
slighter and the more significant, the line where the breast of
the water-fowl meets the water.

水底を見て來た顔の小鴨かな   丈 草
Mizusoko wo   mite kita kao no   kogamo kana

The look on the face of the *kogamo*:
"I have been sight-seeing
Under the water."   Jōsō

The *kogamo* or *takabe* is a kind of small duck, often seen on
ornamental waters. It is smaller, neater, more charming than
the ordinary duck.

The humour and sweetness here is not of a fanciful character.
After diving under the water, the bird comes up with a jerk,
and looks smugly round, as if she had done something clever,
—which she has.

明けがたや城をとりまく鴨の聲   許 六
Akegata ya   shiro wo torimaku   kamo no koe

Day is dawning;
The voices of wild ducks
Are surrounding the castle.   Kyoroku

There is a double figure of the imagination here. The wild ducks are spoken of as enemy soldiers; and it is the *voices* of the birds that surround the castle. For the ordinary man, the crying of the wild ducks round the castle reminds him of the war-cries of the besiegers, but to the man who has attained, the 達人, the military man, the chameleon poet, this is not merely a matter of the association or disassociation of ideas. For the soldier, the poet, there is not so much difference, not so much illusion of separation between the wild ducks and the enemy. His state of mind towards them is not distorted by emotionality, by fear of the one or contempt of the other.

海くれて鴨の聲ほのかにしろし　　　芭蕉
Umi kurete　kamo no koe　honoka ni shiroshi

The sea darkens;
The voices of the wild ducks
Are faintly white.　　　Bashō

Anatole France, in his preface to *On Life and Letters*, Second Series, quotes from the *Progrès Médical*, 1887:

Coloured audition is a phenomenon which consists in two different senses being simultaneously put into activity by a stimulus produced by only one of these senses, or, to put it differently, in the sound of a voice or instrument being translated by a characteristic and constant colour for the person possessing this chromatic peculiarity. Thus certain individuals can give a green, red, yellow or other colour to every noise, to every sound which strikes their ears.

There is a verse by Buson that is somewhat more easily assimilable, in which colour is attributed to motion:

陽炎や名もしらぬ蟲の白飛
Kagerō ya　na mo shiranu mushi no　shiroki tobu

Heat waves of spring;
An unknown insect
Is flying whitely.

A verse by Shiki, in which the motion is black:

A Cowherd returning through the Snow

by Riteki, 李迪, of the Northern Sung; entered
the Academy of Art between 1119 and 1125.

蝙蝠の飛ぶ音くらし籔の中
Kōmori no　tobu oto kurashi　yabu no naka

The sound of the bat
Flying in the thicket,
Is dark.

A verse by Seifu-jo, 星布女, showing the origins of this mixture:

おさな子や花を見せても口を明く
Osanago ya　hana wo misete mo　kuchi wo aku

The baby,
Even when shown a flower,
Opens its mouth.

This poetic confusion of the senses is akin to what is known in Buddhism as "Six senses, five uses," 六根五用, that is, the substitution of one organ for another, or the use of one organ to do the work of all the others; this is a Buddha's power. Another verse, already given, by Shiki:

甲板に霰の音のくらさ哉
Kampan ni　arare no oto no　kurasa kana

The sound of the hail
On the deck
Is dark.

Perhaps the best of such verses, this time by Issa:

鶯や黄色な聲で親を呼ぶ
Uguisu ya　kiiro na koe de　oya wo yobu

The young *uguisu*
Calls its parents
With a yellow voice.

こつそりとして稼ぐなり鷦鷯　　　　一 茶
Kossori to　shite kasegu nari　misosazai

The wren
Earns his living
Noiselessly.　　　　　　　　　　　Issa

One child will make more noise than a wilderness of monkeys

or a jungle of elephants. As distinct from man, Nature works in silence and secrecy, with the minimum of work and commotion. Making much unnecessary noise is useless and dangerous. Issa sees the wren gliding to and fro in the half-twilight of the undergrowth, and feels the mystery of the tiny bird that lives in its world of silence, its world of power.

鷦鷯ちゝといふても日が暮る　　　　　　　一　茶
Misosazai   chichi to iute mo   hi ga kureru

The wren is chirruping,
But it grows duck
Just the same.　　　　　　　　　　　　Issa

There is in this something of the feeling of Burns' *To a Mouse*, which also belongs to the season of winter. Men may work and women may weep, the mouse build its house of "foggage green," but the inevitable hangs over it, old age must come; in the morning the sun rises, in the evening it sets.

馬　光　墓

あら淋し塚はいつもの鷦鷯　　　　　　　一　茶
Ara sabishi   tsuka wa itsumo no   misosazai

Look! this lonely grave,
With the wren
This is always here.　　　　　　　　　Issa

This was written at the grave of the haiku poet Bakō, 馬光, who was buried at Tōseiji Temple in Honjo, Tōkyō, where Issa lived for some time. Bakō died in 1751 when Issa was a twelve year old boy in Shinano. The relation of the wren and the grave of the poet is one indeed of loneliness. Both bird and poet waste their sweetness on the desert and illimitable air.

尾頭の心もとなき海鼠かな   去　來
O-kashira no   kokoromoto naki   namako kana

The sea-slug;
Which the head and which the tail,
God only knows.   Kyorai

The *Encyclopaedia Britannica* tells us:

Marine Pulmonata have in addition to the usual pair of
cephalic eyes, a number of eyes developed upon the dorsal
integument. These dorsal eyes are very perfect in elabora-
tion, possessing lens, retinal nerve-end cells, retinal pigment
and optic nerve.

But the poet, not having read the *Encyclopaedia*, stands aghast
in wonder before the mystery of the sea-slug, its perfect life
lived to the full, eating and drinking, marrying and giving in
marriage, and yet apparently a mere blob of fleshy matter.
There is a humorous verse by Shiki which portrays, not its
lack of form, but lack of youth:

無爲にして海鼠一萬八千歳
Mui ni shite   namako ichiman   hassen sai

Doing nothing at all,
The sea-slug has lived
For eighteen thousand years.

植 物　TREES AND FLOWERS

鷲 の 巣 の 樟 の 枝 に 日 は 入 り ぬ　　　凡 兆
Washi no su no　kusunoki no e ni　hi wa irinu

The setting sun,
Behind the eagle's nest,
In the boughs of the camphor-tree. Bonchō

Such magnificence with simplicity is not easy to attain in seventeen syllables. The blood-red sun, across it the bare black boughs of the enormous camphor-tree with its eagle's nest at the summit,—this is a scene whose Byronic power of description makes it an exceptional haiku, like Bashō's "A wild sea," Vol. III, page 919.

寒 菊 や 粉 糠 の か ゝ る 臼 の 端　　　芭 蕉
Kangiku ya　konuka no kakaru　usu no hata

Winter chrysanthemums;
Rice-bran fallen
Round the hand-mill. Bashō

The day is fine, the sky blue, no wind. In the courtyard, a farmer is pounding rice in his leisurely way. Winter chrysanthemums are blooming in the cold air, and some of the yellowish powder from the mortar has fallen on the ground and on the chrysanthemums near by.

菊 の の ち 大 根 の 外 更 に な し　　　芭 蕉
Kiku no nochi　daikon no hoka　sara ni nashi

After the chrysanthemums,
Besides the long turnip
There is nothing. Bashō

It is a kind of off-season for poetry by the calendar of haiku. After the chrysanthemums have bloomed and faded, no plants remain as a subject of haiku but the *daikon*, a long kind of turnip, which is rather a thing *pour rire.*

This verse is hardly poetry, yet achieves something by reason of its expressing simply and spontaneously the poetical emptiness that Bashō feels.

鞍壺に小坊主のせて大根引   芭 蕉
Kuratsubo ni   kobōzu nosete   daikohiki

Going *daikon*-pulling,
The little boy perched
On the pack-saddle.   Bashō

The father leads the pack-horse, on the wooden saddle of which he has put the little boy, partly to save carrying him, partly to please him. This is a picture of rural life, of family life, of human nature, of the world we live in: the ill-suppressed jubilation of the little boy, the lesser pleasure of the parents, the faint annoyance of the horse, the sublime indifference of the *daikon* waiting in the dark, cold earth.

ふんばりて引けば根淺き大根かな   吟 江
Fumbarite   hikeba ne asaki   daiko kana

Straddling over the *daikon*,
I pulled it up with all my might;
Its root was small.   Ginkō

The disparity of cause and effect (as always when man enters), tumbling over backwards, the loss of self-respect in having made a mistake in overstimating the size of the *daikon*,—the whole is a sudden anti-climax in which the poet perceives the vanity of human wishes, the intractability of matter, the unforeseeableness of life.

大根引大根で道を教へけり   一 茶
Daikohiki   daiko de michi wo   oshiekeri

The turnip-puller
Points the way
With a turnip.   Issa

This turnip is not the round one, but the long, white, sausage-shaped turnip. The man who is pulling up the turnips is so much one with them that he uses a turnip as his own finger, to point the way. And see! the man points the Way with a turnip, of all things!

冬川や誰が引きすてし赤蕪   蕪 村
Fuyukawa ya   ta ga hikisuteshi   akakabura

In the winter river,
Pulled up and thrown away,—
A red turnip.

Buson

There is something comically sublime about this turnip that bobs up and down as it floats in the river. Its redness an affront to the grey sky and murky stream, it goes on its way indifferent to its origin and its fate, and induces in us that same indifference. It was pulled up by *someone* and is going *somewhere*, it is a turnip, and a red turnip, and that is all there is to it. There are sermons in turnips as well as stones, but the sermon is in the turnip, not in the words about the turnip. This is what Wordsworth calls,

The light of things.

麥まきの魍魎長き夕日かな   蕪 村
Mugimaki no   mōryō nagaki   yūhi kana

Demons sowing barley,
In the long rays
Of the evening sun.

Buson

A simpler, and perhaps earlier form of this verse:

麥まきの影法師ながき夕日かな
Mugimaki no   kagebōshi nagaki   yūhi kana

Shadows of men
Sowing barley
In the long rays of the evening sun.

The picture reminds us of the angular figures of the Siamese puppet shadow play. *Mōryō* are spirits of mountains, water, trees, and stones. They have the form of a three-year old child, reddish-black in colour, with long ears and red eyes. They often make fools of people.

冬がれや雀のありく樋の中   太　祇
Fuyugare ya   suzume no ariku   toi no naka

> Winter desolation;
> In the rain-water tub
>   Sparrows are walking.   Taigi

Trees are bare, grasses withered; all around is silent. In the empty rain-butt is heard a faint scuffling, rustling sound. It is sparrows hopping about in it, the sparrows that come closer to us in winter than in the other seasons.

冬枯や芥しづまる川の底   移　竹
Fuyugare ya   akuta shizumaru   kawa no soko

> Winter desolation;
> Rubbish sunk
>   At the bottom of the river.   Ichiku

In winter there is little rain; water decreases, and is clear. All kinds of odds and ends that have fallen into the river appear with a significant clarity. The desolation of winter is seen also under the water.

斧入て香に驚くや冬木立   蕪　村
Ono irete   ka ni odoroku ya   fuyukodachi

> Among the winter trees,
> When the axe sank in,—
>   How taken aback I was at the scent!   Buson

The poet is cutting firewood in the forest, in rather a blank frame of mind. All is silent, except for the sound of the axe. All is colourless, flowerless, leafless, odourless, nothing to see or hear. As he plunges the axe into some insignificant branch, a sweet, powerful odour "assails his nostrils." The meaning of the apparently meaningless is in that strong scent, as inexplicable as the smell is nameless.

からびたる三井の仁王や冬木立   其 角

Karabitaru   mii no niō ya   fuyukodachi

The two Deva Kings
Stand weather-worn,
     Among the wintry groves of Mii Temple.

Kikaku

We have the dreary landscape of winter, snow lying here and there on the leafless branches. The temple of Mii is old with the centuries, and the two gigantic figures from the "far away and long ago" of ancient India stand lonely and desolate as they guard the entrance of the temple from malicious spirits. Everything in the world has withered to this moment of loneliness.

冬木立昔々の音すなり   一 茶

Fuyukodachi   mukashi mukashi no   oto su nari

In the wintry grove,
Echoes
     Of long, long ago.   Issa

Occasionally there is a far-off soughing of wind in the treetops, then silence; a fir-cone falls on the dry leaves. Unnameable sounds, so slight that the ear cannot retain them, a sigh, a rustle, a motion in the air. But these sad sounds are not of today. They belong to a world that is past and dead, to all that lifeless, unchanging world that exists only the mind of man, the world that rises like a phantom when we say the magic words, "Once upon a time...". This is the effect of Issa's words "mukashi, mukashi...," and is heightened by the rhythm and assonance of the verse. Four times we have the end-sounds of a, i:

fuyuko*dachi* mu*kashi* mu*kashi* no oto su *nari.*

散る芒寒くなるのが眼に見ゆる   一 茶
Chiru susuki   samuku naru no ga   me ni miyuru

Pampas grass is falling:
The eye can see
The cold increasing.   Issa

We can see before our very eyes the cold becoming intenser,
—not by reasoning from the fall of the grass to the antecedent
increase of cold, but actually see the cold, see it grow colder.

枯芒むかし鬼婆あつたとさ   一 茶
Karesusuki   mukashi onibaba   atta to sa

Withered pampas grass;
Now once upon a time
There was an old witch. . . .   Issa

Even at the age of fifty five, when he wrote this verse, Issa
had preserved the spirit of fear which is part of the religious
attitude of man to nature. Not to divide man from nature, or
nature from man,—this is the secret of poetry.

葱買ふて枯木の中を歸りけり   蕪 村
Negi kōte   kareki no naka wo   kaerikeri

Buying the leeks,
I came back
Through the withered trees.   Buson

There is a secret relation between the white, chill leeks and
the winter path beneath the leafless trees. The cold and the
silence, the leeks in his hand, the motionless branches that
wheel round him as he walks on and on, these are all one thing
in his mindless mind.

水仙や垣に結ひこむ筑波山 　　　　一 茶
Suisen ya　kaki ni yuikomu　tsukubayama

> The daffodils,
> Embraced in the garden fence:
> Mount Tsukuba. 　　　　Issa

Mount Tsukuba is about a thousand metres high, south of Hitachi, Ibaraki-ken. It is seen rising up beyond the garden fence, which includes, visually speaking, the mountain. The daffodils blooming under the fence are thus embraced into the mountain, and the three things together form a unity of visual impression, though actually separated in distance.

水仙に狐あそぶやよい月夜 　　　　蕪 村
Suisen ni　kitsune asobu ya　yoi tsukiyo

> Foxes playing
> Among the narcissus flowers;
> A bright moonlit night. 　　　　Buson

Buson is a master, perhaps the only one, of this kind of haiku. Though it may be purely imaginary, it is purely so, with no admixture of thought or sentiment, fancy or artificiality. How well the foxes and the moonlight and the narcissus flowers go together.

夜神樂や焚火の中へちる紅葉 　　　　一 茶
Yokagura ya　takibi no naka e　chiru momiji

> Sacred music at night;
> Into the bonfires
> Flutter the tinted leaves. 　　　　Issa

This is a splendid piece of objectivity, worthy of Buson in its colour and scope. The *kagura* is a dance, originating in that performed in front of the cave where Amaterasu hid, by Ame no Uzume no Mikoto. It takes place at certain shrines to the accompaniment of flutes and drums. To give light, bonfires are lit around the platform, and into these fall the leaves that became scarlet in autumn.

百年の氣色を庭の落葉かな　　　　　芭　蕉
Hyakunen no　keshiki wo niwa no　ochiba kana

A hundred years old it looks,
This temple garden,
With its fallen leaves.　　　　Bashō

Not only the stones and trees but the fallen leaves themselves,
fallen only yesterday, "seem" the leaves of a hundred years
ago. Not only to God, but to every poet, and to every man at
some time or other,

A thousand years is as yesterday when it is past.

This is not seeming, or fancy, or illusion; this is enlightenment,
seeing things as they really are, timeless. Everything is in-
finitely old and eternally new.

古寺の藤あさましき落葉かな　　　　蕪　村
Furudera no　fuji asamashiki　ochiba kana

The leaves having fallen,
How miserable the wistaria
Of the old temple!　　　　Buson

While the flowers are blooming, and while the leaves are
green the wistaria is a beautiful sight without apparent affinity
with the weather-beaten and aged temple. But when the leaves
have fallen, the grotesque and writhing stem of the wistaria
looks uncouth and neglected like the discoloured and worn gates
and pillars of the temple buildings.

をちこちに瀧の音聞く落葉かな　　　芭　蕉
Ochikochi ni　taki no oto kiku　ochiba kana

From far and near,
Voices of waterfalls are heard,
Leaves falling.　　　　Bashō

Bashō's feeling here is that of submergence in Nature. All
around is heard the voice of many waters falling from above
into the boulders beneath, with high and hollow sounds. Here

Falling Leaves

by Keishi, 慶子.   The artist and the poet, Richō, 鯉長,
were actors and contemporaries.   Keishi died in 1786.

Isaribi ya   nami no yoru yoru   chiru-momiji

The fishing-fire;

The waves lapping,

Falling tinted leaves.

いさり火や
なみのよる／＼
散もみぢ

and there, withered leaves are falling through the cold, damp
air, soundless, mysterious in their fortuitously destined way.
The one who stands there, what is he? He is the hearing of
the sounds of the waterfall, the seeing of the falling leaves.

焚くほどは風がもてくる落葉かな　　　　　良　寛
Taku hodo wa　kaze ga mote kuru　ochiba kana

The wind brings
Enough of fallen leaves
To make a fire.　　　　　　　　　　　Ryōkan

This is the true and only meaning of Christ's words:

Behold the fowls of the air: for they sow not, neither
do they reap, nor gather into barns; yet your Heavenly
Father feedeth them. If God so clothe the grass of field,
which today is, and tomorrow is cast into the oven, shall
he not much more clothe you, O ye of little faith?

It is expressed more directly, more heroically, with less "wishful
thinking" by Marcus Aurelius:

All that is harmony for thee, O Universe, is in harmony
with me as well....Everything is fruit to me that thy
seasons bring, O Nature. All things come out of thee,
have their being in thee, and return to thee.

猫の子のちよいと押へる木葉哉　　　　　一　茶
Neko no ko no　chyoi to osaeru　konoha kana

The kitten
Holds down the leaf,
For a moment.　　　　　　　　　　　Issa

As the leaf blows past, the kitten stretches out a paw and
holds it down for a moment or two, dabs at it once or twice
and then lets it go. This verse follows on, as it were, another
verse by Issa:

門畠や猫をじやらして飛ぶ木の葉
Kadobata ya   neko wo jarashite   tobu konoha

The flying leaves
In the field at the front
Are enticing the cat.

It is interesting to compare this verse with Wordsworth's *The Kitten and the Falling Leaves*, composed in 1804, and classified by him under Poems of the Fancy. It has one hundred and twenty eight lines, of which two or three are similar to Issa's verse:

With a tiger leap half-way
Now she meets the coming prey,
Lets it go as fast, and then
Has it in her power again.

But even these four lines have not quite got the nerve of life in them that Issa touches so unerringly. Wordsworth is at his best, at his greatest in lines of a philosophic tinge, in something which the Japanese poet (that is, of course, the Japanese mind) eschews, a reaching out from the particular towards the universal, still retaining the warmth that comes from contact with living things. In this poem we have examples of this in such lines as these:

Yet whate'er enjoyments dwell
In the impenetrable cell
Of the silent heart which Nature
Furnishes to every creature...

"Silent heart" is a word of Zen, which has also a philosophic bent, yet praises silence:

叮嚀損君徳、 無言固有功。 (禪林句集)

Many words injure princely virtue;
Wordlessness is naturally effective.

But Wordsworth feels the danger of this generalizing of experience. He wishes

To gambol with Life's falling Leaf,

and, gazing at the kitten and the baby, says,

> And I will also have my careless season,
> Spite of melancholy reason,

in order to get

> Hours of perfect gladsomeness.

Comparing the two poems, we may say that what Wordsworth aspires to do, Issa has done.

水底の岩に落ちつく木葉かな　　　　丈 草
Mizusoko no　iwa ni ochitsuku　konoha kana

> Fallen leaves have sunk,
> And lie on a rock,
> Under the water.　　　　Jōsō

The leaves lie blackish-brown on the rocks in the bed of the stream. Life still runs in them, though a different life from that they knew when they fluttered against the sky of spring. After being hurled through the autumn skies they have settled here under the water,—but not for long. Sooner or later, they will be swept away, and

> Leave not a wrack behind.

But this, the realm of Shelley's leaves in *Ode to the West Wind*, is not the domain of the above verse. In a sense, it is purely that of the picturesque, yet with a poignancy of meaning not derived from personification or symbolism, or even from the lot and destiny of the leaves themselves, but from the mere *fact* of the leaves on the rocks under the water. Somehow or other, the *suchness* of things breaks through these particular leaves in this particular place. That is all we can say.

楢の葉の朝から散るや豆腐桶　　　　一 茶
Nara no ha no　asa kara chiru ya　tōfu-oke

> Leaves of the oak-tree
> Have fallen this morning;
> The bean-curd tub.　　　　Issa

The tub is a very large one, and in the clear water reflecting

the blue sky is seen the milky-white bean-curd. On the top of
the water float two or three leaves of the oak-tree, the crinkled,
serrated, tinted leaves making a contrast with the soft, formless
white of the milky curd under the water. Occasionally the
same wind that has caused the leaves to fall this morning ripples
the surface of the water, and the floating leaves move a little.

鶯 の 口 す ぎ に 來 る 落 葉 か な   一 茶
Uguisu no   kuchisugi ni kuru   ochiba kana

Leaves are falling
For the livelihood
  Of the *uguisu*.   Issa

Issa does not mean, of course, that the leaves are falling in
any way for the sake of the *uguisu*. The flowers do not bloom
for us, the wind does not blow for us, corn does not ripen for
our benefit, nor does the chair stand on its legs for our sake.
The *uguisu* has a deep but chance connection with the leaves.
And it is in this very fortuitousness that life works its unknown
and forever unknowable purposes.

落 葉 し て ぬ か み そ 桶 も な か り け り   芭 蕉
Ochiba shite   nukamiso-oke mo   nakarikeri

Leaves are falling;
Neither have I even
  A pickle-barrel.   Bashō

Nuka-miso is a kind of pickling material made of bran, salt,
and water, kept in a barrel. Even the poorest house has a
barrel of this. Bashō had not even one of these at the time;
but this is stated as an interesting fact, not as a complaint to
anyone in particular or the universe in general. In the *Tsure-
zuregusa*, Chapter 98, written three hundred years before Bashō,
the second of five maxims is:

後 世 を 思 は ん も の は 糟 糠 瓶 一 つ も 持 つ ま じ き 事 な り 。
He who desires the next world must not possess even a
pot of rice-bran bean paste.

西吹けばひがしにたまる落葉かな　　　　蕪 村
Nishi fukeba　higashi ni tamaru　ochiba kana

Blowing from the west,
Fallen leaves gather
In the east.　　　　　　　　　Buson

　All the meaning of Zen is contained in these lines, but only
if no Zen whatever is seen in them. In a sense, it is purely a
matter of cause and effect. The wind blows from one direction
and the leaves collect against the fence on the other side of
the garden. There is no mystery, no spirit of wonder here.
Yet there is a painfully deep meaning of the suchness of things
that has no concern with causality, that stands outside law,
and mocks comparison.

　It is interesting to compare this verse with another that
seems to have been the earlier form:

北吹けば南あわれむ落葉哉
Kita fukeba　minami awaremu　ochiba kana

When it blows from the north,
The fallen leaves fraternize
In the south.

The following two verses are by Buson:

水鳥を吹きあつめたり山嵐
Mizutori wo　fukiatsumetari　yama-arashi

The mountain storm
Blows together
The water-birds.

風一陣水鳥白く見ゆるかな
Kaze ichijin　mizutori shiroku　miyuru kana

A gust of wind,—
And the water-birds
Become white.

人ちらり木の葉もちらりほらり哉　　　　　一　茶
Hito chirari　konoha mo chirari　horari kana

People are few;
A leaf falls here,
Falls there.　　　　　　　　　　　　　　Issa

To know that people are leaves, that leaves are people, without *thinking* so, without making any odious comparisons,—this is the religious and the poetical life. Issa has expressed this life in the most colloquial language, and in doing so, has hidden its depth and wonder under a veil of casualness.

掃きけるが遂には掃かず落葉かな　　　　　太　祇
Hakikeru ga　tsui ni wa hakazu　ochiba kana

Sweeping them up,
And then not sweeping them,—
The falling leaves.　　　　　　　　　　Taigi

At the beginning of winter, we sweep up the leaves with pleasure and conscientiousness, but more and more fall, and nature is too much for us. We submit, and, as the poets say, "Winter reigns."

落葉おちかさなりて雨雨をうつ　　　　　　曉　臺
Ochiba ochi　kasanarite ame　ame wo utsu

Leaves falling,
Lie one on another;
The rain beats on the rain.　　　　　　Gyōdai

This is deeply expressive of destiny, inevitability, one thing following on another with irrevocable fatality, but in it we feel, with Marcus Aurelius,

What a wonderful power is man's to do naught save what will receive the approval of God, and to welcome every dispensation he sends us.

A dead leaf falls, another falls and lies on it. Rain falls on the dead leaves, and other drops fall on those drops dashing them away. This is all there is, yet with what a painful intensity of feeling we watch it happen.

静さや落葉をありく鳥の音　　　　　立 志
Shizukasa ya   ochiba wo ariku   tori no oto

The stillness;
A bird walking on the fallen leaves:
The sound of it.　　　　　Ryūshi

Some lines from *The Task*, speaking of the robin:

Where'er he rests he shakes
From many a twig the pendant drops of ice,
That tinkle in the withered leaves below.
Stillness accompanied with ounds so soft
Charms more than silence.

たおるればたふるるままの庭の草　　　　良 寛
Taorureba   taoruru mama no   niwa no kusa

The grasses of the garden,
They fall,
And lie as they fall.　　　　　Ryōkan

APPENDIX I

SUPPLEMENTARY LIST OF WORKS CONSULTED

(in the author's library)

芭蕉

芭 蕉 俳 句 新 釈	半 田 良 平
芭 蕉 俳 諧 の 根 本 問 題	太 田 水 穂
俳 聖 芭 蕉	野 田 別 天 楼
芭 蕉 雑 纂	菊 山 当 年 男
芭 蕉 集	岩 田 九 郎
芭 蕉 俳 諧	上 甲 平 谷
芭 蕉 俳 句 研 究	沼波瓊音， 太田水穂
	阿部次郎， 安部能成
	小宮豊隆， 和辻哲郎
	幸田露伴
芭蕉句選略解 (秋冬の部)	荻 原 井 泉 水
芭 蕉 全 集 (第一篇)	老 鼠 堂 永 機
	阿 心 庵 雪 人
芭 蕉 (紀行，随筆，書簡)	黒 沢 隆 信
芭 蕉 全 集 (上 巻)	勝 峯 晋 風
芭 蕉 俳 諧 史	吉木燦郎， 勝峯晋風
芭 蕉 句 集	加 藤 楸 邨
芭 蕉	穎 原 退 蔵
野晒紀行評釈 (第三篇)	荻 原 井 泉 水
芭 蕉 一 代 物 語	志 田 義 秀
芭 蕉 読 本	荻 原 井 泉 水
芭 蕉 絵 物 語	内 野 三 廬 二
馬 琴，北 斉，芭 蕉	宇 野 浩 二
芭蕉俳句の解釈と鑑賞	志 田 義 秀
芭 蕉 講 座	穎原退蔵， 加藤楸邨
芭 蕉 研 究	藤 井 乙 男
芭 蕉	菊 田 当 年 男
芭 蕉 講 話	穎 原 退 蔵
旅 行 く 芭 蕉	岡 村 健 三
芭 蕉 展 蕉	志 田 義 秀
俳 句 鑑 賞 (芭蕉七部集)	川 島 つ ゆ
奥 の 細 道 新 釈	三 浦 圭 三
奥 の 細 道 通 解	馬場錦江， 萩原蘿月
蕉門俳諧前集，後集，続集	
(上下巻)	神 田 豊 穂
奥 の 細 道，芭蕉，蕪村	志 田 義 秀

1284 APPENDIX I

芭蕉講座, 第一巻, 発句篇 (上) 　頴原退蔵, 加藤楸邨
芭蕉講座, 第二巻, 発句篇 (中) 　小宮豊隆, 能勢朝次
芭 蕉 講 座, 第六巻, 俳論篇 　小宮豊隆, 能勢朝次
芭 　　　　　　　蕉 　栗 山 理 一
芭 蕉 句 集 新 講 (上下巻) 　服 部 嘶 石

蕪 村　郷 愁 の 詩 人 與 謝 蕪 村 　萩 原 朔 太 郎
　　　蕪 村 夢 物 語 (春, 夏, 秋, 冬) 　木 村 架 空
　　　蕪 村 曉 台 全 集 　大 野 洒 竹
　　　蕪 村 名 句 評 釈 　河 東 碧 梧 桐
　　　蕪 　　　　村 　　　集 　中 村 草 田 男
　　　蕪 村 俳 句 評 釈 　佐 藤 紅 緑
　　　蕪 村 一 代 物 語 　志 田 義 秀
　　　蕪 　　　　　　　村 　暉 峻 康 隆

一 茶　一 茶 俳 諧 史 　中 村 六 郎
　　　一 茶 の 研 究 　高浜虚子, 荻原井泉水
　　　　　　　　　　　　　　　　　　高野辰之, 大江圭虫
　　　一 茶 俳 句 全 集 　荻原井泉水, 大橋裸木
　　　一 茶 読 本 　荻 原 井 泉 水
　　　一 茶 　川 島 つ ゆ
　　　一 茶 の お ら が 春 　勝 峯 晋 風
　　　一 茶 名 句 評 釈 　勝 峯 晋 風
　　　一 茶 論 　浦 野 芳 雄
　　　一 茶 七 部 集 　勝 峯 晋 風
　　　西 行 と 一 茶 　蓮 沼 文 範
　　　一 茶 と 良 寛 と 芭 蕉 　相 馬 御 風
　　　一 茶 文 集 　伊 藤 正 雄
　　　一 茶 　栗 山 理 一
　　　一 茶 俳 句 集 　荻 原 井 泉 水

子 規　正 岡 子 規 　高 浜 虚 子
　　　正 岡 子 規 全 伝 　高橋田 東声規
　　　子 規 俳 話 　正 岡 子 規
　　　子 規 俳 句 集 　高 浜 虚 子
　　　子 規 選 集 　正 岡 子 規
　　　子 規 句 解 　高 浜 虚 子

その他の俳人
　　　俳 人 許 六 の 研 究 　藤井乙男, 鈴木重雅
　　　俳 人 鬼 貫 の 研 究 　鈴 木 重 雅
　　　五 元 集 全 解 　岩 本 梓 石

評釈凡兆俳句全集	高木蒼悟居
俳人漱石論	西谷碧落風
良寛を語る	相馬御讓
其角俳句新釈	高木讓
其角研究	寒川鼠骨, 林若樹
俳僧蝶夢	北田紫水
去來抄評解	岩田九郎
俳人遺墨	金子健二

俳句評釈

俳句鑑賞論	浦野芳雄
和歌, 俳句, 近代詩の評釈	浅尾芳之助
俳句の解釈と鑑賞	岩田九郎, その他九名
俳句の故事解説	宮田戊子
名句の鑑賞	幸崎秋江
句評四季	富安風生
和歌俳句腹力	遠藤隆吉, 河村目呂二
俳句読本	高浜虚子
和歌, 俳句の解釈と鑑賞	加藤一郎
秀句の鑑賞	山口誓子
一人一句	富安風生
俳句評釈	遠藤徳治蔵
名句評釈 (上)	頴原退雲
古今名句評釈	矢田挿天
古俳句評釈	内藤吐男
俳諧評釈	柳田国男
俳諧名作集	頴原退蔵
句作の道 (第一,二,三,四,五卷)	久保田万太郎
俳句史講話 (上卷)	橋間石
俳趣味の発達	麻生磯次
俳句の季節	河野南畦
俳話	内藤鳴雪
連歌, 俳諧俳句, 川柳	能勢朝次, 中村草田男
	麻生磯次
俳句の作り方味はひ方	富安風生
俳談	荻原井泉水月
俳諧七部集 (上)	萩原蘿
俳諧書簡集	山本屋発所子
俳句入門	水原秋桜子
俳句作法 (花,魚,鳥)	水原秋桜子
俳句の道	荻原井泉水子
俳句の復活	山口誓

書名	著者
俳句開眼	大竹孤悠
俳句教程	荻原井泉水
俳諧史研究	佐藤一三
私たちの句集	三好達治

俳句集

書名	著者
新歳時記	高浜虚子
俳家名句集（春夏秋冬）	東盛堂発行
分類俳句全集（秋，冬の部）	正岡子規
類句，作例俳句辞典	大江圭虫
名家俳句集	藤井紫影
俳諧自在	晋永機
四季類題俳句大全	今井柏浦
俳門十哲句集	大橋裸木
新撰俳諧辞典	岩本梓石，宮沢朱明
俳書解説篇	藤井乙男，その他六名
俳諧歳時記	小島伊豆海

近代俳句

書名	著者
現代俳句の批判と鑑賞	飯田蛇笏
現代俳句	山本健吉
現代の秀句	大野林火
近代俳句	栗山理一
現代俳句集	改造社
俳句文学全集	富安風生
全日本新人俳句集	松尾書房発行
新俳句鑑賞	荻原井泉水
新俳句入門	荻原井泉水
新作句辞典	水原秋桜子
花の句作法	水原秋桜子
魚鳥の句作法	水原秋桜子
俳人山頭火	大山澄太
自選句集爽籟集	大竹孤悠
蛇笏俳句選	飯田蛇笏
雲母代表作家句集	雲母発行
句解集	釈飄斉
霜林	水原秋桜子
虚子五百句鑑賞	浜中柑児
俳句の五十年	高浜虚子
虚子の俳句を解く	柏崎夢香

俳画

書名	著者
俳画の描き方	小川芋銭
俳句の書き方	内山雨海
俳画と其の描き方	本方秀

俳		画		法	小川千甕, 横尾深林子
					田中咄哉洲,酒井三良子
俳	草	画	小	径	島　田　忠　夫
俳	人	真	蹟	全	集	野　田　別　天　楼

FOREIGN WORKS

A Year of Japanese Epigrams (1911)　　　William N. Porter
An Anthology of Haiku, Haiku Poems, Ancient and
　Modern (1940)　　　　　　　　　　Miyamori Asatarō
A Bamboo Broom (1934)　　　　　Harold Gould Henderson
A Pepper Pod (1946)　　　　　　Shôson, Kenneth Yasuda
Japanese Literature (1908)　　　　　　　　W. G. Aston
The Literature of Japan (1929)　　　　J. Ingram Bryan
Introduction to Classic Japanese Literature (1939, 1946)
　　　　　　Edited by the Kokusai Bunka Shinkōkai
Japanese Haiku (1955)　Published by The Peter Pauper Press
The Autumn Wind (1957)
　(A Selection from the Poems of Issa)　Lewis Mackenzie
The Japanese Haiku (1957)　　　　　　Kenneth Yasuda
Haikai and Haiku (1958)　The Nippon Gakujutsu Shinkokai
An Introduction to Haiku (1958)　Harold Gould Henderson

APPENDIX II

A CHRONOLOGICAL LIST OF HAIKU POETS

° means a poetess; * a disciple of Bashō;
** one of the Ten Disciples of Bashō;
§ a disciple of Buson; ☆ a disciple of Shiki.

15th Century
Sōgi 宗祇 1420–1502
Moritake 守武 1452–1549
Sōkan 宗鑑 1458–1586

16th Century
Zuiryū 随柳 1548–1628
Teitoku 貞徳 1570–1653

17th Century
Ryūho 立圃 1594–69
Sōin 宗因 1604–82
Ishū 維舟[1] 1606–80
Teishitsu 貞室 1609–73
Shōi 松意 ?
Ryūshi 立志[2] ?–1681
°Chigetsu-ni 智月尼 1622–1706
Kigin 季吟 1623–1705
*Shintoku 信徳 1632–98
°Sute-jo 捨女 1633–98
Ryūsui 流水[3] ?
Ichū 惟中 1638–92
*Tōrin 桃隣[4] 1638–1719
*Suiō 水鷗 ?
*Ensui 猿雖 1639–1704
Chisoku 知足 1640–1704
Saikaku 西鶴 1641–93
*Shara 舎羅 ?
*Rakugo 落梧 ?–1691
Sodō 素堂 1641–1716
*Ranran 嵐蘭 1642–89
Koshun 湖春 1644–97
Bashō 芭蕉 **1644–94**
*Kyohaku 挙白 ?–1698
Gonsui 言水 1646–1719
**Sampū 杉風 1646–1732
*Kakei 荷兮 1647–1716

Wakyū 和及 1648–92
*Sora 曾良 1648–1710
*Shadō 洒堂[5] ?–1737?
*Shōhaku 尚白 1649–1722
*Shihō 史邦[6] ?
*Takuchi 澤雉 ?–1693
*°Sono-jo 園女 1649–1723
Yūsui 幽水 ?
*Senna 千那 1650–1723
*Banko 萬乎 ?–1724
**Kyorai 去來 1651–1704
*Rotsū 路通 1651–?1739
*Uryū 羽笠 ?–1726
°Chine-jo 千子女[7] ?–1688
Isshō 一笑 1652–88
*Yasō 八桑 ?
Raizan 來山 1653–1716
**Ransetsu 嵐雪 1653–1707
Rosen 露沾 1654–1733
**Kyoroku 許六 1655–1715
Saimaro 才麿 1655–1737
Masahide 正秀 1656–1723
**Etsujin 越人 1656–1702
Yasui 野水 1657–1743
Tohō 土芳 1657–1730
*Riyū 李由 1660–1705
Onitsura 鬼貫 1660–1738
**Kikaku 其角 1660–1707
**Jōsō 丈草 1661–1704
*Ryōto 涼菟 1661–1717
Dansui 團水 1662–1711
**Yaha 野坡 1662–1740
**Shikō 支考 1664–1731
*Mokudō 木導 1666–1723
Rogetsu 露月 1667–1751
*°Shōfū-ni-梢風尼[9] 1668–1758
Rōka 浪化 1669–1703

*Sesshi 雪芝 1669–1711
Kanri 冠里 1670–1732
Yasen 野泉[8] ?
*Otsuyū 乙由 1674–1739
*Bonchō 凡兆 ?–1714
*°Ukō-ni 羽紅尼 ?
*Izen 惟然 ?–1710
*Akinobō 秋之坊 ?–1718
**Hokushi 北枝 ?–1718
Senkaku 仙鶴 1676–1750
Hajin 巴人 1677–1742
Kodō 古道 ?–1738
*Bunson 汶村 ?–1713
*Kyokusui 曲翠 ?–1717
*Yamei 野明 ?
*Otokuni 乙州 ?
*Mōgan 毛紈 ?
Fugyoku 不玉 ?–1697
Tōfu 豆富 ?
Keisa 圭左 ?
Kakō 可幸 ?
Teiji 低耳 ?
Seien 晴燕 ?
Rikuto 六渡 ?
Ryūsui 柳水 1691–1758

18th Century
Kiin 希因 1697–1748
Gochiku 五竹 1699–1781
°Chiyo-ni 千代尼 1701–75
°Shisei-jo 紫青女 ?–1751
Yayū 也有 1701–83
Ryōta 蓼太 1707–87
§Shōha 召波 ?–1771
Ichiku 移竹 1708–59
§Tairo 大魯 ?–1778
§Taigi 太祇 1709–72
°Moroku-ni 諸九尼 1713–81
Fuhaku 不白 1714–1807
Tōri 桃李 ?–1779
°Ōshū 奥洲 ?
Aon 阿音 ?
Buson 蕪村 1715–83
Shōzan 嘯山 1718–1800
Ōemaru 大江丸[10] 1719–1805

Rankō 闌更 1726–99
Chora 樗良 1729–81
Gomei 五明 1730–1803
°Seifu-jo 星布女 1731–1814
Katsuri 可都里 1732–1817
Gyōdai 曉臺 1732–93
Shirao 白雄[11] 1735–92
Jūkō 重厚 1738–1804
Seira 青蘿 1739–91
§Kitō 几董 1740–89
°Koyū-ni 古友尼 ?
°Sogetsu-ni 素月尼 ?–1804
Chōsui 長翠 ?–1813
Shirō 士朗 1742–1813
Rikei 李渓 ?–1819
§Gekkyo 月居 1745–1824
§Hyakuchi 百池 1748–1836
Seibi 成美 1748–1816
Jūjō 十丈 ?–1830
°Kikusha-ni 菊舎尼 1752–1826
Otsuji 乙二 1754–1823
Michihiko 道彦 1755–1818
Ryōkan 良寛 1756–1851
Kien 奇淵 1758–1834
Hōrō 鳳朗 1761–1841
Issa 一茶 1763–1827
Isō 惟草 ?–1853
Baishitsu 梅室 1768–1852
Goshin 午心 ?–1817
Tōrin 桃隣 1772–1806
Tanehiko 種彦 1782–1842
Ampū 鞍風 ?
Reikan 鈴竿 ?
Baikin 貝錦 ?
Nangai 南崖 ?
Koshū 孤舟 ?
Jakusui 若水 ?

19th Century
☆Meisetsu 鳴雪 1847–1926
Shosei 初聲 ?
Chōshū 聴秋 1852–1930
Kiitsu 機一 1856–1933
Atsujin 日人 1857–1936
Shōu 松宇 1859–1943

Hashin 芭臣 1864–?
☆Sōseki 漱石 1865–1915
Wafū 和風 1866–?
Shiki 子規 1866–1902
Usen 芋錢 1868–1938
☆Seisei 青々 1869–1937
☆Roseki 露石 1870–1918
☆Kanrō 寒楼 ?
Sazanami 小波 1870–1933
☆Gojō 五城 1871–1915
☆Hekigodō 碧梧桐 1873–1937
☆Rogetsu 露月 1873–1927
Kyoshi 虚子 1874–1959
Kubutsu 句佛 1875–1943
☆Shūchiku 秋竹 1875–1915

20th Century
Arō 亜浪 1879–1951
☆Yaezakura 八重桜 1879–1945
☆Gusai 愚哉 ?
Otsuji 乙字 1881–1919
Kubonta 九品太 1881–1924
Santōka 山頭火 1882–1940
Seisensui 井泉水 1884–1976
Ragetsu 蘿月 1884–1961
Hōsha 鳳車 1885–1954
Kinsai 菫哉 1887–1920
☆Kuson 駒村 ?
Chōi 蝶衣 1886–1930
Ippekirö 一碧楼 1887–1946
Shimpū 晋風 1887–1954
Shūōshi 秋桜子 1892–

¹ Also known as Shigeyori, 重賴.
² There were five poets of this name.
³ Disciple of Baisei, 梅盛 1610–99.
⁴ There were five poets of this name.
⁵ Also known as Chinseki, 珍碩.
⁶ Also read Fumikuni.
⁷ Kyorai's younger sister.
⁸ Pupil of Ryūkyo, 柳居, d. 1748.
⁹ Wife of Ryōhin, 良品, 1668–1758.
¹⁰ Also called Furukuni, 旧国.
¹¹ There is a second Shirao also.

INDEX TO THE FOUR VOLUMES

ENGLISH & JAPANESE LITERATURES (SEE ALSO VOL. I, P. 17)

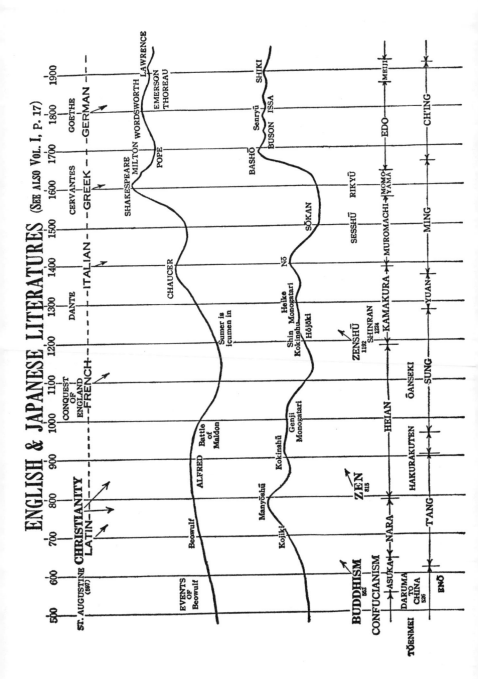

HAIKU Vol. 4

俳 句 第四巻

1982年7月20日　初版発行　　　1997年5月20日　5刷発行

検印省略

著　者　R. H. Blyth

発行者　株式 会社 北星堂書店

代表者　山 本 雅 三

〒113 東京都文京区本駒込 3-32-4

Tel (03) 3827-0511　Fax (03) 3827-0567

THE HOKUSEIDO PRESS

32-4, Honkomagome 3-chome, Bunkyo-ku, Tokyo 113 Japan

◇落丁・乱丁はお取り替えいたします